The Enterprising University

SRHE and Open University Press Imprint
General Editor: Heather Eggins

Current titles include:

Catherine Bargh et al.: *University Leadership*
Ronald Barnett: *The Idea of Higher Education*
Ronald Barnett: *The Limits of Competence*
Ronald Barnett: *Higher Education*
Ronald Barnett: *Realizing the University in an age of supercomplexity*
Tony Becher and Paul R. Trowler: *Academic Tribes and Territories (second edition)*
Neville Bennett et al.: *Skills Development in Higher Education and Employment*
John Biggs: *Teaching for Quality Learning at University*
David Boud et al. (eds): *Using Experience for Learning*
David Boud and Nicky Solomon (eds): *Work-based Learning*
Tom Bourner et al. (eds): *New Directions in Professional Higher Education*
Anne Brockbank and Ian McGill: *Facilitating Reflective Learning in Higher Education*
Ann Brooks and Alison Mackinnon (eds): *Gender and the Restructured University*
Sally Brown and Angela Glasner (eds): *Assessment Matters in Higher Education*
John Cowan: *On Becoming an Innovative University Teacher*
Gerard Delanty: *Challenging Knowledge*
Chris Duke: *Managing the Learning University*
Gillian Evans: *Academics and the Real World*
Andrew Hannan and Harold Silver: *Innovating in Higher Education*
Norman Jackson and Helen Lund (eds): *Benchmarking for Higher Education*
David Istance et al. (eds): *International Perspectives on Lifelong Learning*
Merle Jacob and Tomas Hellström (eds): *The Future of Knowledge Production in the Academy*
Peter Knight: *Being a Teacher in Higher Education*
Peter Knight and Paul Trowler: *Departmental Leadership in Higher Education*
Mary Lea and Barry Stierer (eds): *Student Writing in Higher Education*
Ian McNay (ed.): *Higher Education and its Communities*
Moira Peelo and Terry Wareham (eds): *Failing Students in Higher Education*
Craig Prichard: *Making Managers in Universities and Colleges*
Michael Prosser and Keith Trigwell: *Understanding Learning and Teaching*
John Richardson: *Researching Student Learning*
Stephen Rowland: *The Enquiring University Teacher*
Maggi Savin-Baden: *Problem-based Learning in Higher Education*
Peter Scott (ed.): *The Globalization of Higher Education*
Peter Scott: *The Meanings of Mass Higher Education*
Anthony Smith and Frank Webster (eds): *The Postmodern University?*
Colin Symes and John McIntyre (eds): *Working Knowledge*
Peter G. Taylor: *Making Sense of Academic Life*
Richard Taylor et al.: *For a Radical Higher Education*
Susan Toohey: *Designing Courses for Higher Education*
Paul R. Trowler (ed.): *Higher Education Policy and Institutional Change*
Melanie Walker (ed.): *Reconstructing Professionalism in University Teaching*
David Warner and David Palfreyman (eds): *The State of UK Higher Education*
Gareth Williams (ed.): *The Enterprising University*

The Enterprising University

Reform, Excellence and Equity

Edited by
Gareth Williams

The Society for Research into Higher Education
& Open University Press

Published by SRHE and
Open University Press
Celtic Court
22 Ballmoor
Buckingham
MK18 1XW

email: enquiries@openup.co.uk
World wide web: www.openup.co.uk

and 325 Chestnut Street
Philadelphia, PA 19106, USA

First published 2003

A catalogue record of this book is available from the British Library

ISBN   0 335 21072 4 (hb)

Library of Congress Cataloging-in-Publication Data

The enterprising university: reform, excellence, and equity/edited
by Gareth Williams.
     p. cm.
   Includes bibliographical references and index.
   ISBN 0-335-21072-4
   1. Education, Higher–Economic aspects–Cross-cultural
 studies.   2. Education, Higher–Aims and objectives–Cross-cultural
 studies.   I. Williams, Gareth L.

LC67.6 .E58 2002
378.1–dc21

                                                            2002025804

Typeset by Graphicraft Limited, Hong Kong
Printed by St Edmundsbury Press, Bury St Edmunds, Suffolk

Contents

Notes on Contributors

Eddie Blass is a Senior Lecturer at the Derbyshire Business School, University of Derby. Email: E.V.Blass@derby.ac.uk

D.F.M. Butt is Public Policy Officer, UniSdirect, University of Surrey. Email: F.Butt@surrey.ac.uk

Gilbert Frade was Dean of Engineering Studies at Ecole des Mines de Paris for many years and since October 2001, he has been Dean of Continuing Engineering Education at Ecole des Mines de Paris. Email: doussaid@paris.ensmp.fr

Anne Gold is a Senior Lecturer in Education Management at the Institute of Education. She is interested in the development of management of educational organizations in the UK and internationally. Email: a.gold@ioe.ac.uk

Alan E. Guskin is Co-Director & Senior Scholar, Project on the Future of Higher Education, Distinguished University Professor and President Emeritus, Antioch University. He can be contacted at aguskin@antioch.edu

D.B. Hay is a Senior Lecturer in Education in the School of Educational Studies, University of Surrey. Email: D.Hay@surrey.ac.uk

Scott Hayter is the Director of Development and Alumni Relations at the University of Durham. His team is responsible for coordinating the fundraising and alumni activities of the University.

Ellen Hazelkorn is Director, Faculty of Applied Arts, Dublin Institute of Technology, Ireland. She has published widely on Irish politics; digital technologies, work practices and cultural industries; and media and state relations. She is currently conducting research for IMHE/OECD on processes and strategies for growing research at new and emerging HEIs.

Helen Johnson is Principal Lecturer in Education Management in the School of Education Studies, University of Surrey Roehampton. Email: H.Johnson@roehampton.ac.uk

Mervyn Jones is Director of Continuing Education at Imperial College, where he is responsible for a growing and diversifying portfolio of activities directed towards providing updating for professionals in science, engineering, medicine and management. He has degrees in Physics and Materials Science, and a PhD in Electrical Engineering, all from Imperial College. Email: m.jones@ic.ac.uk

D.A. Kirby is Professor of Entrepreneurship in the Surrey European Management School and Adjunct Professor of Entrepreneurship in the University of South Australia. Email: D.Kirby@surrey.ac.uk

Brenda Little is a projects and development officer at the Centre for Higher Education Research and Information, The Open University. She has worked on several studies involving undergraduates' work-based learning and graduate employment. Email: B.Little@open.ac.uk

Ian McNay is an emeritus professor of the University of Greenwich and now operates as a freelance teacher, developer, researcher and consultant. Email: I.McNay@greenwich.ac.uk

Mary B. Marcy is Co-Director and Senior Administrator, Project on the Future of Higher Education, Antioch University. She can be contacted at mmarcy@antioch.edu

Louise Morley is a Reader in Higher Education Studies at the University of London Institute of Education, UK. She is Director of the Centre for Higher Education Studies (CHES). Recent publications include *Quality and Power in Higher Education* (2003), Open University Press; *Organising Feminisms: The Micropolitics of The Academy* (1999), Macmillan. Email: l.morley@ioe.ac.uk

Rob Paton is Professor of Social Enterprise in the Centre for Comparative Management at The Open University Business School.

Ian Scott is Director of Academic Development at the University of Cape Town. He works at national and institutional level in the area of educational development and widening participation in higher education. Email: iscott@ched.uct.ac.za

Peter Slee is Director of Marketing and Corporate Communications, and Deputy Registrar at the University of Durham.

Scott Taylor is a Research Fellow in the Management Learning Unit and a member of the Human Resource and Change Management Centre at the Open University Business School.

Elaine Unterhalter is a Senior Lecturer in Education and International Development at the Institute of London, University of London. She has particular interests in gender, social justice and education and has written a number of articles which focus on these issues in South Africa, India and Bangladesh. Email: e.unterhalter@ioe.ac.uk

Gareth Williams is Emeritus Professor of Education Administration at the Institute of Education. An economist by training, he has worked for many years on higher education policy especially in the areas of finance and graduate employment. Email g.williams@ioe.ac.uk

Part 1

The Big Picture

Introduction

By now it has been widely recognized that the 1988 and 1992 Education Acts in Britain symbolized a radical transformation in the financial relationships between universities, government and the wider community. In brief the transformation was from institutions subsidized by government to fulfil certain broad academic missions, to suppliers of specific teaching and research services available for direct purchase, or for purchase by government on behalf of student consumers. This led to a rapid growth of 'enterprise' and 'entrepreneurialism' as universities learned the art of financial survival in this new world. Similar changes have occurred in most countries of the world, although the extent and speed of 'marketization' varies very considerably between different countries.

In most countries the changes have been associated with new ideas in the past two decades about the way public services can be equitably and efficiently delivered. Described in the literature variously as the Audit Society, the Evaluative State and New Public Management, they are all essentially solutions to what some economists have called the 'principal–agent problem', that is how does a government as principal ensure that its agents, hospitals, public utilities, schools and universities provide their services in the optimum way from the point of view of society as a whole. Traditionally, this was done through detailed state regulation of the provision of these services, a procedure that reached its apogee in the centrally planned economies of Eastern Europe; but it was also the normal way of delivering most public services, including higher education, in most of the countries of Western Europe.

The new management, based on the ideas of 'resource dependency theory' involved 'steering at a distance' that is the 'principal' devolving detailed decision-making well down the chain of agents, to individual universities and colleges in the case of higher education, encouraging them to behave like market-driven organizations (hence the expression 'quasi-market') and monitoring their activities to ensure that the aggregate outcome is consistent with the principal's aims. Under such a system, those institutions that show most commercial enterprise are usually the most successful both in flourishing as institutions and in meeting broader social objectives, at least those that are encouraged by the principal.

There have also been special features of higher education that have encouraged the application of these ideas. The services provided by universities and colleges are very diverse, meeting a very wide range of needs and interests, which makes standardized provision very difficult – a factor which was exacerbated by the advent of mass higher education. The knowledge industry in which universities and colleges operate is the subject of particularly rapid change with the explosive growth of electronic-based information technology. Finally, there is much concern about costs as higher education systems become bigger and bigger.

This first section explores these ideas in the light of experiences in the United Kingdom, the United States, South Africa and other Commonwealth countries.

1

An Honest Living
or Dumbing Down?

Gareth Williams

The context of enterprise

The 1988 and 1992 Education Acts radically changed United Kingdom universities and colleges. In England and Wales[1] the key was an apparently technical clause in the 1988 Act, which provided for any financial allocations to individual universities to be accompanied by 'Financial Memoranda' that specified within fairly closely defined limits what was expected in return for these financial allocations. On the day they were established, the new Funding Councils received a letter from the Secretary of State setting out the government's interpretation of how the Councils should carry out their responsibilities. One key phrase was that 'I shall look to the Council to develop funding arrangements which recognize the general principle that the public funds allocated to universities are in exchange for the provision of teaching and research and are conditional on their delivery' (DES 1988). This transfer of financial power from the suppliers of academic services to a proxy consumer was extremely far reaching. Henceforward, the only way universities (and now polytechnics) could make much effective use of their cloak of legal autonomy was by continuing to diversify their funding sources. In another passage of the same letter the Secretary of State wrote 'I very much hope that it [the Council] will seek ways of actively encouraging institutions to increase their private earnings so that the state's share of institutions' funding falls and the incentive to respond to the needs of students and employers is increased.'

These changes, along with the financial stringency that accompanied them led to a rapid growth of 'enterprise' and 'entrepreneurialism' as universities learned the art of financial survival in this new world. Similar changes have occurred in most countries of the world, although the extent and speed of 'marketization' has varied considerably between different countries.

Much has been written about the changed culture of universities in the English-speaking world during the 1990s.[2] Some authors interpret the changes as higher education coming to terms simultaneously with massification and with the realities of the information revolution. Others see recent developments as a postmodern *trahison des clercs* in which traditional values have given way to expediency and irony. Most common, however, is the view that they are a regrettable consequence of government stinginess.

The English-speaking university at the beginning of the twenty-first century has been described as, inter alia, the 'entrepreneurial' university (Clark 1998), the 'enterprise' university (Marginson and Considine 2000), 'marketized' university, 'academic capitalism' (Slaughter and Leslie 1997) and 'commodification' of higher education (Rooney and Hearn 2000). All these conceptions are concerned primarily with universities as organizations or institutions that can be managed in various different ways. The present book seeks to probe underneath organizational and institutional theory to explore what is happening to the students and staff who are the real physical manifestation of the university. To be 'enterprising' has undertones of boldness, resourcefulness, originality, creativity and imagination, all of which may be shown by individuals and can be means of both achieving and inhibiting deeper academic values such as integrity, disinterestedness, critical understanding and scholarship.

Enterprise potentially affects far more than the organization and management of universities and colleges. One aim of this book is to explore the extent to which an enterprising university is one in which the spirit and practice of enterprise is taking root in what Clark (1983 and 1998) describes as the academic heartlands. Clark writes of a 'stimulated heartland' in his entrepreneurial universities. But when does a new stimulant become so powerful, or so addictive, that the organism itself changes its nature? If it does, is the change evolution or decay? In terms of the analytical framework proposed by Becher and Kogan (1992), and in contrast to the primacy of normative values of the academic core, which they suggest has helped make the concept of a university meaningful through the centuries, this book aims to explore, through a series of evaluations and case studies, the extent to which an enterprising 'operational mode' is beginning to dictate the value-driven 'normative mode' of universities and colleges in the United Kingdom and a number of other countries. In terms of the four levels proposed by Becher and Kogan, the focus is mainly on the basic units and institutions where students learn and academic staff work, learn, teach and do research; but there is some consideration of some of the effects at the level of individual staff and students and at a broader system level.

In the middle of the nineteenth century Matthew Arnold saw a society 'that distributes itself into barbarians, philistines and populace' with America, the way of the future, being 'just ourselves with the barbarians quite left out and the populace nearly' (*Culture and Anarchy*, 1869). In the tradition of this narrative, we are all philistines now. Universities, which once offered a solid refuge from the tide of philistinism, have instead decided, or been forced, to go with the flow and accept that their survival is determined not so much by their solid foundations of scholarship and culture as by their seamanship in the face of winds and currents created by governments, customers and sponsors. This mood of pessimism is related to, but distinct from the 'more means worse' of Kingsley Amis and other critics of the Robbins Report in the early 1960s. Few commentators today are prepared to attribute present woes directly to the massive expansion of higher education that occurred in the United Kingdom and many other countries in the last two decades of the twentieth century. They prefer instead to blame governments for willing the ends of mass participation but not willing the means to achieve it. Therefore, so this story goes, universities have had to seek money from a growing multiplicity of sources, diversifying and seeking customers wherever they can, even if this means compromising their integrity as centres of long-term excellence in teaching and research.

The university may, in Clark Kerr's frequently quoted passage, be one of the few European institutions that has survived the last 800 years, but the name has survived only by the institution adapting as needs must to political, economic, cultural, social and, above all, technological changes. Theocracies gave way to secular states, religious orthodoxy to humanist enlightenment, oral and hand-written communication to the printed word and interpretation of received wisdom to the discovery of new knowledge. All these changes affected power structures and management arrangements as well as the nature of academic knowledge and the daily lives of individual students and members of staff. Universities have been remarkably successful in managing the tensions between the old and the new, between tradition and iconoclasm, between continuity and change. One common feature of universities over the centuries has been that they are communities of relatively clever people. They may at times have been idle, self-serving, decadent or corrupt, but their institutions have survived and, on the whole, prospered by staying ahead of the game. Although twenty-first-century Oxford is in some sense the same institution that came into existence in the thirteenth century, in every detail, apart from a few remnants of buildings and occasional references to Greek philosophers it comprises a different set of ideas, entities and activities.

However, it is certainly true that the pressures for change today are more powerful and more immediate than ever. The business of universities and colleges is knowledge. A modern university creates and interprets information and ideas and it trades in them. Until the late twentieth century, ideas and information evolved slowly. They could be thoroughly tested in the crucible of experiment and oral and written debate. An accepted paradigm was overturned only when it was clear that there was something better to put in its place. Oral debate required individuals to congregate in one place and written debate depended on the relatively slow physical dissemination of paper. Being enterprising was a rather leisurely process that happened but could proceed through consensus and debate. A paper that missed one issue of a journal could appear in the following issue with little loss. An astronomical observation about which there was some doubt could be checked the next time that comet appeared. An experiment that went wrong could be repeated more carefully. By the middle of the twentieth century, the process was speeding up and it became almost conventional for each generation to reject the dominant ideas of its parents. By the end of the century, it was a cliché that the useful life of much subject knowledge was less than a decade. Many people needed to change their knowledge and ideas several times during a lifetime. People not actively involved in either the advancement of knowledge itself or in frequent professional redevelopment risked finding much of their learning and skills redundant several times in their working lives. The need for enterprise to ensure survival and success likewise speeded up. New ideas needed to be acted on almost immediately or they would be appropriated elsewhere.

One particular development that was at the core of the university emerged very slowly, first with the written word, then with printing[3] has been the capacity to store and access knowledge in a multiplicity of sites. From the hand-written libraries of the monasteries to the public libraries of the nine-teenth century and the cheap paperbacks of the early twentieth century the need to assemble in particular locations to have access to comprehensive and comprehensible knowledge gradually weakened and universities could realistically aspire to be institutions available to everyone. But the accessibil-ity has now reached a stage at which the need for special institutions to permit access to wide swathes of knowledge, even of advanced knowledge, is increasingly open to question. The autodidact has existed ever since the development of cheap printing and self-help groups were a central feature of nineteenth-and early-twentieth-century adult education. However the Internet and email have given a rocket-propelled thrust to these processes. Most knowledge is now accessible by most people from most locations. The key function of the university of the future is likely to be the mediation and the moderation of the knowledge jungle, but even this is unlikely to be location dependent.

In such circumstances, the information industry – the creation, dissem-ination and evaluation of knowledge – becomes something in which enter-prise commands a premium. Decisions need not be made quite so rapidly as those on the trading floors of global financial exchanges, but the raw material of the knowledge business is almost as fleeting. One interpretation of the past quarter century is that knowledge workers are experiencing changes analogous to those experienced by skilled manual workers when mass production became possible in the manufacturing and the entertain-ment industries. While the levels of living and ultimately the jobs of most blacksmiths and music hall artistes went down, standardized methods of production and quality control ensured that many more people were able to have access to high-quality goods and services. Producers who were able to take advantage of the changes became wealthy and powerful. If this inter-pretation is valid, enterprising universities and enterprising people who control them may expect to benefit considerably from the mass production of higher education, while their colleagues form the basis of an intellectual proletariat and not impossibly a rebirth of a new form of Marxism.

The rapidly rising salaries of many vice-chancellors and a few star performers in high-demand subject areas in the United Kingdom alongside the declining relative salaries of most academic staff may give a glimpse of a possible future for the academic world itself.

Enterprise, excellence and equity

Many of the changes of recent years can be interpreted in the light of such an analysis. The term 'mass' higher education, itself problematic, has undertones of the soulless production line (Fordism), tabloid journalism (Murdochism?), the Costa Brava (ClubMedism?) and Hamburger cuisine (McDonaldization). Nevertheless, in contrast to some complaints about commodification, autonomous, enterprising universities competing in a mass market, using appropriate technology may be the most effective way of avoiding standardized production line provision of academic services in the provision of mass higher education. The motor car industry has come a long way in both quality and variety since Henry Ford's customers were able to have any colour they wanted so long as it was black, and the culture of mass eating out means that never has there been more variety or better quality to choose for those who like to eat in restaurants.

In any mass-production industry standardized products are sold because most consumers want them. A middle-of-the-range family saloon meets a certain set of expectations with respect to engine power, safety and comfort: a package holiday from a particular class of brochures can be relied on to meet certain standards with respect to meal availability, toilet facilities, room services, accessibility of leisure and entertainment facilities and so on. The more complex the product, the more valuable to many consumers is the knowledge that there are guaranteed standards. The transaction costs of acquiring information about an individualized product are too great. But there is invariably a range of standards between which consumers can choose. Usually there is a trade-off between quality and price. A room of a particular class in a Holiday Inn is the same anywhere in the world. However, in each hotel there are a range of standards and broadly customers get what they pay for. The difference in higher education, at least in the United Kingdom and many other European countries, is that a standardized product means standardization across the whole system. It is interesting that most countries continue to have at least two explicit higher-education ranges. In the UK and Australia the binary system was abandoned largely because it was believed that two product ranges conflicted with principles of equity if access to the preferred model was rationed.

This has sharpened an intrinsic conflict between the need for diversity in any form of education for adults and the need for a product that conforms to certain easily recognizable standards and criteria. All degrees must meet criteria that are achievable by all institutions. The dilemma can be expressed as a quasi-syllogism. Higher education must meet a great variety of needs and interests. The majority of people should have access to it on an equitable basis. All higher education should be excellent. Publicly funded higher education for all cannot be afforded. Access to the best higher education should not depend on ability to pay for it. Therefore aspirations for both universal excellence and comprehensive equity must be abandoned conclude some observers. Prior to the emergence of mass higher education, this particular circle could be squared by entry requirements. Only people who achieved certain levels of previous educational attainment were considered eligible for entry and high quality and costs could be kept under control by restrictive entry standards. But, by definition, mass higher education cannot restrict entry to meet arbitrary resource limitations.

Mass-higher-education systems must find their own solutions to the problem of excellence and equity in diversity and differentiation. One possibility is for students to pay for what they get. This is very broadly the solution adopted in the United States. Those who cannot afford to pay for it immediately need to be able to borrow the resources to do so. If higher education is a profitable personal investment, the borrowers will be able to reimburse the lenders later on. If it is primarily a consumption good, the question arises of why equitable access to it should be treated as especially desirable.

Another solution in a mass-higher-education system is for universities to cross subsidize some students or some activities at the expense of others. This is broadly what many universities in Australia and the United Kingdom are attempting to do. Enterprise by universities can assist the process in two ways. One is directly. Some universities are able to succeed in one market niche, others somewhere else. The second is by generating a financial surplus through ventures that are not part of the core university mission, but can be used to subsidize it. Thus, students at a university that makes profits from the conference trade, for example, are able to benefit from a more expensive range of services than those at universities that cannot or do not.

However, as soon as either of these happens there is an inherent conflict between diversity and any strict definition of equity or inclusivity. Diversity and differentiation must mean that the missions and clientele of courses differ. Whatever the intentions, some students will get better deals than others. If the prices to students of all courses are required to be equal, some will receive better value for money than others. If the government decided to provide extra subsidy to students in institutions that did not generate additional income, this would act as a deterrent to enterprise and, thus, a net loss of income to the sector as a whole.

Excellence in higher education is also multidimensional. One dimension is the huge range of subjects covered: excellence in clinical medicine involves different costs and different criteria from excellence in literature. Another is the nature of the intellectual challenge for the learners:

excellence in providing for first-generation access students with very poor earlier educational preparation is a very different matter from providing an excellent education to potentially brilliant mathematicians or historians. Enterprise can both promote and inhibit a profile of excellence. An enterprising approach to meeting the wishes of customers inevitably helps to promote excellence if it means providing better courses with the same resources or courses of a given quality with fewer resources. The danger arises if there are other aspects of excellence beside the immediate delight of the customer. If there are aspects of a subject that are inherently difficult but the delight comes after these have been mastered, there is some danger that an enterprising approach towards attracting students to that subject may involve watering down the difficult parts with the result that students never realize the true delights of learning it.

Another case is when it is enterprising to release intrinsically interesting research findings to the popular media before they have been published in a peer-reviewed scientific outlet. If this becomes widespread, there are dangers to the excellence of scientific research as the disinterested pursuit of truth. Truth will out in the long run, but if bad science achieves popular currency it may well give rise to many strands of poor research and wasted resources before the genie can be put back in the bottle.

Enterprise and the idea of the university

If it is indeed the case that the enterprising university is becoming nothing more than a seller of services in the knowledge industry, the question arises of whether its future can be as durable, or as vital, as its past and, more urgently, whether the university as seller of academic services can claim any special prerogative to receive public or unhypothecated private donations to provide these services. If all income is closely constrained to provide particular educational or research services for adult citizens, and if other service providers are able to show that they can provide the same services more efficiently in terms of quality or price, customers will in the long run buy the services from the more efficient supplier, and governments, on behalf of their taxpayers, ought to do the same.

So the emergence of enterprise as a powerful, and possibly dominant, force in universities inevitably raises fundamental questions about their nature and purpose. Many books and articles with titles such as 'The Crisis of the Universities' have assumed at root that the university exists and will continue to exist. Even Ronald Barnett, who proclaimed the death of the university, followed it immediately with the hope of resurrection (Barnett 2000) which, even in a humanist sense, suggests the new daffodil rising each spring from the husk of the old or the family dynasty in which the son (or daughter) carries on the work of the dead parent. 'Continuity and change' is a phrase that any text search of the literature on higher education turns up very many times. Yet what if the university really is dying? The dead flower does not rise again, but is eaten by slugs. The prodigal son does not carry on the father's brave vision, but squanders it on riotous living. Are the genetic engineers not right to try to find ways of prolonging life as we know it, or cloning life so that we know what is being passed on rather than leaving it to the happenstance of probabilistic biology?

To continue Barnett's metaphor, there may be a stage of technological development where the end of the reign of the traditional university is succeeded not by a young invigorated monarch nor even by a republic of letters but by a populism of information. We may find that we all have to navigate our own pathways with nothing to guide us but a myriad of virtual gurus, prophets, help-lines, chat rooms and media hype. Only enterprising universities and enterprising scholars will be able to make durable paths through this jungle without dumbing down and selling out, or retreating into isolated ivory towers.

Learning how to be enterprising

Enterprise in higher education can have two distinct meanings. Most of the rest of this book is concerned with the development of universities and colleges as enterprising institutions, that is organizations that have an eye for the main chance in furthering their aims, whether these are to ensure an excellent learning experience for their students, to widen participation, to advance research or to ensure a comfortable lifestyle for their academic staff. Since the pursuit of all of these aims requires resources, enterprise in this sense is often stimulated by financial stringency, but it was also initiated by the ideological changes about the provision of public services that emerged in the 1980s.

Enterprise can also be something that students learn in higher education. It has long been part of the tacit learning of many students. Those who attain high office in their student unions or any other student club or association, or who spend vacations or gap years doing community work in deprived areas at home or abroad or in exploring remote parts of the world are unlikely to achieve much without a considerable amount of enterprise. It is unlikely that any university would wish it to be thought that its students became less enterprising as a result of their studies. In publicly funded mass higher education, if an attribute is considered desirable, the fuzzy tacit must give way to the well-defined specific. Just as universities and colleges claim to encourage students to learn to be critical, competent, knowledgeable and possibly creative and imaginative, and they can be assessed by quality monitors on the extent to which their courses encourage the development of these qualities, so it is reasonable to suggest that higher-education institutions should actively encourage their students to learn to be enterprising. There are moves in this direction in British universities with exhortations by government and some employers over recent years that in order to support a rapidly changing economy 'enterprise' should become an identifiable constituent of the higher-education curriculum. This forms part of the 'employability agenda', which became very prominent in much of the higher-education debate in the UK during the 1990s.

The Dearing Committee was enthusiastic about the encouragement of learning relevant to a marketized knowledge economy.

> The strongest single message which we received from employers was the value of work experience. This is particularly emphasised by small and medium sized enterprises that need new employees to be able to operate effectively in the workplace from their first day . . .
>
> (Dearing 1997: summary report para 39)

One way of interpreting these pressures is that they are a natural consequence of the expansion of higher education and the emergence of knowledge-based economies. Higher-education curricula have gradually incorporated medicine, law, engineering, economics, social sciences, accountancy, social administration, and since 1970 a huge number of other professional and vocational subjects as the range of occupations that graduates enter has grown. The link of such curriculum broadening with mass higher education is attested by the fact that most of the new disciplines appeared first in the United States, which achieved mass enrolment well before other countries. As more and more graduates enter occupations where enterprise, in addition to professional or intellectual competence and disciplined work habits, is essential for financial and social survival, so the idea of teaching it, or creating a learning environment in which students can absorb a capacity for enterprise is being seen as an important new task for the higher-education curriculum.

A study of employability teaching in universities at the beginning of the twenty-first century (Mason et al. forthcoming) shows that the 'employability' agenda has become very influential in many subjects in English universities during the past decade. However, there is much less evidence of 'enterprise' being treated specifically as one of the employability skills. One exception in the Mason study was design studies in which 'many of their graduates enter a very competitive economic environment with many small enterprises in which graduates will be required to have a range of management and business skills as well as technical proficiency in design (Chapter 3).'

There are doubts, however, about whether it is individual enterprise that employers really want from graduates. In Chapter 13, Little provides some evidence to support the view that team working is valued by commercial employers more than individual enterprise. She quotes one typical graduate recruiter as follows:

> It's amazing how many people (interviewees) when you ask them about team working situations will talk about themselves. . . . don't talk about team work . . . what you're looking for is people who understand what

it is to work in a team, to work with different types of people . . . and make a team effective . . . whereas quite often people will give you a situation where they've achieved something over other people, rather than working in a team situation. . . .

(Graduate recruiter, large computer software company)

Writing of work experience as one of the important ventures by universities to allow students to familiarize themselves with the realities of the market place, Little concludes that 'alongside various "pushes" to help undergraduates gain work experience, it may be time to take stock and ask whether such "pushes" are at least as likely to hinder, as to enhance, access to the labour market for some groups of students'.

The Dearing Committee was particularly enthusiastic about enterprise as part of the content of continuing-education programmes:

We recognise that many higher education programmes, especially short programmes designed in conjunction with employers, and programmes which have benefited from developments under the Enterprise in Higher Education Initiative, already have preparation for employment as one of their key objectives. We have already noted the crucial role higher education will play in our future economy and believe that, over the system as a whole, even greater attention should be paid to this aspect.

(Dearing Committee: para 5.60)

Continuing education is likely to continue to grow both absolutely and in its proportionate share of higher education. Employers will, as now, wish to train their staff. They may undertake this in-house or commission it from external providers, including higher education. There will be a range of needs which cannot be met in-house if, as we assume, there is a significant shift towards self-employment, employment in small and medium sized enterprises . . . and more limited-term contracts.

(para 4.22)

In Chapter 7 Jones takes up a similar theme. He believes that continuing professional development of those who are already in employment will bring higher-education institutions into much closer contact with the realities of industry and commerce:

While it is essential for engineers in their professional development to acquire an appreciation of their professional responsibilities, which for example may entail an appreciation of financial, managerial, ethical, legal and environmental issues, this must be built on a sound initial appreciation of engineering. The pressures of an increasing knowledge base with wider perspective can only be resolved by ensuring that continuing professional development is seen as an essential part of engineering practice. This has not only to be recognized by those involved, but implemented.

Two activities where clearly an institution itself takes a more active role in entrepreneurial activity are, on the one hand, technology transfer and consultancy – with a principal focus on the commercial developments associated with the exploitation of research knowledge – and, on the other hand, continuing professional development – with a greater focus on advanced teaching that is generated by research knowledge.

In Chapter 14 Frade advocates the practical learning of enterprise as part of the curriculum most explicitly. His *Acte d'Entreprendre* makes the creation of an enterprise an explicit part of the curriculum in the *École des Mines* in France. According to Frade, this has proved very successful with students and, after some initial suspicion, is now enthusiastically supported by his academic colleagues. Significantly, the *Actes d'Entreprendre* chosen by students are not all primarily concerned with making money. The examples he cites include community activities such as organizing a tri-Alpine (rafting, canoeing, mountain bike) sporting event and cultural events for handicapped people.

At the moment, however, despite the excitement of some isolated ventures such as those of Frade, the explicit teaching of enterprise in traditional higher education seems to be rather exceptional other than as a by-product of the employability agenda and here, as Little shows in Chapter 13, there are some doubts about the extent to which employers of graduates really want unbridled enterprise to be taken up by too many of their new graduate recruits. The discipline of team working seems to be more valued.

Enterprising organizations

From the viewpoint of existing ideas of what a university is, or ought to be about, Chapter 3 by Guskin and Marcy from the United States presents a challenging but ultimately optimistic picture. Despite these authors' concerns about current challenges, their vision can be seen as optimistic because, although the United States is in most respects far further down the road of massification, marketization, privatization, and community service than other countries and has far more proprietary and corporate universities, they envisage universities continuing to exist in the currently conventional sense of the word.

During the last two decades of the twentieth century, total expenditure on higher education in the United States as a percentage of GDP was roughly twice the OECD average (OECD 2001). Despite this, expenditure per student continued to grow throughout much of the 1990s. Furthermore, although more than half of the United States' expenditure on tertiary education comes from private sources, public expenditure as a percentage of GDP is higher than in most other OECD countries. However, in the untypical good years of the 1990s, according to Guskin and Marcy, US higher education slept. The challenge now comes because 'the new century has brought a rude awakening'. Higher education faces the difficult paradox of being more critical than ever to society's future, but under severe pressure to prove its worth in educating students, especially undergraduates.

The increased resources of the late 1990s in the United States brought encouragement to those who thought that society's support would continue to grow relatively effortlessly to meet the needs of higher education, but:

> ... in the last few years, the pressure for significant institutional change in higher education has reached a crescendo of demands for major reform. These pressures focus on three major issues: 1) the costs of higher education for students and the state; 2) what students are learning and the assessment of student learning outcomes; and 3) the use of new information and computer technologies in the core of the educational process.

> (Guskin and Marcy, Chapter 3)

The solution proposed by Guskin and Marcy essentially amounts to the belief that it is up to the universities and colleges to meet the cost challenges and the student learning challenges. They must take the lead in student-recruitment policies, in staffing policies, in curriculum development and in using new information and computer technologies. A renewed vision, self-confident and effective management taking hold of new technology as a tool to help improve quality and reduce the teaching costs per student, is necessary. This is a model in which the enterprising university or college will be proactive in promoting its vision of what is worthwhile in the knowledge society and will set out to achieve it.

Like any major producer of goods or services, higher-education institutions must obviously take account of their consumers' wishes, but they must also be prepared to promote their own vision of what consumers, individually and collectively, will appreciate from a longer-term perspective. Although Guskin and Marcy do not say this, it is likely that such a strategy will result in a weeding out of some universities and colleges as institutions, but it offers the best hope of survival of 'the university' as a viable organizational form in the twenty-first century.

In a contribution that is on the surface of a very different kind, Slee and Hayter in Chapter 10 make similar points. They are writing from the perspective of development officers in a university that aims to remain in the world league of research and top-quality teaching institutions. The case studies they describe derive from 'selling' such an institution to potential funders, public and private, so that the contributions of the various sponsors complement each other to achieve something that is really worthwhile to the university and its students. It starts with a shared vision. 'With regard to strategy: the whole institution needs a clear vision and strategic objectives to which everyone subscribes ... the best enterprise teams will focus on major projects for big-picture ideas in areas that have the critical mass in top-quality staff, teaching and research.' Enterprise, for Slee and Hayter, is a collective university activity that 'takes advantage of existing strengths and provides strategic support for the institution's long-term future'. It is a process through which their university can promote its image of what a first-class university should be and not merely a way of responding to the wishes of those who have money, whether they be students, private donors or governments.

Ian Scott in Chapter 4 is more cautious about the role of enterprise in the higher-education system of a less industrialized country, in his case South Africa.

> International thinking on higher education is dominated by the trends and driving forces prevailing in the developed world. Under pressure from rapidly-changing demands and limited capacity, 'less-industrialised' countries (LICs) are inclined to adopt first-world approaches and models without sufficient critical analysis which carries a substantial risk of unforeseen consequences.

He goes on to say that:

> . . . a case in point is the spread of enterprise in higher education in many developing countries, where public provision has been precipitately exposed to market forces and private provision has taken root. Equity and excellence, in their various manifestations, have long been the key contending challenges in higher education in LICs; . . . The emergence of enterprise as a significant force in higher education has added new dilemmas and possibilities. Balancing these forces in the interests of development should be a central challenge for policy makers and practitioners . . .

The South African policy environment when enterprise emerged as a significant force in higher education was one where old forms of regulation were disappearing while the post-apartheid policy framework was still being formulated. The conditions that fostered the growth of entrepreneurialism in public higher-education institutions and the spread of private higher education came about more as a result of broad national developments and macro-economic policy than a widely debated development strategy by the education authorities. As in several other countries, university enterprise was seen primarily as a way of filling gaps resulting from shortage of public funds.

The rise of entrepreneurialism on this foundation has had some unintended consequences. Growth in enterprise-related provision certainly shows that there are some demands that traditional public provision is not meeting. However, Scott doubts 'whether the way in which the demand is being met is in the long-term public interest'. For him, 'enterprise is not an end in itself but of value insofar as it is a means to meeting developmental goals . . . A key question, then, is to what extent enterprise, as the major new force in higher education, can be harnessed to meet critical output goals, in the interests of national development'. He sees a tension between the short-term revenue-generating purpose of enterprise and the need to invest in long-term development, and he expresses particular concern 'that aggressive entrepreneurialism in the private sector and a few public institutions could draw in a disproportionate share of profitable programmes and fee-paying students, leaving the core development and equity responsibilities to the remaining public institutions while at the same time reducing their resources'. Scott concedes that unregulated enterprise might successfully increase overall participation in higher education, but considers this has 'limited value in itself' if national development and equity issues are not addressed as an integral part of the enterprise solution.

For Scott, and for several other authors in this book, enterprise in higher education, as in any other activity, is a means to an end and is not an end in itself. The fact that in many areas of economic and social activity, including some in higher education, the end is the enrichment or the empowerment of the entrepreneur has led many academics and observers of the academic scene to be suspicious of enterprise as a feature of higher education. According to McNay, enterprise 'provokes . . . an image of shady villainy, a fifth column gnawing away at the basic values that define a university, a wolf masquerading as a milch-cow'. Private proprietary universities are thought to be in it to make a quick buck. Corporate universities are seen as part of the investment strategy of large companies in a global knowledge society. (See the contributions of Scott (Chapter 4), Paton and Taylor (Chapter 8) and Blass (Chapter 9)). Conventional universities are enterprising in order to try to replace shortages of public funds or donations. However, it is not necessarily so. The saint can be as enterprising as the sinner.

Enterprise, excellence and equity in practice

There are practical questions about the part commercial enterprise should play in a higher-education system's portfolio. If a corporate university is providing services that a conventional university is unable to supply, or if the conventional university finds that some of its regular activities can be income-generating, then the threat to the excellence is small and indeed it is likely that the quantity and quality of the service provided will be enhanced. An example of quality improvement in the United Kingdom is the treatment of students from overseas since they became full-cost fee-paying customers 20 years ago. The university response to this sudden policy change was one of the first examples of commercial enterprise becoming a prominent feature of the management of many universities. Some universities soon realized that foreign students now brought with them significant income that was free of government constraints. They abandoned their previously passive attitude to foreign student recruitment and undertook vigorous recruitment drives. The dip in recruitment in 1982 and 1983 immediately following the fee increase, was soon recouped, and by 1987 there were more foreign students in British universities than in 1979.

While there have certainly been some examples of sharp practice, there is little doubt that most universities with an active overseas student recruitment policy make great efforts to ensure that their customers' special needs are met in matters ranging from learning skills to dietary preferences and religious observation in a way that certainly was not the case when such students were subsidized and marginalized.

Equity, however, is a more complex matter. If the result of the income generation is that more of the service is provided, then more people are able to benefit from it. However, whether this makes the provision more equitable depends on interpretations of the word 'equity'. High fees inevitably benefit students from families who are able to pay them, and even if they are fully covered by loans, it is far easier to take out a large loan for those from a secure financial background than those with little experience of the considerable sums of money involved. In Chapter 5 Morley et al. show that expansion of higher education in several Commonwealth countries, often through the growth of private universities and colleges, has increased women's participation considerably. Yet they express doubts about whether this has really made higher education more equitable in other respects.

Enterprising ventures that are undertaken by universities in order to generate additional income raise complex issues. Some are practical. One of the most useful privileges of conventional higher education institutions in most countries is their special tax status. They are exempted from many of the taxes that commercial enterprises and private individuals have to pay. If a university undertakes a non-educational activity that is directly competitive with a commercial organization, it has an unfair advantage. In most countries with partly marketized higher-education systems the tax authorities are usually aware of such possible abuses, but the university that allows its primary focus to become purely commercial and short term may find it is skating on very thin ice.

The most difficult issues arise when income generation requires a university to depart from its core mission. Various cases can be identified. If there is peripheral capacity that is underused for some of the time – a swimming pool or student residences, for example – then it obviously makes sense to hire the facility out and generate income at times when the university's regular clientele are not using it. A second case is the non-academic services the university uses, such as catering, bookshops and printing. The current orthodoxy is that the enterprising university out-sources such services to specialist suppliers. However, this is not clear-cut. I have been told by a senior administrator in one extremely successful and enterprising university that he took the view that if an outside company could make money out of providing such services, then the university too ought to be able to create a surplus out of it if it is managed properly – his university does it very profitably.

The third case is where staff are not used to their full capacity on regular university or college business. This is the meaning of enterprise that is implicit in some of the chapters in this book – those of McNay (Chapter 2), Hay et al. (Chapter 11) and Jones (Chapter 7), for example. Here the first question a well-managed university should ask is why it should seek peripheral business if there is insufficient demand for its core products. If the university is unable to recruit enough students, or the staff it has is unable to do worthwhile research, then there are serious questions about whether it is really in the university's interest to retain such staff. Universities do not exist merely to provide employment for their staff. Supplementary work may be a legitimate short-term measure or it can possibly be a way of enabling some people, for example postdoctoral students, to earn a living while they are building up their research or teaching profiles. However, it is unlikely to be a viable long-term solution for a university in financial difficulties. Guskin and Marcy describe how, in the United States, there has been a very rapid rise in the numbers of part-time and temporary staff for specific tasks. They doubt whether this is viable in the long term.

The most common case, at least in the United Kingdom, is where, even if all staff *are* fully employed on the core business of research and teaching, the funding available is insufficient to maintain a viable institution. One solution is for entrepreneurial activities to subsidize the core income of the institution. Yet this raises very delicate management issues. If regular university staff are expected to spend a significant proportion of their time on what they see as non-academic work and surrender a significant part of the income generated to their institution, some will decide that it is preferable to do such work in a genuinely commercial environment. Possibly even more seriously, there are risks in this approach for the quality of both teaching and research as well as to the physical and mental health of the staff concerned.

However, the university often sets up a commercial arm to sell academic services, different from, but related to, its core academic mission, at a profit. The surplus goes to the university instead of to shareholders. Provided the activity is properly accounted for and any cross subsidy is fully understood, this is a valid venture for an enterprising university. The university itself, or at least its management, becomes the entrepreneur in the sense proposed by Slee and Hayter (Chapter 10). One danger is that unless it ensures that it has legal protection for the ventures, the university risks losing control of spin-out and similar companies and there are many examples of this. Another problem is the relationship of the staff of the subsidiary company to the regular academic staff of the university. The function of the company staff is to make a profit for the university. If they work alongside regular university staff who have equivalent qualifications and experience but better employment conditions, there is likely to be pressure from them to be taken on to the regular university payroll which is self-defeating from the point of view of the generation of profit to help the university with its primary mission.

The underlying fear of those who remain suspicious of enterprise as an attribute of universities is that it will drive out their other more fundamental university qualities, such as intellectual integrity, critical inquiry and commitment to learning and understanding. Are such fears justified? The broad answer is that in the experiences reported in this book the problems are real, but not insurmountable. The enterprise culture has not yet penetrated the university heartlands to the extent that it can seriously be seen as a vice rather than a virtue. There are danger signs – corporate universities and other private ventures are beginning to cherry pick some of the more profitable market niches and public funding everywhere is under severe pressure. Higher education is being seen in some political circles as primarily a worthwhile private investment. There is a widespread view that universities are badly managed and could stand further cost reduction if their management improved.

However, the main claim of this book is that enterprise is an enabling process through which the more fundamental aims of universities can be protected and pursued in mass-higher-education systems. Competitive enterprise can certainly result in dumbing down, but it can also lead to great works of scholarship and artistic and intellectual creation. Research at the boundaries of knowledge, as well as great artistic, literary and musical works are all produced and made widely available as a result of enterprise. It is the challenge facing those who manage and work in universities to ensure that the dominant outcomes of their enterprise are the proven virtues of exciting teaching and discerning research and not the transient rubbish of the mass media or the mass instant-food industry.

Notes

1. There were very similar developments in Scotland and Northern Ireland.
2. Indeed there have been similar changes in other countries, especially in the former Soviet bloc and in China. However, this book arises out of a conference in an English-speaking country and all the papers were based on work in English-speaking countries and almost without exception cited literature in English on experiences in English-speaking countries.
3. It is helpful to recall the struggles that accompanied the invention of printing, censorship and the attempts at preventing the translation of the Bible into vernacular languages.

2

The E-factors and Organization Cultures in British Universities

Ian McNay

Introduction

'Excellence' and 'equity' are rosy-cheeked, apple-pie terms; in higher education, 'enterprise' provokes a much more ambivalent response: an image of shady villainy, a fifth column gnawing away at the basic values that define a university, a wolf masquerading as a milch-cow. Institutional cultures can reinforce those stereotypes. So can policy perspectives, initiatives and agencies at a national level. The result is a narrow interpretation of the three terms and the adoption of a single, dominant understanding that is not helpful to development. I want to try to redress that imbalance, and consider other 'e-factors' affecting the three that are of primary concern.

This chapter builds on my previous work modelling organization cultures in higher education (McNay 1995, 1999). That, in turn, drew on Clark (1983) and Weick (1976). I want, first, to summarize that work as a context for the rest of the chapter; then to relate the cultures to the concepts of equity, excellence and enterprise while glossing those concepts, and then consider issues of conflict and complementarity among the cultures and concepts. The conclusion commends a concept of 'enterprise' as essential to the development of universities and can be seen as a commentary on Clark's later work (Clark 1998), as well as arguing for a move forward from a previous reductionist regime of economy, efficiency and effectiveness.

Clark's (1983) 'triangle of coordination' identified three pressures acting on higher-education systems at a national level. They were the academic oligarchy, the market and the state. He then saw the state as double headed and I developed (McNay 1999) a quadrilateral that separated the state bureaucracy from the state as policy maker. In an open-systems approach, those four elements penetrated across institutional boundaries. Within institutions, I developed (McNay 1995) four cultures extending Weick's view of universities as 'loosely coupled systems' (Weick 1976). They related to the degree of looseness/tightness in control of policy development and control of policy implementation and operation, leading to four quadrants

Table 2.1 Concepts summarized

System coordinates (Clark/McNay)	academic	state oligarchy	state bureaucracy	market policy
Values (Clark)	liberty	social justice	loyalty	competence
Cultures (Handy)	individual	role	power	task
Cultures (McNay)	collegium	bureaucracy	corporation	enterprise
E-factors	excellence elitism?	equity equality	economy? efficiency? effectiveness?	enterprise

of collegium, bureaucracy, corporation and enterprise. In turn, they related back not only to Clark's adapted triangle, but also to the chapter in the same book on values that treated another foursome – liberty, equity/social justice, loyalty and competence (Clark 1983). Those familiar with the work of Handy (Handy 1985) will see relationships to their four organization cultures of individual, role, power and task.

The three concepts of concern here then map on to this model. 'Excellence' is usually seen as deriving from the collegium, with its stress on the academic freedom of the individual (Becher and Kogan 1992, Russell 1993). 'Equity' and equality are embraced by Clark within social justice, and bureaucracy is seen as having as a main aim the establishment of due process so that all are equal under the regulations. 'Enterprise' has a cultural quadrant already labelled. The fourth quadrant will be treated later. The concepts and labels are summarised in Table 2.1.

The e-factors in practice

This section considers the concepts further, linking each to its cultural 'home'. One concern is to examine the risk of too narrow an interpretation of each and the danger of overemphasis on the priority each may claim within an institution. Each has a set of advocates who, at an extreme, risk turning a culture into a cult. The adherents of any one develop suspicions of the others as they strive for supremacy in the political model of the university as an organization (Baldridge 1971).

Excellence

Excellence in the collegium often relates to a 'golden age' view of academic life. Some years ago, as part of an international programme on the entrepreneurial university, I led a study group to the University of Cambridge. Members of the group were interested in the university's research policy.

'We think it is a Good Thing' was the reply. 'What about your research committee?' 'We don't have one.' 'How, then, do you ensure excellence?' 'We appoint the best people and let them get on with it.' That view of intrinsic motivation of dedicated autonomous academics as the key to excellence assumes degrees of trust and procedural autonomy that do not fit with the management culture in many universities – even Cambridge is changing (Baty 2002).

There are dangers. Concepts of excellence can be restricted by an exclusivity of definition promoted by an established elite. Given the need to test new knowledge before acceptance into the canon, there is a conservatism in much of academic life.

Bell and Gordon (1999) offer evidence that some feminist models of research present a challenge to the academic hierarchy and that current definitions of scholarship prevent the advancement of women in the academy. The weighting of factors in newspaper league tables promotes a single traditional concept of excellence through the ranking that emerges. When the University of Durham developed University College, Stockton – an outreach campus linking more equitable access to an enterprise skills curriculum (the aim of the government initiative 'Excellence in Cities') – concerns were expressed in Senate about the impact on average A level entry scores and consequent league-table ranking (Hogan 2001). The 'bureaucratization of quality' (Rowland 2001), through peer-review processes, incorporates many who may have a collegial-based view of excellence, but are required to discount the individual basis of that culture or adopt criteria that emphasize a particular interpretation of excellence. The Research Assessment Exercise (RAE) in the UK has provoked charges of preference to lab-based psychology, to econometrics within economics and challenges to the criteria and processes in clinical dentistry.

For the 2001 RAE, there was considerable debate as to whether impact, relevance and 'fitness for purpose' were indicators of quality in the Education Unit of Assessment, on an equal footing with academic publications or the vitality of a department's research culture. Initially, they were relegated to a supplementary, third, criterion applicable only to research judged to be of national or international quality (Higher Education Funding Council for England 1999a). After a vigorous consultation, it was accepted that the 'educational significance of the research and its relevance for the academic community, policy makers and practitioners ... *may be* among the characteristics of both the quality of research outputs and the vitality of research culture' (Higher Education Funding Council for England 1999b, emphasis added). This reinterpretation was probably more the result of political sensitivity to the high-profile debate over research on schools (Hargreaves 1996, Tooley and Darby 1998, Hillage et al. 1998) as to representations from those committed to Mode 2 research approaches in a professional domain (Gibbons et al. 1994). For me, such approaches can be seen as entrepreneurial, derived from and developed with the community served, rather than the enclosed world of the invisible college. Such exposure to the operational world challenges academics and enhances quality through the rigour of application. There is, though, a history of challengers being resisted by those deemed excellent under established norms – the animal and human health fields have seen several such in recent years.

Equity

Equity is about more than equality. It is contingent. It addresses previous inequities and aims at just rewards. The danger is that it drifts to an ideo-logically 'hard' concept of equality that aims at standardized treatment of all, regardless of circumstance. Bureaucratic cultures sponsor such standard approaches since they are easier to manage and administer. Exceptions pose a problem, and yet excellence often derives from the exceptional, and entre-preneurial responses recognize diversity. Homogenization has often followed massification in an industrial model of delivery of higher-education services that disregards individual difference. Academic staff may often consent to such a culture, commit to it as a default option, because attempts to do otherwise are frustrated and frustrating and exhaustive of effort.

Several examples from my own experience may help illuminate the issues that arise from inflexible approaches based on good intentions and prin-ciples of equality of treatment.

When I became Head of a School at the University of Greenwich, I learned that there was an accepted boycott of the university's scheme for promotion through excellence or exceptionality in teaching. The view was promulgated that all the School's teaching staff were equally excellent and deserved enhanced salaries, and that until all could be so rewarded none should seek recognition for personal excellence through the scheme developed by 'management'. I encouraged individuals to apply, and, 3 years later, the School had the highest proportion of teaching staff promoted through the scheme, and the gender balance of staff in promoted grades had moved from 8:1 to a more equitable 6:6 out of 29.

There was, at times, a similar attitude – it might be labelled 'negative equity' – to students' exceptional circumstances. There was resistance to allowing, say, a third attempt at an assignment because of particular factors notified by a student, unless all students who might have similar circum-stances, but had not made a case, could be contacted. In a graduate profes-sional School, the range of circumstances can be extensive. That example highlights the traditional tension between equality of opportunity (to sub-mit a case for consideration) and equality of outcome for all in a particular population. The SRHE annual conference, 2001, saw an interesting paper from Salford University, where policy aimed at increasing equity in degree classification by introducing a standard marking scale and a uniform method of classification (Rivlin and Roberts 2001). The good intentions are obvious; the consequences may be unexpected. The differences among disciplines do not lend themselves easily to such standard prescriptions and the tensions between promoting equality and coping with curricular diversity may not be creative tensions but combative ones.

Those examples draw on activities that might be seen as located in the collegium; two more link to the enterprise quadrant. At Anglia Polytechnic University, I gained several external grants for work outside the UK. One was for a major project in the Ukraine. I accepted that three people had to sign a form before I could spend part of the grant on buying an air ticket to get there – I had had problems in some countries getting recognition of payment processes that avoided the risk of corruption. In Kyiv, I stayed in a flat and went to the local farmers' market to buy bread, eggs and fruit. I then submitted a claim for £10 a day for subsistence – to set against the several hundred pounds per day I was earning for the university (this was late 1980s). The claim was rejected. Receipts were needed. The controls against corruption, against excess, allowed no exception – and getting a receipt from an old woman with a bucket of eggs posed challenges beyond those of language! The preference was for me to have stayed at an expensive hotel, losing the university income. The failure to manage exceptions meant that extra rules were applied to all, with negative controls imposed – equally, but inequitably – on the innocent. The Good Shepherd managed the exceptional stray, and the flock trusted him and followed. In the UK, our model derives from a television programme where two dogs drive the flock, directed by a man (usually) with a crooked staff.

The final example comes from Greenwich. The university had no strategic planning at corporate level. In this respect, it reflected Coffield's (2002) view of government approaches to lifelong learning – 101 initiatives, but no strategy. Within the School, in anticipation of national policies that have since emerged, we invested in development of resource-based distance learning supported by email and computer-mediated tutoring, which was in line with the university's mission statement and, in principle, encouraged by senior management . . . I think. It was an entrepreneurial approach to enhancing equality of access to high-quality professional training. The cost profile of distance provision for professionals is, however, different from full-time, campus-based, undergraduate courses (Rumble 1999): a more intensive demand on School resources such as staff time, including travel to observe and assess teaching, and preparation of printed material, and less on corporate resources held at the centre. The formulaic approaches to internal resource allocation treated all students as equal in their demand on resource. That meant that students who never came near the campus had the same top-slice (over 60 per cent) applied to the income they generated as those who used the campuses that swallowed up so much of the university's costs. It took considerable effort by staff in the School to ensure an equality of excellence in the student experience. There was subsequent resistance to extending flexible modes of delivery and support beyond the original programme.

So, approaches based on equality of treatment risk undermining efforts at equity, entrepreneurial innovations or excellence in curriculum processes.

The due process involved in committee procedures characteristic of the bureaucratic culture may be seen by defenders as the administrative equivalent of scientific method, but, as Brew (2001) points out, rationality may be a defence against knowing differently (and acting differently, too?). The creativity essential to both excellence and enterprise may, therefore, be stifled.

Enterprise

Enterprise, narrowly interpreted, risks corruption of basic ideals, too. Constant chasing after income can be wasteful of effort (Williams 1992), can lead to 'mission drift' through dispersed control, and loss of coherence and continuity. Core activity can be displaced, disrupted or distorted: undergraduates find classes rescheduled to free a room for short courses which are generating supplementary income. Yet Warner and Leonard (1997) underline the importance of student care for the 'core business' income base. Funding for a chair in, say, commercial law or international law is easier to find than for one in family law, so development becomes imbalanced and some areas of study better protected under financial pressure. Cost imperatives and target achievement may make curiosity in research less acceptable as commercial sponsors expect to control agendas and research councils penalize late completions. There may be a risk to excellence from such pressures.

A broader concept of enterprise would balance those risks. It would recognize creativity, initiative, flexibility and responsiveness as key elements, as they are for excellence and equity initiatives. The increase in participation rates in the late 1980s may have been driven by economic imperatives as government funding reduced, but there was a confluence of interest with those committed to the access movement, and imaginative approaches to supporting transition. The emphasis in entrepreneurial approaches is on the client, and their prominence in this culture counters criticism of universities as ivory towers. It opens up institutions to their community constituencies, so enhancing their credibility and political support. Recommendation 57 of the Dearing Report (National Committee of Inquiry into Higher Education 1997), if implemented, would require each governing body to do exactly that: to 'systematically review ... the arrangements for discharging its obligations to the institution's external constituencies'. Within the teaching process, conservative complacency is challenged as utilitarian students confront and judge knowledge with different criteria of quality. Academics and other staff may also become conscious of costs, although accurate costing of activities is still elusive since data are not transparent.

Some staff still resist such language. They resist selling themselves. Often they undervalue themselves and certainly under-price their services. Yet Henkel (2000) describes the emergence of 'research entrepreneurs' who set and control their agendas, but also get funding to pursue them. Teachers may be reassured by the language of a text aimed at those running small businesses:

> Delighting customers means continually coming up with something unusual, which takes the customer by surprise, and which makes your [university/college] and its people stand out from the crowd . . .
>
> It is about understanding and anticipating their needs, constantly seeking out problems and quickly solving them for the customer.
>
> It is about building up long term relationships, not quick fixes and is undoubtedly the route to competitive advantage
>
> Customer delight is essentially personal and spontaneous, aimed at raising the self-esteem of the person experiencing it. For that reason, it must be done in such a way that the recipient does not feel threatened, nor under any kind of obligation.
>
> (Gilliland 1993: 47)

That is not only good business, it is good teaching practice, and will improve retention and completion rates for the league tables.

Conflicts and complementarities

There is an atomization of policy at national and institutional level that sets the three cultures in opposition. There are different structures with responsibilities for each, so that, for example, staff in units reaching out to the business community as part of enterprise do not articulate with those reaching out to the community to promote access by learners. The tribalism of their adherents and the allocation of institutional responsibilities can reinforce this and provoke clashes. Some have been described above. Others include:

- 'equitable' exploitation of intellectual property derived from excellence in individual, often entrepreneurial, research and allocation of subsequent income;
- disruption of teaching from staff priorities accorded to research in pursuit of excellence;
- standardized structures for diverse curricula – modularity as a Procrustean bed; and
- inequitable weighting of performance indicators of 'excellence'.

Yet they can complement and enhance one another and each can reduce the risk of isolated interpretations of the other two:

- enterprising approaches can enhance outreach to promote equity of access;
- excellence in the collegium is necessary to renew the knowledge base of entrepreneurial activities and products, to establish standards and to theorize the knowledge gained in the field of practice . . . and to improve the chances of success with research bids;

- enterprise adds to traditional excellence the rigour of relevance and responsiveness and recognizes the contribution of the student client – a key concept of andragogy;
- equity approaches can moderate the elitism and exclusion that excellence may drift into;
- excellence in teaching allows all students to add to value through their learning as equitably as possible; and
- equity in reward systems promotes criteria, whereby diverse manifestations of excellence and enterprise are recognized.

Leading the academic enterprise

In her study of university structures, Sporn (1999) identifies factors enhancing and impeding adaptation by universities to changing environments. Enhancers include not only an entrepreneurial spirit, in the broader sense developed above, but supportive leadership, professional management, collegial governance and differentiated structures. The impeding factors include resource dependence, legal regulations, a culture of 'perseverance' (plodding on), weak integration and missing goals and strategies. Clark (1998) has five factors enhancing the entrepreneurial university: a strengthened steering core; a diversified funding base; an integrated entrepreneurial culture; a stimulated academic heartland and an expanded developmental periphery.

My research suggests that those positives are not prevalent in many UK universities and that the impeders can be found in many places. Slaughter and Leslie (1997) have identified the risks of too narrow an interpretation of enterprise, some of which accord with those above derived from my studies. The strong steering core was a dominant element in those institutions I studied, but it was a control dominance, not a developmental one. All four universities had a corporate-bureaucratic culture and in development workshops for higher-education staff this comes through as common across the sector. The picture is one where equity, excellence and enterprise risk being stifled by the culture of the fourth quadrant in my model. The holders of corporate power use the bureaucracy as a control device in the elusive pursuit of economy, efficiency and effectiveness. There is a lack of full understanding even of those terms and a risk-averse approach to innovation.

The integration, or, at least, balancing of equity, excellence and enterprise is best done at the developmental periphery. Centralization and standardization do not work. Handy (1985) calls my corporate quadrant a power-based crisis culture that is destructive in the longer term. The loyalty and conformity demanded do not allow the debate, disputation, dialectic essential to development, or the diversity to ensure 'fitness for purpose'. Nor is their integration across issues, even in the small directorate group where holders of different portfolios protect them and, in return, do not interfere with those of colleagues.

Comments from senior staff in a modern university in the north of England in a project to evaluate the work of the Executive will illustrate these issues of control and lack of integration. They are representative of many more such comments.

> The Executive makes the realisation of any vision difficult due to the bureaucracy and constraints that they impose upon creativity/flexibility. Devolution is frequently done without fully letting go, so Deans and Heads of Department are hamstrung in their efforts [but criticized if they do not deliver].
>
> They have, by autocratic means, goaded us into far too many initiatives too quickly. They cannot understand that change needs time. They believe that bureaucracy will result in quality. They will not take responsibility for the problems they create.
>
> The Executive members may be highly talented in their respective fields, but the whole is distinctly less than the sum of the parts. It is quite difficult to give the whole a 'character' because they often do not gel as a unit.
>
> The Executive does not function correctly as a 'group'. It remains a collection of individuals who are concerned to promote their individual concerns, prejudices and sectional interests.
>
> (McNay 1998)

In a mass system, if a thousand flowers are to bloom, the industrialized model is unfit for purpose. We must cultivate our own gardens. This is not a plea for a return to the secret garden of the curriculum, nor for unaccountable autonomy, but for recognition that best practice in all three areas is contingent. Local determination of its definition is essential – not within a closed system, but relating to, and responsive to a diverse, complex and ever-changing environment. That is how the academic enterprise will survive another 800 years.

3

Facing the Future in the United States: Faculty Work, Student Learning and Fundamental Reform

Alan E. Guskin and Mary B. Marcy

Higher education in the new century faces the difficult paradox of being more critical than ever to society's future, but under severe pressure to prove its worth in educating students. Higher education has come under close scrutiny for its use of financial resources. This is in part because it is a huge business which costs taxpayers and students immense amounts of money, and in part because its product – student learning – has been questioned by employers and governing bodies. In addition, it is partly because it is not subject to systematic outcome measures. Yet it is also recognized as a primary means of personal and societal advancement, and a major driver of the economy. Expectations of and pressures on colleges and universities are high.

In coming decades, colleges and universities will face significant pressures that may well disrupt educational and administrative practices and, in particular, undermine the quality of faculty work-life. The key to overcoming the severity of these potential problems will be a fundamental reform of how colleges and universities educate undergraduate students.

The opportunity to transform colleges and universities in the USA is aided by the fact that over 50 per cent of the faculty presently teaching are 50 years old or older. With the likelihood of huge numbers of faculty retirements over a 10- to 15-year period, we can face financial and other accountability pressures by creating fundamental changes in how faculty work and students learn, while minimizing layoffs and human pain.

Pressures for change

In the last few years, the demands for major reform in higher education in the USA have reached a crescendo. They focus on three major issues:

1. the costs for students and the state;
2. what students are learning and the assessment of learning outcomes; and
3. the use of new information technologies in the core of the educational process.

Costs

It is generally accepted within higher education that the expenses involved in educating undergraduate students will continually increase. Faculty salaries, the costs of educating increasing numbers of students by hiring new staff members, increasing costs of materials and facilities, and, more recently, the huge and continually increasing investment in new information technologies, all contribute to escalating costs. As a result, even with the considerable savings from painful cuts made in the last decade or so, the costs of maintaining the present academic structures require fiscal resources surpassing those that societal institutions and individuals are capable of and/or willing to provide.

The Higher Education Price Index (HEPI) rose more than six-fold between 1961 and 1995, much faster than inflation as measured by the Consumer Price Index (CPI). Between 1980 and 1995, the annual average rate of growth in the costs of providing higher education exceeded the CPI by a full percentage point. A sector whose costs grow faster than inflation for an extended period ultimately reaches the limits of available resources, as has been demonstrated in the healthcare industry.

> [While] public support per student has just kept pace with inflation ... real costs per student have grown by about 40 percent ... Until now, institutions have been paying for [these] rising costs by sharp tuition increases; however, such increases will shortly begin to keep Americans from pursuing higher education.
>
> (Council on Aid to Education 1997: 11)

Most institutions have tried to face these challenges with escalating fund-raising efforts along with tuition increases and cuts in non-academic areas. But these initiatives, while adding some important resources, cannot address the fundamental operating costs of institutions.

Student learning outcomes

The need for colleges and universities to focus on student learning has become a rallying cry for many who are demanding the reform of undergraduate education. Over the last decade, the six regional higher-education accreditation associations have increasingly pressured colleges and universities to assess the outcomes of student learning as part of their accreditation reviews. There has also been a growing emphasis among states to tie part of the annual allocations for higher education to institutional performance, as measured in one way or another by the outcomes of student learning. Because of the lack of well-developed student learning outcomes measures, institutional performance tends to be viewed in terms of crude measures of learning such as attrition and graduation rates. As learning outcome measures become available, it is likely that the funding of institutional performance will focus more on actual demonstrations of learning than on these gross measures.

Use of new information and computer technologies

There have been significant improvements in information technologies over the last few years and these innovations are likely to continue to develop at an increasing pace over the years ahead – especially in the area of sophisticated content-oriented software. These advances will enable colleges and universities to further integrate technology into the core of the educational process. This point is emphasized in a recent article:

> As the inexorable improvement in digital technology continues, and we gain a better understanding of how to use it, we will experience further improvements in the capacity, reliability, cost effectiveness and ease of use. Soon it will be impossible, even with great effort, to achieve the same learning results without the use of technology that we can achieve with it.
>
> (Newman and Scurry 2001: 87)

As a result, pressures will mount from inside and outside the traditional higher-education sector – including competing institutions, funding agencies, policy makers, governing boards and students themselves – to utilize technology as key parts of the learning process. Like many revolutionary innovations, the influx of technology cannot be adequately accommodated by traditional means. As Twigg (1996) argues:

> As you design mediated programs, you will find that the more you replicate the traditional campus model, the more your operating costs will resemble or exceed traditional campus costs. . . . You will save money only if you substitute one function for another function at less cost. This isn't a matter of research; it's a matter of logic and common sense.

Technology does offer tremendous promise for higher education. But it is a promise that can only be realized through innovation and significant change.

A good example of expectations for reform is indicated by one of the conclusions of the National Commission on the Cost of Higher Education (1998: 28):

The commission believes significant gains in productivity and efficiency can be made through [alternative approaches to] the basic way institutions deliver most instruction, ie faculty members meeting with groups of students at regularly scheduled times and places . . . [We] should consider ways to focus on the results of student learning regardless of time spent in the traditional classroom setting.

In effect, the Commission, governors, the Council on Aid to Education and many others are recognizing that there must be fundamental changes in how education is delivered at our colleges and universities. Ignoring future fiscal realities and student learning can, and probably will, have a devastating impact on colleges and universities.

How the educational delivery system undermines the quality of faculty work-life

Over the last 50 years, colleges and universities *have* made adjustments and changes in the face of difficult educational problems. There have been many evolving undergraduate academic reforms as colleges and universities have struggled with student attrition, the arrival of new generations of academically and demographically diverse students, and the explosive growth of new information technologies, among others. But these changes have not been fundamental; rather, the reforms have, with a few exceptions, maintained the traditional academic and financial structures, in which

educational quality is assumed to be determined by the nature of faculty and institutional resources, not what students have learned,

creditable student learning is thought to occur primarily – or solely – in classrooms with faculty members teaching groups of students; and courses in the USA continue to be taught primarily in semester or quarter time periods.

This educational delivery system – composed of courses, quarter or semester calendars and faculty teaching classes – is assumed to be unchangeable and has contributed to continuing increases in institutional costs. Further, because these academic structures have been maintained while costly new computer technologies and the necessary support infrastructure have been introduced, the escalation of expenses has been enormous.

The task for faculty and administrators at almost all colleges and universities is to deal with these pressures by reviewing and challenging the educational assumptions of their own institution. Present forces in higher education will either lead to significant reform in the undergraduate educational environment, or to a major diminution in the quality of faculty work-life resulting from sharp increases in faculty teaching loads and related work.

If the latter occurs, we will surely have the worst case possible – significant decreases in the quality of faculty work-life *and* in student learning.

As fiscal and political pressures increase, academic administrators will reach deeper and deeper into faculty positions to continue to maximize the financial flexibility and viability of their institutions. In the past, such pressures were met by increasing tuition fees beyond the growth of inflation, by deferring maintenance and cutting administrative and support staff and expense budgets. But each of these solutions has been or is becoming exhausted.

The present system limits our ability to reduce per student costs of education without major diminution in the work lives of faculty. This educational delivery system is based on two interlocking assumptions:

1. in order for students to learn they have to be grouped together in courses taught by faculty members; and
2. therefore, in order for a college or university to increase academic productivity (ie reduce per student costs), faculty members need to teach more courses or teach more students in their classes.

Short-term faculty hiring strategies

Many colleges and universities have had to develop short-term strategies to deal with financial stress in the last decade or so. Since little thought is given to fundamentally reforming the process by which education is delivered and there is significant pressure to maintain the present arrangements for existing faculty, the short-term strategies for dealing with the need to increase academic productivity tend to focus on hiring inexpensive faculty to serve the same (or an increasing) number of students with reduced resources. The strategy includes:

- hiring full-time non-tenure track faculty members who are expected to teach more classes per year, often at lower annual pay, rather than filling open positions with tenure track faculty;
- hiring part-time faculty members who teach individual classes at very low cost, rather than filling open positions with tenure track faculty.

The use of these two alternatives is reflected in the data presented in Table 3.1 based on the National Study of Postsecondary Faculty in 1987, 1992 and 1998. It shows that from 1987 to 1998 the number of full-time non-tenure track faculty more than doubled. At the same time, during this 11-year period there was a substantial *decrease* in tenure track faculty members (about 12 per cent or 12,000). This *reduction* in tenure-track faculty and *increase* in full-time non-tenure track faculty occurs across all institution types. Most of these data reflect the increasing number of faculty retirements and lack of replacement of vacated positions with tenure track faculty members. And, from all indications, this pattern is likely to continue.

Table 3.1   Distribution of full-time faculty from 1987, 1992 and 1998 in tenured, tenured track and non-tenured positions (does not include Community Colleges)

Tenure status	1987 (N = 397,443)	1992 (N = 393,723)	1998 (N = 423,329)	Change in % 1987 to 1998
Tenured	59%	56%	55%	−2
Tenure track	24%	24%	20%	−12
Non-tenure track	9%	13%	21%	+149
No tenure system	7%	8%	4%	

Source: This table was developed from data in the National Study of Postsecondary Faculty, 1987, 1992 and 1998. United States Department of Education, National Center for Educational Statistics.

In their recent book, Baldwin and Chronister (2001: 30) summarize the underlying issues:

> A host of external and internal forces is encouraging colleges and universities to rethink their staffing policies and patterns . . . Collectively, these factors have required colleges and universities to look at new ways to utilise limited resources more effectively to fulfil their multiple missions. As institutions try to cope with demands for greater account-ability and responsiveness, new technologies and competitors, and stri-dent criticism of the tenure system, faculty appointments off the tenure track have become increasingly attractive.

What seems apparent is that given the present financial strains and uncer-tainty about future fiscal resources, university leaders have considerable anxiety about the future of higher education. Since every thoughtful aca-demic administrator knows that laying off tenured faculty is not good for their professional health or that of their institution, the hiring on limited-term (2–3 year) contracts of inexpensive full-time non-tenure track faculty who have good academic credentials remains a desirable option. While this is not a happy solution for most institutions, or many of the faculty members hired, it does appear to solve immediate problems in a time of slow deterio-ration of the fiscal health of a college or university. These faculty members have lower salaries and, especially at research and doctoral universities, teach more classes than those on tenure track.

Fiscal pressures and the long-term impact on faculty

The assumption behind the short-term faculty hiring strategy is that present fiscal conditions will not get worse and are likely to get better. Therefore, at a minimum, the present balance between financial resources and costs must be maintained over time. However, this will be very difficult. On the cost side, there is every indication that without fundamental changes college and university costs will continue to increase beyond inflation – as they have done for many decades. On the financial resource side, colleges and universities will have to continue to increase their tuition beyond the level of annual inflation and receive increased funding beyond inflation levels from state and federal governments.

Neither seems likely. First, the pressure to reduce the rate of tuition increases has been growing for some time and is not likely to abate, nor will it be possible for many people to afford higher education if tuition continues to rise at too high a rate. Moreover, government support for higher education is not likely to exceed inflation given the intense competition with other public programmes. Hence, the combination of tax cuts and rebates, the predicted slowdown in the economy, state spending priorities and the inability of students to afford substantial increases in tuition will limit the financial resources available to both private and public colleges and universities.

Given the cost structure of higher education and the unavailability of adequate public and private funds, the short-term strategy of protecting the work of tenured and tenure track faculty and the status quo in educational practice by hiring inexpensive faculty is not a viable long-term solution. The tendency over time will be for universities to reduce faculty costs by not rehiring part-time and full-time non-tenure track faculty members. These actions will be consistent with the basic rationale for hiring most of these inexpensive faculty on limited-term contracts in the first place. For the most part, the policy was created *both* to immediately decrease faculty costs and to have the capability for dealing with future decreases in financial resources by terminating the services of those limited-term contract faculty, something that could not easily be done with tenured and tenure track faculty. By hiring short-term faculty, colleges and universities may have delayed this crisis, but they have not avoided it.

Faculty and the need for reform

The danger is that administrative and faculty leaders will continue to choose the short-term strategy in the next few years and will not heed the call for fundamental reform. In doing so, they will be following the common human tendency to avoid the difficulties and struggles of significant institutional change and take the path of least immediate pain. Quinn (1996: 5) dramatically sums up this tendency and its implications: 'Within our organisations, we have spent many years learning how to routinize and control things, how to build equilibrium [but] we are very unskilled at altering organisational structures that have outlived their usefulness . . .'.

When a system faces the challenge to make a deep change, individuals will usually create an alternative scenario. It is usually the scenario of the painless fix. It is an early stage on the road to slow death.

Over the next few years, the hope is that this tendency will be avoided and the short-term strategy of faculty hiring will be seen as part of a transitional period to significant reform, rather than as desirable practice for the long term. If used wisely, this transitional period of hiring full-time non-tenure track faculty could, as Baldwin and Chronister (2001: 30) write, 'buy institutions time and flexibility to respond to the diverse forces that are reshaping higher education'.

The message is clear: we must look carefully at how the education delivery system can be transformed to enable both faculty work-life and student learning to be enhanced. Except for the relatively small number of extremely wealthy colleges and universities, higher-education institutions and the faculty themselves face, at best, a very difficult future.

Transforming higher education: the joining together of faculty and institutional interests

To accept the present model of educating students and allowing the work-life of faculty to deteriorate serves no one's interests. Faculty will be dispirited by very heavy teaching loads that provide scant time for professional development or scholarship, as well as by a sense of insecurity about their future. In turn, as a result of low faculty morale and a burdensome teaching load, students will experience deterioration in the quality of education. The public will not be pleased with the learning environment students face and will intensify their demands for accountability.

However, there is a lever for creating significant changes in the role of faculty and the way student learning takes place while also dealing with institutional financial realities: the faculty themselves. If faculty realise that the present educational delivery system severely limits options for dealing with the future economic difficulties of their institutions and, therefore, will be the primary reason for undermining the quality of their work-life over the next decade and beyond, then there is hope that they will be open to the creation of new educational structures and processes.

Faculty resistance to change is quite reasonable if reform leads to a significant amount of disruption and pain without clarity on how the outcomes will benefit their professional work-life and the institution's educational goals. But the converse may also be true: linking a negative projected future to adherence to unchanging basic assumptions and institutional systems creates avenues for thinking anew about these issues. In these circumstances, faculty professional interests – that is protection of the quality of faculty work-life – can join with institutional interests (especially in the fiscal area) to help create the conditions for a fundamental change of the educational environment. With such openness and the availability of some viable models of fundamental reform, the faculty and administrative talent exist to create alternative faculty roles and new educational delivery systems that could enhance student learning while maintaining or enhancing the quality of faculty work-life.

Reform, students and the goals of undergraduate education

To this point, we have argued for fundamental reform, based on a confluence of both external and internal pressures, and the assumption that
our institutions have the capacity to respond creatively to these pressures.
Yet fundamental reform is meaningful only if it is able, in the process of
bringing about change, to maintain or enhance the core mission of colleges
and universities. We need, then, to envision the future of undergraduate
education by understanding the nature of our students and by affirming
our educational goals.

Most existing undergraduate educational models were formed decades
ago, and their underlying assumptions envisioned a very different student
from those we see today. While the model student around which we built
our educational delivery system and curriculum was assumed to be aged
18–22, in residence on campus, not employed outside of school, and orig-
inating from a particular educational, socio-economic and ethnic background, the reality of contemporary students is very different. Seventy-one
per cent of contemporary students are employed, an ever-increasing number
represent a diversity in background that is new to higher education,
and many have family responsibilities and fall outside the traditional age
range for undergraduates. They face more life pressures, and bring with
them a greater array of life experiences, than our original models ever
imagined.

While our students may look different from those our educational delivery
models anticipated, the basic *goals* of undergraduate education are still consistent with those we imagined a number of years ago. In an environment
that is placing such enormous pressures on colleges and universities to
fundamentally reform, it is necessary to maintain a clear focus on these
undergraduate educational goals. Without such a focus, there is a danger
that fundamental reforms can be undertaken which undermine an institution's educational integrity.

The general goals of undergraduate education, while not absolutely uniform across all campuses, are still generally consistent and familiar to most
who work in higher education. We attempt to develop students' abilities
to reason and think critically and analytically, to have effective written and
verbal communications skills, to be able to apply theory to practice and to
have a fundamental quantitative and scientific literacy, while understanding
some of the major forces that shape society. Students are expected to grow
personally and intellectually in college, develop an ability to work with a
wide range of people with differing perspectives, be cross-culturally sensitive
and have an appreciation for those who are ethnically or culturally different. With these personal and intellectual capacities, college graduates can
become contributing members of a diverse and democratic society.

Research and a good deal of thoughtful analyses give us a good indication of how we might succeed in reaching these goals: we are more likely to
succeed through small, intense, diverse, experienced-based programmes,

courses and activities that emphasize reflection, application and a close relationship to faculty members. The problem is, in too many cases, students do not experience this type of education. And, as indicated by the previous discussion of faculty workload and external pressures, the likelihood that students will not receive such an education will increase, unless we are able to fundamentally reform the ways in which we deliver undergraduate education.

To address these issues we need to explore the best existing ideas about the nature and practice of undergraduate education and ask a basic question: 'Given what we know and likely future social, technological and economic realities, if we were creating a college or university today, what would it look like?' To answer this question, we need to create educational models that incorporate the best existing conceptions, programmes and directions, while balancing the need for fiscal integrity with maintaining the quality of faculty work-life and enhancing student learning. In order to do this, we need to look beyond existing university structures and processes.

However, it is a challenge to move beyond well-worn responses to such big-picture questions. Rawls (1971) suggests that one means of imagining such new systems is for those creating the system to be ignorant of their eventual position within it – in this case, Rawls is imagining a just society. He invites us to create a society in which we do not know if we might be rich or poor, black or white, male or female, straight or gay, talented, average or below average. The result, he argues, would be a just system, because those creating the system might assume any place within society; everyone within the system would be treated fairly.

This is an intriguing method for visualizing the future of our colleges and universities. What would higher education look like if we envisioned new models for colleges and universities utilizing Rawls' device for envisioning change? Can we imagine that we might be a student, or a faculty member, or an administrator, or a member of an accreditation team, or a parent, or a legislator, or a member of the local community within one or another new model of undergraduate education? What would we want a college or university to look like if we were in any of these roles?

This is the framework being used by the Project on the Future of Higher Education, a grant-funded initiative at Antioch University which is co-directed by the authors of this chapter. While the Project is just beginning, the work on creating models for the undergraduate college and university of the future is already emerging. The Project has developed a consensus on the core assumptions about what will be essential in undergraduate education of the future. These assumptions include:

- *mission* – a focus on student learning and learning outcomes;
- *student learning environments and student learning processes*, which include diversity of learning environments, environments which value diverse communities and people, assessment through a demonstration of learning outcomes, learning from practice and technology;

- *new faculty roles* – aligning faculty rewards with roles that reflect a new academic professional (faculty and others involved in coaching and mentoring as well as new non-classroom learning); and
- *new structures* – remove traditional barriers, de-emphasize traditional structures (such as departments, divisions, schedules, calendars and credit hours) and emphasize fluidity and permeable boundaries.

With this framework of assumptions, the Project will work with creative thinkers and practitioners in higher education to discuss, write about and present to others potential models for the undergraduate college and university of the future. Essential to this process will be an evolving dialogue on the ideas and models generated, to create a vision for the future that builds on the success of higher education, while responding to the ever-increasing pressures we all face in the new century.

4

Balancing Excellence, Equity and Enterprise in a Less-industrialized Country: the Case of South Africa

Ian Scott

Introduction

The trends and driving forces prevailing in the developed world dominate international thinking on higher education. Under pressure from rapidly changing demands and limited capacity, 'less-industrialized' countries (LICs) are inclined to adopt first-world approaches and models without sufficient critical analysis (Subotzky 2001: 107), which carries a substantial risk of unforeseen consequences.

A case in point is the spread of enterprise in higher education in many developing countries, where public provision has been precipitately exposed to market forces and private provision has taken root. Equity and excellence, in their various manifestations, have long been the key contending challenges in higher education in LICs; the tension between them has had far-reaching socio-economic effects and is now being intensified by globalization. The emergence of enterprise as a significant force in higher education has added new dilemmas and possibilities. Balancing these forces in the interests of development should be a central challenge for policy makers and practitioners as the outcomes will affect the society at large and the life-chances of many individuals.

Every context is different, and South Africa has some particularly unusual features. It does, however, share key developmental issues and needs with other developing countries. This chapter is concerned with the educational rather than the knowledge-production function of higher education, and thus with its direct role in human resource development. Focusing on South Africa, the chapter (a) offers an interpretation, from an educational perspective, of some implications of the emerging forces of globalization and enterprise for higher education and its capacity to meet pressing developmental needs, (b) presents a view on key approaches required for meeting these needs, and (c) problematizes the role of enterprise in enabling higher education to fulfil its responsibilities.

The current position

Key factors affecting higher education in developing countries

Unsurprisingly, participation in higher education in LICs is lower than in developed countries: the average participation rate in middle-income countries is currently about 20 per cent as opposed to 40 per cent in high-income countries (Ministry of Education 2001: 2.2). While the value of such figures can be disputed, correlations between participation in higher education and economic development (Sadlak 1998) have persuaded a range of governments to see increasing participation as a priority.

There are, however, some significant obstacles to increasing participation that prevail particularly in LICs. Resource shortages combined with social inequalities result in only a narrow band of the population having access to effective secondary education. Consequently, a very small proportion of school-leavers are adequately prepared for direct entry to conventional higher-education programmes. This means that, to increase participation, the higher-education system must have the capacity to cater successfully for students who have potential but who are seriously disadvantaged and under-prepared for traditional higher education.[1] In other words, increasing participation beyond even a modest level means genuine *widening* of participation, with all the implications this has for provision and resources.

Widening participation entails accommodating diversity, which is now commonly seen as a desirable goal in its own right. However, while cultural and intellectual diversity is clearly enriching, the same cannot be said of diversity in the quality of prior learning and thus in preparedness for higher education, which is instead a major problem and obstacle to equity.

In South Africa, these problems are sharpened by the fact that its socio-economic disparities still run largely along racial lines. The transition to democracy has been achieved politically and a small proportion of black people have advanced rapidly, but for the majority, access to education that makes a significant difference to life-chances has not materialized.

Inequalities and resource shortages are not confined to the developing world, but they occur in many LICs on a scale that is unfamiliar to advanced countries, and fundamentally affect higher education. In South Africa, the persistence of historical-educational disparities has been central to the under-performance of the higher-education sector as a whole and the continuation of skewed patterns of access, participation and success. Socio-economic inequalities are set to remain a key factor affecting development.

While the problem of educational disadvantage is commonly seen as a failing of the school system, in the South African context it is not justifiable or productive for higher education to decline to share responsibility for addressing it. Apart from the fact that the parameters of the system were shaped by apartheid, deep-rooted problems in schooling mean that the student intake will continue to be inadequate unless higher education arranges its own structures in order to enlarge the pool of entrants, as discussed later.

The tension between equity and excellence

Particularly because of endemic resource shortages, higher education in LICs has experienced a chronic tension between equity and excellence or, in current policy terms, between widening participation and quality and standards. These challenges have been the two main contending forces in South African higher education in the transition to democracy, and managing the tension between them is continuing to be a key developmental dilemma.

On one hand, after a lengthy period of semi-isolation from global economic forces, there has been rapidly growing pressure to 'open' and modernize the economy and for higher education to deliver provision that is rigorous, efficient, appropriate for contemporary conditions, and of an 'internationally comparable' standard. On the other hand, redress of historical racial inequalities is vital for stability and progress. Government has classified equity and redress as a 'fundamental principle' that should guide the development of higher education (Republic of South Africa 1997a: 1.6).

It is important to recognize that a range of interpretations of 'equity' have arisen, including, in Subotzky's (2001: 100) formulation, 'equity as parity and formal equality versus equity as the transformative recognition of difference – the principled basis for redistribution'. Higher education has been perceived as vital for individual advancement, and access to it has carried high stakes for youth in impoverished communities. This led in the early 1990s to radical 'equity of access' demands from black youth, and consequently to uncontrolled growth in several institutions, with the great majority of the new students being seriously under-prepared. The pressure this put on resources and standards brought the equity–excellence tension into sharp relief, and was the context in which Wolpe et al. (1993) made a major conceptual contribution in their analysis of the relationship between 'equality' and 'development'.

There are also differing conceptions of 'development' in South Africa, in respect of both compass (economic, social, cultural) and focus (on 'global competitiveness' or local 'redistributive reconstruction and development') (Subotzky 2001: 107). The tension between equity and globally orientated development is similar to the tension between equity and excellence.

Notwithstanding the theoretical debates, equity and excellence (and hence development in its 'global' sense) have in practice been treated as independent, usually competing, goals. Traditional concepts of academic excellence, along with teaching practices predicated on a traditionally well-prepared student intake, have remained the central driving force or aspiration across the system. By contrast, the wide range of equity-orientated initiatives that have spread across the system since the early 1980s – originally in opposition to apartheid policy – have largely remained on the margins of mainstream provision, financed predominantly from donated or non-recurrent funds.

At national level, although the importance of equity in higher education has been clearly acknowledged since the democratic transition and government has committed itself to funding equity-orientated provision, the policy has remained largely 'symbolic' (Subotzky 2001: 108). While it is core policy to convert the higher-education sector into a planned and integrated system, deregulation has in fact come first. Racial categorization has been removed, but not the historical disparities. Ironically, the continuing absence of an effective quality-assurance system has strengthened perceptions of conflict between equity and excellence as mistrust between institutions and of alternative programmes goes unchecked. Substantive policy and actionable strategies for balancing equity and development have not yet been put in place.

The emergence of enterprise in higher education in South Africa

The local policy environment in the mid-1990s, when enterprise emerged as a significant force in higher education in South Africa, was one where old forms of regulation were disappearing while the new, post-apartheid policy framework was still being formulated. In fact, the conditions that fostered the growth of enterprise in both its manifestations – that is entrepreneurialism in public higher-education institutions and the spread of private higher education – came about more as a result of broad national developments and macro-economic policy than a widely debated, carefully formulated development strategy on the part of the education authorities.

In 1996 the National Commission on Higher Education supported the expansion of private provision, in the interests of widening participation at low cost to the state, but recommended that legislating this be deferred until effective planning and quality-assurance systems could be established (National Commission on Higher Education 1996: 163). However, the right to establish 'independent educational institutions' was established in the new South African constitution in the same year (Republic of South Africa 1996: 29(3)) as part of the negotiated political settlement, and a rudimentary legal framework for private higher education was accordingly provided in the 1997 Higher Education Act (Republic of South Africa 1997b).

While there had been a long history of private provision in some areas of post-secondary education, it was marginalized and offered mainly commercial certificates and diplomas (Mabizela 2001). After 1996, however, there was a mushrooming of private providers, ranging from foreign universities and substantial for-profit companies to single-owner operations with dubious capacity. Reliable data on size are not available: enrolment was at one stage estimated at up to 500,000 a year (Cloete and Bunting 2000: 26). Of the (approximately) 90 private institutions registered in the first wave (there are currently 36 public universities and technikons), the great majority concentrate on basic (usually sub-degree) business-related programmes.

Rapid growth in entrepreneurialism in some public institutions occurred in this same environment and period, stimulated by decreasing state funding as well as opportunities presented by the partial vacuum in policy and regulation. In the 1990s some institutions (notably historically white Afrikaans-medium universities) achieved extraordinary enrolment growth through distance-education programmes, partnerships with private providers, and the acquisition of satellite campuses (such as former Teacher Education Colleges) offering basic business and education qualifications (Cooper and Subotzky 2001: 36–9 and 78–81). In so doing, the institutions made good use of South Africa's current higher-education funding formula, which rewards overall growth without reference to agreed targets.

Being essentially unregulated in extent, shape and quality, the 'enterprise-related' growth in private and public institutions raised concerns about the protection of the public interest, and government placed a moratorium on the expansion of distance provision by contact institutions, pending further consideration of policy. It has subsequently restricted public–private partnerships.

The rise of entrepreneurialism has clearly had consequences that were not intended by the policy makers. Growth in enterprise-related provision shows that there is demand that traditional public provision is not meeting. However, it is debatable whether the way in which the demand is being met is in the long-term public interest. Critical assessment of the implications of enterprise for equity, excellence and development is essential, as is discussed later.

Current patterns of access, participation and output

The current performance and outputs of the higher-education sector can provide a summative assessment of the effectiveness of existing structures, approaches and policies. Some key indicators are as follows.

• *Overall participation in public higher education* – South Africa's gross participation rate was 15 per cent in 2000, compared with an average of 20 per cent for comparable middle-income countries (Ministry of Education 2001: 2.2). While the comparability of participation rates is problematic, government recognizes that overall participation is inadequate.

- *Secondary–tertiary articulation* – there are too few people who meet the traditional entry requirements for higher education. In recent years, in a population of 40 million, fewer than 80,000 school-leavers have achieved the statutory minimum university entry requirements annually, and only about 20,000 have met the minimum mathematics requirement for admission to good-quality science, engineering and technology programmes (Ministry of Education 2001: 2.1.2).
- *Efficiency rates* – the sector is characterized by poor throughput and completion rates, particularly in 'numerate' fields and among students from disadvantaged backgrounds (Council on Higher Education 2000; Ministry of Education 2001: 2.1.2–3). The wastage of human and material resources involved is recognized as a major obstacle to equity and development.
- *Participation and output patterns* – higher-education participation and outputs remain severely skewed in terms of race (and social class) and fields of study (Cooper and Subotzky 2001). There is disproportionately low enrolment in science, engineering and technology. While there were major overall increases in black participation during the 1990s, much of the growth was in 'soft' fields where there is no shortage of graduates. The under-representation of black people (and in some cases women) in science, engineering and technology or professional and graduate programmes is both a socio-political problem and the main contributor to the 'endemic shortage of high-level professional and managerial skills . . . [particularly] in the science and economic-based fields . . . in which future demand is likely to be the greatest' (National Commission on Higher Education 1996: 2, Ministry of Education 2001: 2.1.1).
- *Quality and standards* – there are major concerns about differentials in quality and output standards across the sector, and whether graduates are acquiring appropriate skills. In the absence of a mature national quality-assurance system, deficiencies and prejudices cannot be addressed, to the detriment of equity and development.

It is fair to conclude from such indicators that there is not enough excellence or equity in the higher-education sector, and this means there is not a firm enough base for meeting contemporary demands. Given the pressure for development, it is essential to improve output through concrete action based on clear goals. The following section offers a view on what the broad goals should be.

What is most needed from higher education in South Africa?

Changing demands on higher education in LICs

The increasing significance of higher education in enabling any country to be competitive in the global economy is common cause. The effects of the shift to the knowledge economy and economic globalization on the 'North–South' divide have become an international issue, and differential capacity to produce and retain people with relevant high-level skills is increasingly recognized as a major cause of the widening gap between developed and developing countries.

Economic globalization is thus placing LICs under increasing pressure to improve their production of highly skilled personnel in terms of quantity, quality and appropriateness for contemporary conditions, or risk falling further behind in international competitiveness. In South Africa – with its troubled history, its own wide gap between rich and poor, and its consequent vulnerability to social conflict – it is vital to develop a modern economy in which the majority of the population can participate. Higher education clearly has a collective responsibility to deliver the quantity and kinds of graduates needed, which, alongside knowledge production, must be its essential contribution to development. The state, for its part, must be accountable for establishing the conditions in which higher education can fulfil its responsibilities.

National development as the central goal

Analysts have shown that, in the turbulent post-apartheid period, South African higher-education policy-making has had to hold conflicting imperatives (particularly equity and development) in tension, and has achieved this by keeping key commitments at the symbolic level (Subotzky 2001: 109), resulting in a system 'with no clear direction and without a major policy-driver' (Cloete and Bunting 2000: 79). If policy remains symbolic or fragmented, there will not be a sound basis for meeting key contemporary challenges. What is needed in the first instance is an overarching goal and 'a clear statement of the problem which the policy is designed to remedy' (Brown 2001).

Establishing a viable place in the global economy is of such importance to the future of South Africa (and other LICs) that national development – particularly in the sense of building international competitiveness – should be accepted as the central goal for the higher-education system at this juncture. This is not to suggest an exclusive focus on economic development or that other social goals are not important, but rather to contend that the progressive marginalization and impoverishment likely to result from failing to find a viable place in the global order would severely impede all forms of development.

The performance of the higher-education system is showing that it is not effective to treat forces like excellence, equity and enterprise as independent issues. Excellence will always have intrinsic value, but will mean little for the country as a whole if it exists only in isolated enclaves. Equity in participation in higher education will be an empty achievement unless the education gained brings real benefit to the individual and the society.

Enterprise is not an end in itself, but of value insofar as it is a means to meeting developmental goals. National development, although a broad concept, can currently provide a defensible and unifying goal against which substantive policies and plans can reasonably be assessed.

If national development is the central goal, the 'statement of the problem' is that the graduate output of higher education is deficient in quality and appropriateness as well as quantity, and is not meeting essential needs. This is the central problem as it is the output that makes the difference to development. It follows that improving graduate output in line with developmental needs should be the central policy-driver (and the focus of resources) for the educational function of higher education.

Output goals for higher education

What the goal of national development should demand from higher education in terms of specific output is not simple to determine, particularly in view of the failings of human-resources planning. However, there are certain clear deficiencies in capacity that severely impede development. Analysis of these needs can readily generate a cluster of high-level output goals to guide operational policy. Various goals have been identified by different analysts (for example Cloete and Bunting 2000) and in the Ministry's National Plan for Higher Education (Ministry of Education 2001). Given the developmental needs, the core goals should be the following:

- a steady increase in successful overall participation;
- sound quality and 'internationally comparable' standards in all programmes;
- a substantial increase in the number and proportion of graduates with 'high-level professional and managerial skills . . . [particularly] in the science and economics-based fields' (Ministry of Education 2001: 2.1.1);
- progress towards representivity in all main fields, particularly science, engineering and technology and professional programmes, not just as an end in itself but as a key to sustainable growth; and
- ensuring that graduates are adequately prepared to function effectively in the knowledge society, which has major implications for curricula and the ethos of institutions.

Output goals at this level of generality may seem self-evident and simplistic, but collectively they are critical for development, and can be used to generate strong criteria for assessing policy options. Goals of this kind are present in current policy documents, but are unfortunately not clearly prioritized or distinguished from a multiplicity of other goals that should be seen as a means towards improving output rather than ends in themselves. Moreover, it has to be recognized that although these broad goals are individually not new, the system is not showing any significant progress towards achieving them. This indicates the presence of underlying systemic flaws, which will continue to undermine outcomes until they are identified and corrected. The real challenge, then, is to identify the key obstacles to progress, and to develop concrete, implementable approaches to overcoming them. A view of some essential developmental requirements is given below.

In evaluating policy options, it is also important to be clear about what must be avoided. In current circumstances, in South Africa and other LICs, a temptation to be resisted is sacrificing quality, standards and relevance for the appearance of equity, particularly through accrediting qualifications that lack real substance or utility. In the context of globalization, this could only have negative consequences for competitiveness.

What will it take to achieve the output needed for development?

Implications for the relationship between equity and development

Since globalization is increasing pressure on LICs to improve higher-education performance in terms of both quantity and quality, there is need for fresh thinking on the tension between equity and development.

The performance of the South African system indicates that treating equity and development as separate goals will not produce the higher-education outputs needed. There are two key considerations. First, the pool of traditionally well-prepared students is far too small to provide for the required graduate output. Second, as long-standing performance patterns show, the traditional curriculum structures and teaching approaches in use are not effective for the great majority of students from disadvantaged backgrounds, who are under-prepared for conventional higher-education programmes. Consequently, as long as current educational approaches prevail, output growth can be achieved only at the expense of efficiency and essential standards. The apartheid legacy is such that there is a low probability of significant improvement in the output of pre-tertiary education (see Cloete and Bunting 2000: 13), leading Jansen (2001: 5) to assert: 'It is clear to most analysts that participation rates will not increase even in the medium- to long-term.' Unsurprisingly, the shortages of well-prepared candidates are most acute in the fields where there is most need for growth.

Achieving the outputs needed for national development therefore depends on the system's capacity to cater successfully for students from disadvantaged backgrounds. South Africa's two decades of experience with equity-related educational development programmes has strongly affirmed that, with appropriate forms of provision, 'talented but disadvantaged' students can succeed in higher education. The demands of globalization are now calling for these equity-related approaches to be recognized and utilized as key means of improving graduate output. In these circumstances, progress with equity is not in competition with development goals but is integral to meeting them.

Without effective use of equity-related approaches, then, it will not be possible to successfully widen participation or improve representivity. Such approaches are also necessary for pursuing the other key goals, namely quality, relevance and changing the 'shape' of the output, as discussed below.

Focusing on the educational process in higher education: the need for systemic solutions

The challenge of developing latent talent, particularly in disadvantaged communities, is a central one for the third world as a whole, intensified by globalization. Educational development work in South African higher education has produced substantial evidence that the generally poor performance of students from disadvantaged groups is not due to shortage of talent, but has much to do with the incapacity of the existing higher-education structures and approaches to cater for diverse educational backgrounds. Similarly, many disadvantaged students who might succeed never enter higher education because standard selection methods see only achieved performance rather than potential, or in Miller's words 'predict the past' (1992: 101).

Structural problems are at the heart of the shortcomings of the educational process in South African higher education. The curriculum framework exemplifies this. The basic curriculum structures used by the universities were established before the Second World War. The assumptions underlying these structures – particularly about students' prior learning – were naturally normed on a relatively elite and homogeneous student intake. While the intake has subsequently undergone major changes, particularly in terms of diversity in background and preparedness, no corresponding flexibility has been introduced in fundamental parameters such as entry level, duration and expected rate of progression. There are substantial variations between programmes in selectivity, difficulty and status (which tend to cluster disadvantaged students in lower-status courses) but the lack of structural flexibility *within* programmes is, in practice, a major obstacle to access and success for disadvantaged students (Scott 1995). This applies especially in the most selective science, engineering and technology and professional fields, where there is most need for representivity and growth.

One far-reaching outcome of this structural problem is that many disadvantaged students experience a debilitating 'articulation gap' between their prior learning and higher education, a result of which is that they never develop sound academic foundations. This has a pervasive effect, being a primary cause of mediocre performance, inability to progress to graduate studies, or outright failure, all of which tend to reinforce racial stereotypes. Poor foundations also have a particularly negative effect on kinds of learning that are most valuable in the information society, namely a strong conceptual base, problem-solving and research skills – in general, the capacity for learning-to-learn.

By contrast, since their introduction in the 1980s, educational-development programmes that circumvent the rigidity of traditional curricula have enabled many disadvantaged students to succeed in higher education. The key to effectiveness is substantial additional provision of a foundational nature, offered in the universities and technikons and closely articulated with the mainstream courses concerned. This design provides, in effect, an extended curriculum, one or two semesters longer than the traditional version, that offers differential entry levels and directly addresses the articulation gap and related obstacles to the quality of learning. Given the iterative relationship between curriculum and student selection, extended curriculum programmes also enable many 'talented but disadvantaged' students who do not meet traditional entry requirements to be responsibly admitted to full degree programmes. Initiatives of this kind are successfully used in science, engineering and technology in particular, and, by improving both access and success rates, have produced a high proportion of the black graduates in these key fields.

While the effectiveness of educational development programmes has been acknowledged up to government level (Ministry of Education 2001: 2.3.2), they are still commonly treated as supplementary provision, as if they were needed only for small numbers of students on the margins of the intake. This is not acceptable in the LIC context, where educational disadvantage is not a minority issue. Successful widening of participation calls for equity-related approaches such as extended curricula to be incorporated as integral elements of mainstream provision.

In theory, diversity in preparedness can be accommodated by institutional differentiation, a direction that various countries, following the United States, appear to be taking. This policy option is the topic of a major debate in South Africa, which is outside the scope of this chapter. In addition to the binary divide, *de facto* institutional differentiation already exists owing to apartheid inequalities. Some degree of differentiation is inevitable, and a positive form of 'complementary' or mission differentiation could no doubt be productive. Statutory differentiation, however, runs the major risk of entrenching stratification, to the detriment of development as well as equity. If stratification is not curbed, there is the prospect of the great majority of students from disadvantaged communities being consigned to under-resourced community colleges and, in conditions where student mobility is impeded by institutional inequalities, forced to go via sub-degree courses and additional selection filters if they are to progress to substantial qualifications. The problems of stratification can be much reduced if existing institutions improve their capacity to accommodate diversity through flexibility in the curriculum framework of individual programmes.

The importance of 'educational fundamentals' in higher education

What all of this points to is the centrality of fundamental elements of the educational process – such as curriculum structures, articulation and forms of delivery – in determining the outcomes of the higher-education system, and who benefits. On the analogy of Biggs's (1999) theory of 'constructive alignment', ensuring that these fundamentals are well aligned with conditions and needs in a given context is an essential condition for optimizing output. Public policy and attention habitually focus on high-profile features of the system, such as governance, institutional categorization or student financial aid, yet it is the character of the educational process that principally shapes the performance of the system and hence its contribution to national development. Where output is unsatisfactory, reorganizing the superstructure of the system will not help much if the educational process remains flawed. Given the importance of higher-education output for development, ensuring the fitness for purpose of the educational process should be the primary policy aim.

While the arguments for reform of traditional structures and approaches in higher education may be recognized by government, shortages of human and material resources, along with the demands of day-to-day management of a system in transition, limit the capacity of the state to take responsibility for all the necessary changes in provision. A key question, then, is to what extent enterprise, as the major new force in higher education, can be harnessed to meet critical output goals, in the interests of national development.

The potential of enterprise to meet key higher-education goals

Arguments in favour of promoting enterprise in higher education, particularly through sanctioning private higher education, have focused on expanding access and choice, increasing responsiveness and relevance, and filling gaps in standard public provision.

However, the experience of enterprise in South African higher education in the 1990s has raised significant concerns. While the spread of short vocational courses offered by private providers no doubt met a need, a high proportion of the enterprise-generated growth in the public and private sectors was in sub-degree programmes in education and 'soft' business-related fields, which are not priorities. The concerns about quality and unplanned growth that led to the government moratorium on certain forms of entrepreneurial activity presumably arose mainly because of the lack of regulatory mechanisms. In any event, enterprise in this period clearly fulfilled its income-generating purpose but, by reproducing undesirable output patterns, evidently contributed little to development or equity in the full sense.

Besides this experience, there are some factors embedded in the LIC context that raise reservations about the potential of enterprise and market forces to help meet the central challenges for higher education, particularly the following.

- *Enabling disadvantaged students to realize their potential* – The kind of intensive foundational provision that is needed to foster the long-term development of disadvantaged students is resource-intensive and not lucrative, and the students concerned are often the least able to pay fees. Expanding this form of provision is, however, among the system's greatest needs.
- *Improving quality and appropriateness* – The provision required for this demands greater staff capacity and is more expensive than traditional provision. Elite private institutions could doubtless match or surpass public institutions in this, but private institutions in developing countries are unlikely to be Harvards.
- *Changing 'shape'* – The programmes in which growth is most needed are often the most expensive to mount. Entrepreneurialism has most commonly targeted programmes that are popular and inexpensive to run.

This brief analysis points to a tension between the short-term revenue-generating purpose of enterprise and the need to invest in long-term development. There is a particular concern in South Africa that aggressive entrepreneurialism in the private sector and a few public institutions could draw in a disproportionate share of profitable programmes and fee-paying students, leaving the core development and equity responsibilities to the remaining public institutions while at the same time reducing their resources. The only core goal that such unregulated enterprise might successfully meet would be increasing overall participation, which has limited value in itself.

Analysis of the policy options will need to consider why positive features of higher education enterprise that some (for example Clark 1998) have identified in the first world might or might not apply in LIC contexts. As a start, it is important to acknowledge that key contextual variations – in factors such as general educational attainment, levels of consumer sophistication and protection, state regulatory ability and the capacity of the economy to absorb a widening range of (especially non-essential service) occupations – may make for significantly different outcomes. As there are long lead-times in establishing the value and utility of education, reliance on market forces and a *caveat emptor* approach carry high risks for countries where there is no room for wastage of resources.

Despite the caveats, enterprise can clearly not be dismissed as a powerful force in higher education in South Africa.[2] Local experience and reflection suggest that there are two key conditions for maximizing the positive effects of enterprise. First, there needs to be an effective framework of state regulation that aligns with the core goals of higher education. Extending regulation would appear to be contrary to world trends but it should be recognized that basic statutory and collegial regulatory mechanisms

– particularly relating to quality, accreditation and consumer protection – are taken for granted in developed countries but are not in place in many LICs. Second, incentives must be created for enterprise to manifest itself in innovation, in creative approaches to meeting core goals, rather than in pursuing income-generation primarily through 'more-of-the-same' provision. These conditions would be fostered by, inter alia:

> prioritising the improvement of the educational process in public higher education, to set benchmarks for the system; this should be the first call on public resources; establishing accreditation and quality assurance approaches that focus on outcomes; providing financial incentives for enterprise initiatives – in private and public institutions – that are linked to value-adding and shape targets.

Conclusion

The challenges for higher education in South Africa and other developing countries appear daunting, yet it is probably more important now than ever before that the system should live up to its responsibilities. Facilitating this will require a holistic view and willingness to see excellence, equity and enterprise in relation to overall national priorities. In particular, efforts to 'transform' higher education should go beyond high-profile organizational features, and recognize that the fundamental educational process is a major determinant of the outcomes of the system, and consequently deserves to be a key focus of energy and resources.

Notes

1. The term 'disadvantaged' may be regarded by some as undesirable labelling. In South Africa, however, the expression 'disadvantaged students' is widely used to refer to people whose preparedness for higher education has been (seriously) negatively affected by structural inequalities in schooling.
2. Apart from provision for private higher education in the South African constitution, it is possible that education will be defined as a service under World Trade Organization agreements, which would greatly limit the state's ability to control private higher education.

5

Enterprise Culture, Equity and Gendered Change in Commonwealth Higher Education

Louise Morley, Elaine Unterhalter and Anne Gold[1]

The chapter considers whether the growth of an enterprise culture in higher education in selected Commonwealth countries has eclipsed or promoted equity discourses. Enterprise culture is linked with transformations of state welfarism in higher education, new approaches to state funding, the acknowledgement of new competitive markets and the shift from concerns with production to consumption in policy-making. The chapter examines some of the contradictions involved in the introduction of markets and enterprise culture in higher education. For example, while there has been some expansion of access for women and other historically under-represented groups, new formations and management processes, such as borderless universities and quality assurance, tend to universalize participants and overlook power relations both within and outside higher-education institutions. In particular, discourses surrounding the location and experience of women in Commonwealth higher education have tended to be silenced or marginalized.

The chapter also draws attention to the paradox that increased democratization and sustainable equity strategies in the wider society generally have not accompanied greater access to higher education. For example, quantitative change in higher education is not necessarily accompanied by a redistribution of material, social, economic and political rights. Nor are there significant qualitative organizational changes that take account of social justice. In conclusion, we examine the conditions under which equity and enterprise may be able to co-exist through a closer theorization of both aspects of justice and the nature of markets.

The chapter draws on a review of published and semi-published literature in this field. Our intention is to begin a dialogue across different bodies of literature in order to enrich the examination of issues relating to gender and higher education in high-, middle- and low-income countries. The methods we have used are standard literature search techniques. We used a range of bibliographic tools, both text and web based, to identify writing and datasets in the field of gender and higher education. In addition, we wrote to 30 researchers, writers or project directors in this field requesting assistance in identifying literature.[2] Major themes and trends were analysed in the literature and the datasets. Significant gaps were also noted. While the writing and statistical information surveyed is extensive, it is not comprehensive, as we have used only secondary literature and published compilations of statistics. In addition, because much of the writing in this area is grey, or semi-published, there is still a considerable task to complete, which involves identifying material on gender and higher education held at a local level.

Policy drivers for change

Commonwealth higher education has changed over the last 10 years in response to changes in the political economy and the emergence of new discourses. Throughout the Commonwealth, higher-education institutions have been key organizations legitimating state authority. They fulfilled this role initially in the guise of establishing practices that equipped rulers to rule. They inducted elite groups into prevailing ideas of citizenship, enabling them to enact the ways in which civil, political and social rights were to be interpreted (Marshall 1992). As pivotal institutions, universities influenced the professional development, values and knowledge bases of a range of public- and private-sector employees. Writing on Kenya, Manya (2000) observes that African universities were established to nurture an African male elite, who would make possible a politics of independence that could relate well with the concerns of Europeans. Surveying African universities generally in the early 1990s, Ade Ajayi et al. (1996) saw these as bastions of knowledge, guardians of the future and an indispensable tool of development. This conception raised no questions regarding whose knowledge was to be protected, whose future guarded and how development was to be defined, and by whom.

New formations of the university

These confident assertions of state-led development through a form of higher education, with many links to British models, came under scrutiny in the 1990s. An aspect of enterprise culture has been that the concept of the university is changing. With the development of e-learning, lifelong learning and the learning society, the university is no longer a place, but a space. Within the Commonwealth, as elsewhere, new competitions, markets and new sites of learning, including the workplace and the community, are emerging. The enterprise culture and the rapid expansion of private education are providing opportunities and threats. Internationally, private higher education is 'one of the most dynamic and fastest-growing segments of postsecondary education at the turn of the 21st century' (Altbach 1999: 1). The University of Phoenix (based in the United States) now has over 40,000 students in 25 different countries, many in Commonwealth countries (Manicas 1998). Sadlak (1998) estimates that there are approximately 300 colleges and universities offering virtual degrees with a total of more than a million students online. In countries and regions where governments are unable to provide sufficient funding for higher education, such as Sub-Saharan Africa, private education and distance learning are flourishing.

This explosion is accompanied by a conceptual shift that suggests that higher education is a private, rather than a public good (Singh 2001). Higher education is being more overtly opened up to market forces. On the one hand, this could be a healthy challenge to archaic state monopolies. On the other hand, it could reinforce class privileges and elitism. The expansion of private education and the growth of distance education travelling from the west to lower-income countries are sometimes new forms of colonialism. The inclusion of lower-income countries in the new global reach of powerful western universities is more linked to exploitation of market opportunities than a concern with democratization and enhanced participation rates of previously excluded groups and communities. In this market discourse, the social identity of the purchaser of private education is left untheorized. In borderless education, there is a disembodied representation of purchasers and providers of the higher-educational product.

There is a context to the emergence of these new forms of university globalization. The enormous expansion of information communication technologies (ICT) throughout the 1990s began to change both the world economy and the place of higher-education institutions in that economy. As Castells (2000) points out, the emergence of a network society and the importance of information flow in that society provided new openings and challenges for higher education. Commentators in low- and middle-income countries have begun to document the complexity of the processes entailed in engaging with Castells' vision (Yates and Bradley 2000, Muller, Cloete and Badat 2001). Many highlight how some women, particularly those with higher levels of education, have become the beneficiaries of the new political economy (Mitter and Rowbotham 1997, Rathberger and Adela 2000). In this context, the policy climate some Commonwealth countries (notably Malaysia, South Africa and India) have encouraged increased enrolment in higher education in order to underpin increased international competitiveness.

Yet the network society does not hold out an unambiguous promise for higher-education institutions. Globalization also presents threats to nation states, still the major funder and policy maker in higher education. These threats cohere around the untrammelled competition inaugurated under the regime of the World Trade Organization and limits on key areas of state sovereignty. A consequence of this new context can be a decline in national resources for higher education. Often the growth of enterprise cultures in higher education are attempts to make up for a decline in the real value of state subsidy, management's inability to fund increases in staff pay or the expansion of resources as the economic downside of globalization bites.

The context of globalization and changing forms of higher education in the 1990s was extremely complex. While the conditions were excellent for corporate growth, an international agenda on poverty eradication and an expansion of human rights also emerged supported by powerful West European governments and influential Commonwealth countries, such as South Africa, Nigeria and Canada (Klug 2000, Fine et al. 2001). Side by side with this came a growth of international concern with good governance and the accountability of the state sector. As international opinion swung away from neo-liberalism and free-market economics, a consensus emerged on the importance of the state, possibly in partnership with other providers, for the delivery of health, education and social welfare. Higher-education institutions were included in a discourse of accountability and good govern-ance, and often compelled into regimes that scrutinized their practice as a condition for the receipt of state grants.

One outcome of the new policy agenda was an attempt to build interna-tional consensus on rights and higher education. UNESCO hosted the first World Conference on Higher Education in Paris in 1998. Representatives of 182 countries endorsed the *World Declaration on Higher Education for the Twenty First Century: Vision and Action* with its commitment to in-depth reform of higher education throughout the world. Article Four of the Declaration is specifically concerned with gender (UNESCO 1998). The UNESCO con-ference had been preceded by concern within the Commonwealth on this issue. The under-representation of women in Commonwealth universities was seen by the Commonwealth Secretariat (1994) as a human-rights issue and one the most important issues facing universities. Discursive links started to occur between poverty and access to higher education (Makhubu 1998).

Thus, on the one hand, in the era of enterprise culture the university has been viewed as ungendered, a site for knowledge to serve national interests and ungendered notions of the network society. In this guise, it was open to quantitative change primarily with regard to the inclusion of some formerly excluded groups. On the other hand, the university was viewed as an insti-tution complicit with the social divisions of the society, but nonetheless open to qualitative change and transformations concerning gendered and other forms of inequity. In the next section we identify how both these themes emerge in writings on gender and higher education in the era of enterprise culture.

The access agenda

Enhancing access and participation has been a powerful policy objective throughout the Commonwealth. It is linked to economic rationales and those of democratization and social inclusion. It invariably takes the form

Table 5.1   Female students in higher education as a percentage of all higher education students in India and South Africa, 1980–98

	1980	1985	1990	1994	1997
India (% students who are female)	26.7	33.0	33.3	34.0	34.8

	1980	1988	1990	1995	1998
South Africa (% of students who are female)	35	45.0	48	49	55.0

Sources: Swainson 1991, Seager 1997, Government of India 1998, Cooper and Subotzky 2001, UNESCO 2001

of a small expansion of places to members of under-represented groups (sometimes on a quota system). In Britain there is a government objective to expand the age participation rate to 50 per cent by the year 2010 (Higher Education Funding Council for England 2001). In this policy context, the emphasis is on representation of students from lower socio-economic groups. As women currently constitute over 50 per cent of the undergraduate population, gender is not perceived as a priority category. Furthermore, in the first burst of expansion in the early 1990s, when participation rocketed from 15 to 30 per cent, a major new market was that of mature women. Ironically, 'New Right' legislation in Britain, based on an ideological commitment to markets and the enterprise culture, produced a more significant demographic shift in higher education than three decades of equity legislation (Morley 1997). However, questions can be posed about whether the inclusion of this new group was a result of a commitment to equity and democratization or the exploitation of a profitable new market. Elsewhere in the Commonwealth, there has also been gendered change in terms of enhanced access, as Tables 5.1–5.5 demonstrate.

There has been a significant increase in the numbers of women who enrol as students in higher education and the gender gap has either not increased significantly or has declined in all parts of the Commonwealth. Table 5.1 documents this increase in two Commonwealth countries that experienced significant political and economic change in the 1990s, India and South Africa.

It can be seen that in both countries there has been a significant increase in the proportion of women students over the last 20 years. The trend for expanded participation by women in higher education is evident worldwide, even though there are considerable differences in levels of participation between high- and low-income countries.

Table 5.2 shows there are significant differences in the gross enrolment ratio in higher education (that is the proportion of the age group 18–30 enrolled in tertiary-level institutions) between developed and developing countries, but in both locations the proportion of women under the age of 30 in higher education has increased significantly more than the proportion of men. While in 'developing' countries there is a lower proportion of women

Table 5.2 Trends in tertiary gross-enrolment ratios by country group and gender, 1980–95

	1980	1995	Relative change (%)*
Developed			
Males	36.2	47.6	31.5
Females	36.2	54.7	51.1
Developing			
Males	6.7	10.4	55.2
Females	3.7	7.2	100
Sub-Saharan Africa			
Males	2.5	4.6	84.0
Females	0.7	2.5	257

* The difference between 1995 and 1980 calculated as a percentage of the 1980 ratio.
Source: Katjavivi 2000

Table 5.3 Tertiary gross enrolment ratio by gender: Africa

Country	1987 male	1987 female	Gap in 1987	1996 male	1996 female	Gap in 1996	Change between 1987 and 1996
Mozambique	0.3	0.1	0.2	0.7	0.2	0.5	0.3
Tanzania	0.5	0.1	0.4	0.9	0.2	0.7	0.3
Lesotho	1.2	1.8	−0.6	2.2	2.6	−0.4	0.2
Uganda	1.3	0.5	0.8	2.6	1.3	1.3	0.5
Botswana	2.6	2.2	0.4	6.1	5.5	0.6	0.2
Mauritius	1.8	1.2	0.6	7.7	6.1	1.6	1
Zimbabwe	6.5	2.4	4.1	9.4	3.9	5.5	1.4

Source: UNESCO 2001

of the relevant age group in higher education, compared to men, there have still been enormous increases in the proportion of women, although admittedly from a very low base. Even in Sub-Saharan Africa, where there are huge gender gaps in primary and secondary education, there has been great growth in the proportion of women in higher education since the 1980s.

Tables 5.3 and 5.4 look in more detail at selected African and South Asian countries. They show that while participation rates are under 10 per cent for all the African countries in the tables, the gender gap has grown at higher-education level except in two countries, namely Lesotho and Botswana.

In South Asia a similar pattern is evident in India, and while in Sri Lanka the gross enrolment ratio of women was higher than for men in the 1980s, a gap was evident in the 1990s. It is evident how significant the participation

Table 5.4 Tertiary gross enrolment ratio: Selected countries Asia

Country	1987 male	1987 female	Gap in 1987	1996 male	1996 female	Gap in 1996	Change between 1987 and 1996
India	7.2	3.6	3.6	8.4	5.3	3.1	−0.5
Sri Lanka	1.2	3.4	−2.2	5.9	4.2	1.7	3.9

Source: UNESCO 2001

Table 5.5 Men and women as a proportion of academic staff in selected Commonwealth countries, 1999–2000

Country	% female	% male
United Kingdom	33	67
Australia	48.4	51.6
South Africa	45	55
Malaysia	45	55

Sources: Australia 2000; Higher Education Statistics Agency 2000, Cooper and Subotzky, Singh and Gill 2001, UNESCO (2001)

rate of women has been and how, in fact, the gender gap reflects higher female compared to male participation.

Yet these dramatic increases in participation by women as students over two decades across the Commonwealth have not been accompanied by a concomitant expansion in employment opportunities for women in higher education in all Commonwealth countries. Table 5.5 indicates how women remain a minority of staff employed in higher education, although the gaps have narrowed over the last 20 years. However, at senior levels of employment – professors, deans and vice chancellors – women are strikingly under-represented (Lund 1998, De La Rey 2001, Onsongo 2001).

The access agenda focuses on quantitative representation rather than qualitative change, but has been accompanied by moves to vocationalize aspects of higher education and respond to certain dimensions of what are seen as consumer choice. In this framework the university tends to remain an elite organization, transmitting what is deemed to be high-level knowledge and professional competencies to a select few. Groups that have historically not had access to higher education are often allowed access to less elite institutions (Modood and Acland 1998). Access implies a universal, value-free 'body of knowledge', or canon, to be transmitted to a slightly changed composition of the student body. In the policy discourse of the learning society, access to higher education is seen to have redemptive power as it promises social inclusion and cohesion as well as national prosperity (Morley 2000). However, access ignores the radical agenda for recognition of identities and redistribution of rights and entitlements. The numbers change as women are counted in, but the different forms of knowledge that women bring are not given epistemic privilege. Power is not challenged and transformation is within set limits. This approach is concerned with women, not gendered power, feminist theory or practice, or masculinities. The onus is on the new constituencies to adapt and adjust (Edwards 1993).

Other major themes that emerged from the literature review indicate that the increase in women's access to higher education as students has not been accompanied by a simultaneous development of an organizational culture concerned with gender equity issues in relation to pedagogy, curriculum or organizational management (Marshall 1997, Mayberry and Rose 1999). There is horizontal and vertical segregation in the academy throughout the Commonwealth with women under-represented in senior posts and often over-represented in faculties concerned with education, arts or healthcare. In higher-education institutions where case-study research has been conducted it is evident that the organizational culture does not foster women's advancement into management. Thus, Lamptey (1992) found that women at a university in Ghana were perceived to lack the social skills and personality traits that made an effective manager. Onsongo's study (2000) of Kenyan academics indicated how men drew on important professional and micropolitical networks to secure their promotion, resources to which women had no access. In a number of countries women's skill as managers in higher education have been noted (Gill 2000, Ramsey 2000), but the implications for women of taking management posts in organizations that do not take gender equity seriously are often severe (Morley 1999, Ramsey 2000).

A number of studies draw attention to women academics' internalized narratives of lack and deficit. Their failures to engage in prestige research projects (as opposed to the more feminized roles of teaching) or take management positions were depicted by them as a result of their inadequacies, rather than shortcomings in the institution (Lamptey 1992, Morley 1999). Side by side with this, and a feature of the same framework, women academics in South Africa attributed their success to luck, chance and factors external to themselves, rather than their own work or the quality of their thinking (De La Rey 2001).

An indication of the hostile climate women encounter as students and staff emerges from the growing literature on violence and sexual harassment in higher education. Studies are beginning to emerge of high levels of sexual exploitation of female students by male staff (Zindi 1998) and of female staff by male colleagues (Mlama 1998).

The published literature to date is predominantly quantitative and the qualitative studies still too patchy to present a comprehensive picture. Yet much of the literature on higher education in Commonwealth countries contains problematic assumptions, which obscure the possibilities of a refined account of gendered dimensions of the institutions. The first assumption, often made by advocates of increased women's access to higher education, is that a growing quantitative representation of women is sufficient to facilitate change (Commonwealth Secretariat 1994, Lund 1998). A second assumption in many studies (for example Ade Ajayi 1996) is that effective nation-building carried out by higher-education institutions is gender neutral and thus that men and women's interests must be equally represented. This often goes together with the assumption that there is consensus regarding what effective nation-building entails. This flies in the face of much literature on gender and nation (Yuval-Davis, 1997). In the final section we engage with some of these assumptions and their bearing on understanding enterprise culture, through a discussion of some of the theoretical literature on social justice, equality and markets.

Theorizing enterprise culture

To date, much of the writing on enterprise culture has proceeded by describing some of its effects on increased access for previously excluded groups, such as women. Alternatively, emphasis has been on new cultures of management, including new forms of accountability or partnership (for example Marginson and Considine 2000). As yet, little analytical work has considered whether enterprise culture entails the emergence of a new set of political and economic relations governing the allocation of information, goods, labour and time and thus forcing changed practices in higher-education institutions. While some important beginnings are to be found in the work of, for example, Altbach 1999, Barnett 2000, Jarvis 2000, none of it takes the gendered politics of the new institutional formations seriously.

There are a number of ways in which gender can be theorized at the institutional level:

- it can be viewed as merely a descriptive category of sexual difference, as much of the mainstream literature on expanding women's access to higher education does (for example Lund 1998).
- it can be viewed as structuring the relations of the organization excluding women from both central and diffuse centres of power (Marshall 1997).
- it can be viewed as a polysemic category, always expanding beyond the boundaries of the words used by academics to explain gendered relations (Williams 1993, Spivak 1999).

It seems to us that none of these theorizations adequately capture the simultaneous inclusion and exclusion of women that we have noted as a feature of higher education in the era of enterprise culture. Instead, we follow Nancy Fraser (1996, 1997) in regarding gender as a bivalent category. Fraser identifies two dimensions to injustice – maldistribution of resources and misrecognition of identities – and argues that social justice requires correcting both. Gender is, for her, a bivalent category because women suffer both kinds of injustice. Examples of maldistribution would include the underemployment of women in higher education, particularly at senior levels. At the same time, a gender analysis also needs to take account of examples of misrecognition and include the ways in which scant attention is paid to women's scholarship in a particular discipline. An example is documented in Delamont's history (1996) of the Chicago school. Other examples are the way the language used by women managers is subjected to scorn by male colleagues (see Hearn 1994). Very little detailed theoretical work has been conducted as to whether the advent of a more market-oriented enterprise culture in the management of higher education signals a new politics of cultural change in institutions that facilitates new forms of redistribution and recognition with regard to gender.

Fraser diagnoses two different ways of addressing injustice. She terms these affirmative and transformational reform strategies (Fraser 1996). Affirmative forms of redistribution might entail admitting women in larger numbers into higher education and increasing the number of women staff employed at all levels. Affirmative forms of recognition might entail one session in a particular course on women's contribution to a particular field or the appointment of a student welfare officer to deal with issues of sexual harassment.

Transformational strategies, by contrast, aim radically to alter the ways in which the politics of institutions work. Whereas under current systems of governance senior professors take crucial decisions, a transformatory politics might seek wider participation so that much more attention is given to the representation in senior decision-making bodies of those at the bottom of the hierarchy. This is where women cluster as students and junior staff. Other transformative redistributive strategies might have a bearing on the labour market in higher education, so that feminized work (often unpaid) in community organizations or in family care is considered useful preparation side by side with scholarship for a career in higher education. Indeed, the enterprise culture provides openings in this direction given that partnerships with community bodies are a key element of many enterprise strategies in higher education (see Coate et al. 2000). New approaches to management often emphasize the importance of 'working with people'; skills often learned (either willingly or unwillingly) by women in their socialized roles as carers and facilitators of others. Transformative recognition strategies would require the establishment of different cultures of working, where sexual harassment was seen as a problem for the whole institution, not just the victims. To take forward such strategies there would need to be a commitment to forming new languages in disciplines to take account of the forms of gender and other intersecting exclusions relating to race, class and sexuality of the past. Some examples of putting feminist pedagogy into action in higher education in New Zealand and Canada have begun to be documented, but they emphasize the considerable institutional difficulties these innovations face (Mayberry and Rose 1999).

The growth of enterprise culture in higher education has led to limited forms of affirmative redistribution with regard to access of women to higher education. Yet even this has been taken forward weakly with regard to the employment of women staff and little attention has been given to affirmative forms of recognition. We have no documented studies of transformative redistribution or recognition strategies in higher education linked to the enterprise culture. Indeed, weak affirmative strategies and a minimum set of demands are sometimes seen as the maximum that can be achieved.

At a theoretical level, if enterprise culture is about transforming relations both inside higher-education institutions, and between higher-education institutions and government, business and the community, there is nothing to prevent it instigating further affirmative forms of recognition and transformational forms of redistribution and recognition.

Enterprise culture is often linked disparagingly with the growth of markets in education, which signal reduction in state investment in higher education and the growth of inequities between institutions. However, in defence of markets, Sen has pointed to the ways in which they facilitate the free movement of labour and information and how these have been of considerable importance in facilitating many women's escape from patriarchal family relations and limited access to information (1999: 112–16). He argues that markets might be an efficient form to secure capabilities, the substantive freedoms to do and be that people have reason to value, but only to the extent that markets observe egalitarian distributive constraints. In addition, consideration must be given to the provision of non-marketable public goods (such as clean air or universal education) for which the state must take responsibility (Sen 1999: 122–34).

What are the implications of Fraser's and Sen's work for evaluating enterprise culture and gender equity in Commonwealth higher education? Enterprise culture has facilitated greater access of women to higher education, but has not paid careful attention to the distribution of equity or the expansion of recognition. It is questionable whether capabilities have been expanded, given the evidence of high levels of sexual and micropolitical harassment and the narratives of deficit and failure women students and staff report. This is not to say that enterprise culture could not facilitate an expansion of capabilities and an expansion of equity in redistribution and recognition, but it has not done so to date. Indeed, it may bring into being conditions of competition and selfishness that militate against building capabilities linked to equality goals.

However, in spite of the growth of private higher education, the state remains the key funder of this sector. Much greater attention to affirmative and transformational agendas could be an aspect of contract compliance with regard to the state subsidy. This is already underway in South Africa where higher-education institutions have to provide detailed 3-year plans, as part of securing funding from the state, regarding how they are working to gender and race equality strategies (De la Rey 2001). Indeed, contract compliance brings aspects of the ethics of the market into the public sphere, as a means of ensuring the advancement of equity agendas.

The growth of enterprise culture might provide the openings not just for increased access by women to higher education, but also for increased democratization and transformation with regard to gender equity. There is nothing in enterprise culture in and of itself that would prevent this. However, the ways in which it intersects with older forms of organization in higher education, in which gendered forms of inequity are deeply etched, make us somewhat pessimistic. It remains to be seen whether global conditions changing the institutional form of higher education will facilitate the emergence of a new generation of leaders in higher education able to take forward a transformational agenda for redistribution and recognition.

Notes

1. The authors wish to thank the Association of Commonwealth Universities for funding the research on which this paper is based. Edwina Peart acted as research assistant in the early stages of this project. Versions of this paper were presented at the SRHE conferences on Globalization and Higher Education in Cape Town, April 2001 and on Excellence, Enterprise and Equity: Competing Challenges for Higher Education in Cambridge, December 2001. Thanks are also due to participants at those conferences, Christine Porter and Harry Brighouse for useful comments.
2. The initial study was conducted by Edwina Peart. The bibliographic searches were completed by Penny Burke and Christine Porter.

Part 2

Organizational Changes

Introduction

The pressures from resource stringency and the methods of new public management have brought various institutional responses as universities and colleges have struggled to survive or to improve the services they are able to offer students and other stakeholders. In the language of the mass media, they have tried to rise in the league tables or the pecking order.

Broadly, there are four ways a higher-education organization can seek to improve its academic and economic standing. One is to improve efficiency so that academic services of a given quality can be offered at a lower price to governments and other consumers. A second is to offer better quality service. If this is done at the same cost as others, this is an alternative definition of efficiency improvement. However, the institution may decide to offer a better quality service at a higher price in the belief that this can be offered at a given price. Another possibility is to market the institution and the services it offers actively. For almost all universities and colleges the higher the quality of staff and students it can attract, the higher will be its academic standing and its economic success. An institution may try to sell specific services to a wider range of clients or, what is often more attractive, although more difficult, it may decide to exploit the charitable status enjoyed by most universities and colleges and seek donations from individuals and organizations. Finally, the institution, probably in collaboration with all or some other higher-education institutions, may try to lobby governments politically to try to attract more public funds.

This section tells the story of some of these attempts. Ellen Hazelkorn describes how and why many of the newer universities and colleges have attempted to build up their research in order to improve their academic and economic standing. She concludes that new institutions argue that research and scholarly activity are integral to their mission, and that new understandings of knowledge production and dissemination favour new structures and frameworks. Interdisciplinary teamwork is strongly favoured, and new institutions often seek to formalize interdisciplinary research into clusters supporting academic work. Hazelkorn claims there is little dispute that innovation, application and knowledge specialization have increasingly become primary indicators of competitive advantage, performance and survival.

Mervyn Jones explores one rapidly expanding new venture in many universities – continuing professional development – and, in particular, the importance of new technology in assisting universities to acquire credibility in offering career development training to experienced professionals. Enterprise is essential to identify market opportunities and to act on them once they have been recognized.

Finally, there are two chapters on corporate universities that are not bound by the academic traditions of conventional universities and aim to meet very specific economic demands.

6

Challenges of Growing Research at New and Emerging Higher-education Institutions

Ellen Hazelkorn

Towards a political economy of higher education

There is little dispute amongst policy makers or in the literature that the post-Second-World-War, post-Sputnik era ushered in a period of rapid and tremendous change in higher-educational structures, provisions and demand across almost all OECD countries. Indeed, the import of these changes has been marked by terms such as massification, democratization, diversification, harmonization, internationalization and globalization. Several factors are indicated, including the economic and demographic boom, the significance of scientific discovery, the heightened importance of educational attainment and career opportunity, the birth and subdivision of academic disciplines and the professionalization of academic careers. A combination of domestic and external pressures and actors, including the active engagement of supra-national agencies such as the EEC/EU, OECD, UNESCO and World Bank, have played a part in fostering these changes. Between the Second World War and the late 1970s, the number and type of students seeking higher education accelerated rapidly alongside the number of academic and support staff, and public investment.

The history of this rapid growth in the range and type of educational opportunities and institutions has been well documented. Polytechnics, Fachhochschulen, advanced colleges of education, institutes of technology and community colleges, as well as *ab initio* universities, emerged to cater for a wider range of socio-economic groups, and educational and employment requirements. Policy-makers and educational managers talked of a higher educational *system*. Universities offered advanced postgraduate study and conducted research, answerable to a worldwide academic community; teaching focused on the abstract and was less concerned with immediate needs. In contrast, non-university institutions catered variously for vocational or undergraduate needs, often with a regional or community bias;

their emphasis was on training, and academic staff were expected to concentrate on specific workplace needs. The difference was 'not so much inherent as secured by fiat, since colleges were not funded for research and only some were permitted to enrol a few coursework masters students' (Meek and O'Neill 1996: 65). As part of an integrated national system, (elite) universities and (mass) colleges and institutions enhanced social mobility, met the needs of the labour market and offered opportunities for innovation. Its comprehensiveness provided opportunities for most students. Some transferability between 'sectors' was permitted, but the awarding of advanced degrees and the title 'university' were strictly monitored. The 'binary', whether *de jure* or *de facto*, was enforced.

By the late 1970s, however, strains and countervailing pressures began to appear. Two inter-related factors are particularly important for the purposes of this chapter. First, the emergence of the knowledge-based or information society has undeniably transformed the mode of production and social organization of advanced societies. National governments now purposively attach great strategic importance to capacity-building decisions and investment, and the necessary management and 'institutional arrangements that enable individuals and societies more fully to appropriate its material benefits' (David 1999. xiii). Research expenditure is seen as critical to national geopolitical positioning, and higher education has been required to respond accordingly. Second, institutional existence is no longer guaranteed. Government and public support for the financial underpinning of public services has waned. Higher education is being asked why it exists and 'to grapple with the fact that we are not an ends, we are a means . . . through which our society educates itself and shapes itself' (1988 Australian White Paper, quoted in Adams 2000: 69). Public funding is tied to measurable outcomes, students are demanding assurances about educational quality, and the role of academics and content of academic work is being redefined and restructured. Intra-institutional tensions have surfaced, and inter-institutional rivalry is prevalent. Inevitably, there are winners and losers in this process.

At the beginning of the twenty-first century, the once benign higher-education system is being transformed into a competitive marketplace. Aspects of national 'higher-education systems' and the role that different institutions play are being reshaped. Previously sharp boundaries between elite and mass education, vocational and academic, technological and traditional, and undergraduate and (post) graduate have come under scrutiny, and in some instances have broken down or been altered. Traditional universities are no longer the sole, or in some instances, the primary site for advanced learning or research. In line with a broader understanding of the production of knowledge, there has been a 'relative decline in the attraction and prestige of the academic paradigms represented by conventional universities with a growing emphasis on "employment relevance"' (OECD 1991: 72). Many of the new institutions have charted significant careers in applied or industrially relevant research and consultancy, and have begun to win a sizeable share of government and industrial funding. There is also evidence of innovative new courses and disciplines. New fields of knowledge, such as business and management, engineering and applied sciences, nursing and social care, the media and the creative arts, have gradually become professionalized, fuelled by, and in turn fuelling, a rapidly expanding academic literature. As staff become more involved in advanced-level teaching, they have begun to spend more time on research and to compete for research funding. The rationale for dual sectors or the binary system continues to be argued, but 'over time the division . . . [is proving] difficult to maintain, and the boundaries between the classical and the technical institutions . . . blurred' (OECD 1999: 16).

To some observers, these developments represent a breakdown in national higher-education systems via a process of convergence or dedifferentiation. Newer institutions are accused of adopting the accoutrements of traditional universities, actively copying their research profile and teaching programmes, and engaging in 'academic' or 'mission' drift. For others, however, these changes are part of the natural or inevitable process of institutional development and historical change, or a further step in the democratization of the 'Humboltian ethic' (Neave 2000: 265). If massification and expansion in the 1960s differentiated the second stage in higher-educational development from its elite origins, then the late 1990s marked the beginning of the third stage. By then, it was clear that a broadly educated population could no longer be formed by and within universities alone. In societies where knowledge and knowledge creation are highly privileged and integral to both national and institutional prestige, advanced learning and research capacity are allied and critical. Paradoxically, by seeking to conform to their mission, new and emerging higher-education institutions soon outgrew the straitjacket of their birth.

Institutional mission and strategic choices

There is little disputing the fact that external forces are influencing in a much more directive way both the structure of higher-education systems, and the way in which individual institutions are organizing and managing themselves. Drawn from preliminary data collected from case studies of higher-educational institutions from across 15 countries established or reconstituted since about 1970, this section focuses on issues of institutional mission, strategic choice and organizational structure. In particular, it looks at issues of research management and capacity-building, asking if there are particular characteristics and experiences that new and emerging institutions share.

Research as mission and strategy

For new and emerging higher-education institutions, the case-study evidence highlights two primary forces fuelling their research ambitions: mission and survival. First, many new institutions were established as part of a regional economic strategy. They were required to focus on local and regional needs, and specifically to develop and help 'retain an *educated* manpower in the area'. Initially, they were allowed to undertake only limited research activity – often the emphasis was on development and consultancy – with a specific commitment to relevant knowledge and applied learning. In this respect, their role was primarily viewed as 'teaching only'. Yet, over time, and commensurate with the global omnipresence of the knowledge-based economy, their commitment to providing 'economically useful skills with industrial relevance' and ensuring that 'academic activities are aligned with the economic development of their region' has become inextricably bound to growing research capacity. Moreover, many of the disciplines they parented now require a more sophisticated response to economic and labour-market pressures; hence institutions state that they engage in research to ensure 'academic excellence in a professional context'. By obeying their mission – to serve and respond to specific training and more general needs at the local and regional levels – new higher-education institutions have needed to adopt policies, practices and strategies that paradoxically strain their original role.

Second, research or 'scholarship' is increasingly related to institutional status and, in turn, to students, staff and facilities. Reductions in block government funding, the geo-political significance of knowledge for national prestige, and the emergence of benchmarking and other evaluative criteria across OECD and non-OECD countries have had a powerful impact on the behaviour of higher-education institutions. In this respect, new institutions are no different from their older colleagues; they are acting as rational organisms by responding to 'specific funding opportunities'. As institutional status becomes more and more linked to survival, inter-institutional competition has sharpened. Almost all participating institutions state that research activity and priorities are directly related to their competitive position: it is necessary to 'sustain academic and professional reputation in a knowledge-based economy' or to 'retain and improve their position' vis-à-vis their competitors. Participants variously describe the factors influencing their research ambitions and strategy as follows:

> The fundamental factors influencing research strategy, as listed in the order of importance, are: excellence and reputation; recruitment and retention of faculty, students (graduate and undergraduate); research and scholarly activity being an inseparable part of the academic function of the university.

> To foster the development of technology and research, . . . innovation and technology transfer [within a specific region of the country].

> The necessity to integrate education and research . . . , [attract] researchers . . . [and] diversify funding . . .

For some, their research reputation is so important that they have provided funds from their own block grants, often contrary to government approval.

These comments are mirrored in other studies; for example American 'universities found that enhancing their reputation for research paid dividends in terms of attracting better students, projecting a positive image of public service, and enlarging voluntary support (Geiger 1993: 321). A study of UK polytechnics argued similarly; research activity was necessary 'to sustain academic reputation, to attract the right sort of staff, to enable course development, to attract students (undergraduate as well as postgraduate) and to provide an extensive consultancy service for the region' (Pratt 1997: 142). Even less prestigious and teaching-oriented colleges have accommodated research, not to compete with the research elite, but rather to 'try to secure a small group of scholarly distinction to give their campus national visibility so as to compete with others at levels similar to their own' (Lipset 1994: 222).

'Sheer underdevelopment of profile'

New and emerging higher-education institutions vary in origins and context; many developed as a result of the transformation or amalgamation/merger of smaller, regional/community or vocationally oriented, colleges, while others were established as *ab initio* institutions. Some are called universities while others fall within the broader category of 'tertiary', 'alternative', 'postsecondary', 'new generation,' or 'non-university' higher education. Many of these institutions share common experiences with respect to funding and infrastructure, and human resources and research capacity.

The most frequent remark is that the process of conversion or formation has ignored their status as either 'late-developers' or 'newcomers'. Participants point to the fact that they were not traditionally resourced for research and, as a consequence, they have poor institutional infrastructure and technical support. The funding gap between new higher-education institutions and older universities continues, and over time differences between the two groups has widened; indeed, one person described the difficulties of trying to keep pace as running as if a lead ball were attached to one's ankle. Moreover, because academic staff at new institutions were hired originally to teach, they often lack the necessary prerequisites – a research postgraduate qualification, for example – and the necessary research experience. In addition, academic workloads are significantly greater than their university colleagues; hence, research is being built on the back of relatively heavy teaching commitments, producing, in some instances, internal tensions and morale difficulties. These conditions are compounded by salary and career differentials, which inhibit faculty-building strategies. As the parent of many new disciplines, many of which had no research tradition, institutions face particular difficulties achieving recognition and funding, and navigating from successful applied and professional teaching programmes to research postgraduate activity.

Many of these issues may not be unique to new and emerging higher-education institutions, although some participants expressed the view that older universities often act as a 'cartel', intentionally or not and with or without government endorsement, to inhibit the activities and progress of newer institutions. Older universities resent sharing 'research spoils' with new institutions (Meek and O'Neill 1996: 74). They argue that criteria and rules for research funding are introduced and altered to meet the needs of the established universities and are 'deliberately' disadvantageous to new institutions. There is some support for this view; UK and Australian institutions, for example, experienced an 'overnight' conversion to university status, but without the requisite funds to enable them to compete directly with other/older universities. Some ground was 'grudgingly' made up in the latter case, but ultimately market forces are being used crudely to delineate between research and teaching universities. One participant stated forcefully that:

> It is difficult for the smaller, newer universities to compete with the larger, older ones in at least two respects: less income and poorer infrastructure ... Governments like institutions to share, but this is usually at the disadvantage of the smaller one.

Clark concurs, stating that while governments muddy the waters by:

> calling all higher education institutions by a single name ... the river of reality runs in the other direction, fed by the massive tributaries of differentiation ... and [sic] by government policies that deliberately encourage operational differentiation (1996: 22).

Building a 'culture of scholarship'

According to Clark (1995), the nexus between research and teaching too narrowly describes higher education's role as a place of inquiry. A few years earlier Boyer had also rejected the dichotomous view of research versus teaching to pose a broader understanding of 'scholarship'. Scholarship, he argued, embraced a more integrative understanding of knowledge production and dissemination: discovery, application, integration and learning (Boyer 1990). Gibbons et al. (1994) provided another leg to this frame, recognizing and amplifying the intellectual and strategic importance of collaborative and interdisciplinary work via the concept of Mode 2 research. Given the particularities of their history, many new and emerging higher-education institutions have, often unwittingly, adopted these concepts.

Participating institutions talk of 'adjusting ministerial criteria' to fit their disciplines and embracing the wider conception of scholarship, most notably in reports from Australia and New Zealand. In this respect, research includes innovation and creativity, traditional publications and creative/ professional practice, and cross-disciplinary and industry-relevant work. Definitions of research and focus are variously explained as follows.

The main focus is on applied research . . . with its outcomes applied in consulting and experimental production.

Research is defined as critical and creative activity undertaken on a systematic basis in order to extend knowledge and understanding and/ or solve practical or theoretical problems.

For the statistical report to government, we use the distinction of basic and applied research and development. However, our daily research activities are so much diversified, we do not strictly distinguish [between] these categories.

The emphasis is on applied or relevant research with a local and regional dimension, although local does not necessarily mean the immediate vicinity; it can refer to local development anywhere, e.g. in Africa.

Institutions aim to conduct research which 'informs and is informed by learning, teaching and professional practice' and is 'tightly interwoven with the region' via innovative partnerships and commercialisation.

Given their histories, most new institutions have adopted a pragmatic view of achievement. While some institutions have embarked on formally rene- gotiating academic contracts to either include research or to create research- only positions, others are focused on recruiting experienced researchers directly into academic departments or into (semi)autonomous research units/centres. Institutions, and the literature, have mixed views on whether it is possible to grow research from their existing base or whether they need to rely more heavily on recruitment strategies; there is also some debate around whether staff development plans and flexible workload schemes should be focused selectively (Hoare 1995, Jones and Lengkeek 1997). In some instances, funding is targeted controversially at research-active staff only, while others are eager to ensure that new ideas and new researchers are not neglected. Nevertheless, all institutions emphasize that growing a critical mass or community of scholars, based on interdisciplinary teams, is essential to success. This includes increasing the number of postgraduate research students and experienced supervisors. Infrastructure supports and services are significant elements of all strategies.

The process of growing a culture of research and scholarship can be lengthy and challenging. One author suggests that the process of change can be so long that many good researchers leave out of frustration (Berrell 1998: 277–93). Accordingly, institutions signal the need to attune their research ambitions to institutional reality. Skoie similarly advises that the task of introducing research should be 'approached carefully to generate an effort with reasonable standards. The time horizon should be carefully set' (2000: 418). Hence, with careful planning of academic activities, new institutions can realize the appropriate scale and foster an ethos which reinforces their mission of research and related teaching (Johnston et al. 1995: 47).

Institutional organization and research

Management and productivity are two issues of critical importance in the current climate of competitive funding, evaluative criteria, and monitoring and reporting requirements. The move towards greater accountability for public funds has been matched by greater attention to managerialism: 'Research expenditure – whether by industry or government – is an investment that demands a return. It should not be a discretionary expense' (Turpin et al. 1996: 19).

Not surprisingly, new institutions, like their older colleagues, are investing much time and effort in issues of research management, internal structures, facilities and support services. The research office is now virtually 'ubiquitous' within institutions seeking to grow research. Led most often by a deputy or pro vice-chancellor or vice-president for research or research and development, it has an explicit role to manage, organize and improve the competitive performance of research. The formulation of a research strategy or research management and training plan is the primary starting point, on the basis of which each institution seeks to identify a selected number of research priorities or 'interdisciplinary' themes. Depending upon the institution, the deputy/pro vice-chancellor or vice-president for research is the institutional link and coordinator between and across faculties and management, via deans and/or research committees. Institutions vary on whether they consider postgraduate activity – some make no distinction between taught and research – under this ambit.

The research planning process invariably involves elements of top-down and bottom-up, albeit that the balance differs across participants. Compare the following two examples.

The office of the vice-president (research) chairs a committee of associate deans of research . . . [which represents] the members of faculty as a whole and perform strategic outlook exercises to determine future priorities. Faculty members contribute to the exercise via departmental or faculty sessions and in some cases through participation in university, enterprise-wide priority-setting exercises. Individual researchers overall are a crucial part of this process.

The strategic planning committee sets the broad strategy for every university function for the next 6 years, once every 6 years. The research committee then sets strategy and policy for research and research programmes. The president is consulted on important matters. Researchers' views are heard on relevant matters.

How and where research activity is currently organized within institutions also differs; yet, the majority of participants were clear that they wished to shift the locus of activity away from individuals and towards clusters. Whether that new focus is departments, units or centres, the desired outcome is critical mass, with grant-awarding reputations and timely outcomes. Priorities are determined by a combination of factors; national priorities, funding, competencies and evaluation are mentioned frequently. The overwhelming majority of institutions, however, cited competitive advantage as the most important factor influencing their research agenda.

Most participating institutions have a process for internally allocating research funds; in some instances this mechanism is quite formal, such as through an office of research, and via faculties/departments or according to other criteria. The latter variously involves financial support for staff development, sabbatical leaves, grants to areas less likely to receive external funding, travel grants, start-up grants, matching funds and research students. Operationalizing the distribution model is potentially contentious and divisive, as the debate at participating institutions about top slicing to support central services or institution-wide research activities/centres revealed. Other participants described their approach as follows:

> Internal finance as far as possible supports an up-qualification of the teaching and/or generates external allocations and cross-institutional research cooperation.

> The basic research allocation model [seeks to] stimulate the ability to attract external funding.

> We use a performance-based model to determine what amount of resources each department gets for research projects or research student programmes. This approach has forced departments to improve their performance. For other activities like supporting research infrastructure or postdoctoral fellowship, an allocation to departments is not made and applications are considered on a competitive basis by the research committee.

Greater emphasis on research has raised intra-institutional tensions. One institution acknowledged the 'difficulty in reconciling individual, college and wider institute objectives and aspirations' while another stated that the 'review of research concentrations . . . involved significant uncertainty' and that 'developing a strategy to codify research active staff experienced strong resistance'. A third stated that they:

> are facing a generational change among the academic staff . . . , newly recruited staff come with a new view of the necessity for research as well as cooperation with the trades and industry. There is also some concern that the increased research activity will be at the expense of the teaching. On the other hand, the research offers a possibility for professional development for the benefit of the teaching.

Growing research and establishing a nexus between teaching and research is not without personal costs in terms of time required; squeezing 'research out of people and departments that have no training, aptitude or inclination' (Skoie 2000: 416) inevitably generates tensions. Participants are drawing various lessons from their experience and the ever-growing literature on the changing academic workplace:

1. not everyone needs to be involved in research;
2. policies which enhance the nexus between research and teaching should be encouraged;
3. a range of services, awards and rewards to encourage and facilitate should be introduced; and
4. a wider definition of scholarship, rather than a traditional dichotomous view of basic and applied, would help provide a more encouraging environment.

Theorizing late-development and research structures

Case-study methodology is often criticized for its lack of rigour and generalization from a small sample. Individual experiences involve several interrelated factors often unique to the institution, society or context and comparisons are far from direct and unproblematic. Yet, such studies can contribute uniquely to our knowledge of individual, organizational, social and political phenomena by enabling us to generalize from specific experiences. This section will seek to draw some tentative theoretical propositions from the specific experiences of new and emerging higher-education institutions.

Theorizing late-development

The academic literature and higher-education policy has tended to discuss recent changes in higher-education systems in one of two ways. Van Vught (1996), Huisman (1998) and Morphew (2000), for example, have variously described the process whereby newer institutions have developed a research agenda as a 'problem' of academic or mission drift. Drawing upon the very large literature on differentiation and diversity, Van Vught has likened higher-education institutions to other organisms that grow and change in response to external factors: the 'nature, number and distribution of organisations at any given time is dependent on resource availability and on competition within and between different species of organisations' (1996: 51–7). To survive, higher-education institutions need to secure a continuous and sufficient supply of resources. In an era of decreasing public funds, competition for scarce financial resources has encouraged institutions to copy each other rather than develop distinctive profiles (Huisman 1998: 94). Because research is perceived as more highly valued than teaching, institutions have converged on a single model of a 'university'. Likewise, reflecting on the Carnegie classification system, McCormick (2000) suggests that '[t]here are strong incentives for institutions to conform to particular models of institutional activity, and indeed to particular indicators of activity'. In this scenario, institutional homogenization or de-differentiation is an inevitable result of competition. Terms such as 'mockers and mocked', 'pseudo-universities', 'institutional chameleons' and a 'contagious effect' are often used to describe this rush towards uniformity.

An alternative view is presented by Geuna (1999), Dill and Teixeira (2000) and Pham (2000), who seek to explain the changes as an outcome of rational choice theory. Borrowing from economics, they argue that in a competitive environment, institutions will search out their own niche and develop their own mission and institutional profile. The emphasis here is on innovation and the development of 'new products, new ways of delivering or organising them, and the use of new resources' (Dill and Teixeira 2000: 108). For example, because reputations for teaching and research are becoming intertwined, universities are positioning themselves and re-organizing their institutional structures accordingly (Zubrick et al. 2001). Research is also necessary to ensure that vocational/professional disciplines keep pace with sophisticated labour-market demand. As social and economic organizations, higher-education institutions are focusing on building unique competencies in order to position and differentiate themselves. Finding a specific niche in the research market is one such approach. In this scenario, competition leads to diversity not conformity.

Evidence from the case studies, however, suggests a third interpretation. Borrowing from the literature on late- or newly industrializing countries and competitive advantage (O'Malley 1989: 8–31, Porter 1990), this view sees the changes and challenges discussed in this chapter as part of the inevitable process of historical change and institutional development rather than as the result of misguided mission drift or product diversification. New higher-education institutions can be viewed as 'late-developers' or 'newcomers' established in response to different events and circumstances. As such, they are experiencing all the disadvantages of starting late from a poor base, and competing against the strength of established providers who have built up a firm relationship with policy makers and dominant groups. Responding to this new environment, governments have often maintained an ambiguous attitude towards their higher-education system, and particularly newer institutions. Endorsing diversity while demanding knowledge production and industrial relevance, they have variously favoured statutory instruments or market forces, in the conventional (neo-liberal) belief that intervention would undermine efficiency or productivity and lead to underperformance. However, the impact on new institutions has been at best benign and at worst devastating. Thus, in this scenario, late-developers and newcomers come up against open and hidden barriers to entry or what Geiger (1993: 295) refers to as the 'insuperable advantage of established institutions and the immutability of the university hierarchy'.

In response, new and emerging higher-education institutions have sought to devise strategies for survival, selectively adopting policies to help overcome barriers or restricted barriers to entry. Similar to the experience of late- or newly industrializing countries, they have proactively sought to attract external funds and providers – for example, buying-in well-established researchers or research projects or forming strategic alliances – and to develop their resource base. Of most relevance to this chapter, new and emerging higher-education institutions have sought to identify and exploit exceptional and niche advantages based on their particular experiences and expertise. Despite differences in origins and context, and the obvious challenges (Curran 2001: 223–51), every participating institution is attempting to build a research culture as the proceeding section illustrated. If recent developments are understood as the next stage in the evolution of higher education or a 'delayed catching-up process' (Berry 1999), then barriers to entry can be recognized as such and appropriate action taken. There are important policy issues that emerge from this analysis.

Theorizing research structures

New and emerging universities, like their more established counterparts, are actively grappling with the complexities of research management and capacity building; for late-developers and newcomers the challenges are that much more difficult, not least because many of them have not traditionally been resourced for research activity. While newer institutions have not fared as well as traditional universities in competing for research funds, this has not deterred them. They 'have found it necessary to strengthen their research capabilities, and . . . have gone about it in a variety of ways' (Turpin et al. 1996).

The growing literature in support of Gibbons' Mode 2 concept reflects research practice within universities, across higher education more broadly, and across national research/science systems. Coupled with arguments drawn from Boyer, new institutions in particular have been able to develop research strategies which more accurately reflect their experience, expertise and mission. In fact, it could be argued that Mode 2's emphasis on inter-disciplinary team work focused on useful application, moving non-hierarchically across the 'boundaries' of basic, applied, strategic, industrial research and professional/creative practice, more aptly suits their profile. Perhaps not surprisingly, many of the participating institutions mentioned these issues specifically in their responses, while, at the same time, emphasizing the importance of priority-setting and niche areas. 'The key question is how to structure and organise teaching and research in the universities, given that research practices are changing' (Gibbons 1995: 101).

It is self-evident that there has been a dramatic transformation in the relationship between knowledge production, higher education/institutional mission and society. While research and scholarship is still grounded on the activity of individuals, it is conceived of less and less as an individual activity. In recent years there has been a rapid progression from knowledge as an individual activity to maintain intellectual rigour to the production and dissemination of knowledge as responsive to the social/regional economy and national/global research and development policies. Indeed, it is arguable whether the former can any longer be distinguished from the latter.

Table 6.1   Model of institutional teaching/research relationships and structures

Type 1	T = R → Inclusive departments
Type 2	T & R → Departments + units/centres
Type 3	T | R → Departments + autonomous centres
Type 4	T ≠ R → University + autonomous institutes

Source: Adapted from Clark as quoted in Coaldrake and Stedman 1999: 22–3.

One participating institution referred to its mission as a 'global orientation with a regional responsibility'.

Depending upon their stage of development and preferred nexus between teaching and research, participating higher-education institutions appear to be introducing the following organizational and strategic research arrangements (see Table 6.1). In the early stages (Type 1), institutions and academics favour a very close relationship between teaching and research, perhaps spawning small research groups, which are retained within the department. As a critical mass develops, the needs of the research team and the strategic needs of the institution favour a more formalized structure for research; existing academics may move seamlessly between teaching/departmental commitments and the centre (Type 2). The ability of institutions to attract substantial external research funds is increasingly conditional on highly productive teams and timely outputs, factors which are potentially inhibited by normal academic workload issues. Hence many of the institutions have acknowledged the need to renegotiate contracts and strategically recruit. Autonomous research centres or campus companies (Type 3), located either within the institution or in science/industrial parks, are favoured when the research group has reached a size effectively incompatible with the routine academic demands of the institution. Type 4 suggests a clear separation between teaching and research, for example the establishment, usually by government, of independent research institutes only some of which support postgraduate students. Perhaps not surprisingly, this strategy was not widely favoured by participants.

The model in Table 6.1 works on two levels:

1. a structural and organizational manifestation of the nexus between teaching and research; and
2. a developmental and strategic relationship between each of the 'types'.

Several issues arise. First, while there is a 'natural' progression, there are many strategic and academic reasons and issues of context and timing to explain why institutions might favour one relationship and arrangement over another. For example, new institutions wishing to develop a 'culture of scholarship' from a green-field site might retain larger groups within departments. On the other hand, institutional tensions, academic contracts and reward systems might favour the formation of autonomous centres or 'outreach' entities much earlier. Second, the idea that the 'structuring of research activities must serve to reinforce the academic role of the university' remains strong (Gutiérrez 1996: 19ff). Hence, there is concern that research activity removed from the academic core and graduate education have contributed to an incremental fragmentation of universities as places of inquiry, as expressed via Derek Bok's 'over-extended organisation' (in Geiger 1993: 327). The more an institution moves down this road, the more it encourages 'two parallel structures within universities: one for teaching and another for research' (Coaldrake and Stedman 1999: 23)'. Third, case-study evidence suggests that growing research is a process: individual → cluster (unit) → larger cluster (centre). If there is a developmental relationship between each of these positions, can the process be shortened, and if so, by what mechanisms: staff development, strategic recruitment or buying-in large-scale projects? Drawing upon the late-development literature, buying development off-the-shelf has been tried with varying degrees of economic success around the world. Important policy issues emerge from this analysis.

Summary

This chapter has examined some issues facing new and emerging higher-education institutions. Four main points emerge. First, based on case-study evidence, the problems these institutions face are arguably associated with the challenges of late-development not mission drift. Second, the latter argument is often based on the view that research activity is an accoutrement of universities. In contrast, new institutions argue that research and scholarly activity is integral to their mission; these are attributes of higher education in general not specific to 'universities.' Third, new understandings of knowledge production and dissemination favour new structures and frameworks. Participants strongly favour and encourage interdisciplinary teamwork, and are strategically seeking to formalize this work into clusters supporting academic work. And finally, there is little dispute that innovation, application and knowledge specialization has increasingly become a primary indicator of competitive advantage, performance and survival. While research management and research capacity are high on the strategic agenda of all higher-education institutions – as signalled by the participation of a few well-established universities in the study – new institutions as late-developers and newcomers encounter barriers to entry.

7

Achieving Excellence: Changing Paradigms, Cultures, Entrepreneurship and the Role of Continuing Professional Development in Science and Engineering

Mervyn E. Jones

Introduction

Universities are one of the oldest institutions in modern society, some being able to trace their history to the twelfth century or even earlier, when the curriculum was dominated by philosophy and theology, with instruction in Latin. They have evolved to the diversity of modern higher education, with its multiplicity of institutions, departments, qualifications and standards. Inevitably, during this period many changes have occurred. Today, however, the changes in society, and the impact that these have on the universities, are greater and probably more rapid than at any time in the past. At the same time, there are both huge changes to the knowledge base, especially in science, engineering and medicine, together with increasingly stronger linkages between education and economic prosperity. Maintaining a competitive edge in an increasingly global framework is dependent on a workforce that is appropriately educated. Despite the thought being devoted to enhancing the effectiveness of the educational process, expectations as to what can be achieved in an undergraduate curriculum are limited, especially with the changes in initial education, in society and in professional requirements. Against this background it is somewhat surprising that the driving forces for continuing professional development (CPD), although well established and widely recognized, do not generate the response from academic institutions that might be expected. It is suggested this may need to be reconsidered. Although currently we do not have appropriate mechanisms with which to recognize and make CPD an integrated reality, some thinking is already beginning to move towards changing structures, for example Lee and Messerschmitt (1999), Midwinter (1999).

In most countries higher education has changed from being for the elite (less than 10 per cent of the age group) to a mass system (more than 30 per cent of the age group) and in the UK the growth of institutions and of student numbers has reflected this, with political pressure to increase numbers yet further to a target of 50 per cent. Such changes have not occurred without problems. These have affected the very nature of the institutions in the expanded sector, together with the level and mode of funding – a change in quantity can also result in a change of quality. In the UK, central government has been the major source of sector funding and, by whatever criteria it might be judged, for many years there has been a progressive decline in the unit level at which this has been allocated. Funding for research and for teaching is usually directed by different routes, resulting in concerns about whether one activity is subsidizing the other. (There has also been concern that the funding for research from some quarters does not necessarily cover adequately the full overheads associated with the activity.) Many employers no longer assume that the graduate, although educated, may need a period of 'apprenticeship' to become of appropriate value to the company, but, in these more stringent times, look for precise matches between requirements and skills. So in both teaching and research, the ground rules are changing.

In the disciplines of science, engineering and medicine there are additional factors. Engineers and scientists play a crucial role in driving forward the technical progress of society and are faced simultaneously with two challenges. Technologies continue to develop with unabated speed in response to the progressive increase in the body of knowledge associated with a subject. At the same time there is a need for professions in these fields to acquire an increasingly diverse range of competencies, which are required throughout a professional career. For example, in addition to extended technical skills, engineers are expected to have language skills and increased awareness of managerial, financial, environmental and legal issues, and to be able to be deployed flexibly to meet changing and competitive market conditions. For many reasons that lie beyond the scope of this chapter, the skills of school leavers are also changing. Thus, taken together, changes in initial education, in society and in engineering requirements are putting unrealistic pressures on student curricula.

Clearly, the education and training of scientists and engineers should be of great concern to society. Many factors influence this education, from the nature and focus of the curriculum through to the needs of employers and the changing patterns of professional employment. The initial degree, although essential, realistically cannot be seen as sufficient in itself to equip an engineer throughout a working life. This poses huge problems for curriculum design – what to include and what to omit. There can be a credibility gap between the expectation and realization from the different perspectives of students, academics and employers. It should not be forgotten that today, as never before, academic institutions, which have the prime responsibility for the initial training of scientists and engineers, have come under increasing resource pressures, with rising student numbers, declining staff/student ratios, and reduced pro-rata funding support from central government.

Two cultures

In 1959 in the UK, C.P. Snow (1905–80), a former scientist, senior Civil Servant and novelist, caused widespread controversy that is not usually associated with a university public lecture. His Reed Lecture, given at the University of Cambridge and entitled 'The Two Cultures and The Scientific Revolution' (Snow 1964), was an examination of the cultural gaps that exist between the sciences and humanities and the limitations of educational systems that have perpetuated and exacerbated this divide. At the time, the lecture provoked an intense and sometimes acrimonious debate, and even personal when involving the acerbic English literary critic F.R. Leavis (1962). In the years that have followed, the phrase 'The Two Cultures' has survived. Although more than 40 years later, this lecture and the subsequent discussions that it provoked, continue to make pertinent observations on key issues within society, which transcend what might initially appear to be the anachronistic and arcane discussions of academics. We have moved a long way from the Renaissance, when it was realistically possible for polymaths to be knowledgeable in many fields.

That particular debate, important and relevant though it is, should not be seen just in its narrow context. The cultural schism between the humanities and sciences identified by Snow is only one of several that run through society. On the one hand it can be extended by exploring its relevance to engineering education and, on the other, by looking at an additional cultural divide, not explored by Snow, which is equally, if not more, relevant today. This is the divide between industry and academia. It is important to identify the traits that characterize these two cultures, what is lost by a failure to appreciate their differences and where appropriate to bridge this specific gap, a gap surely as important as that between arts and sciences. Historically, in many ways, these cultures (that is the academic and industrial) have been very distinct, and therein may lie the seeds of many past troubles and the potential for losing future opportunities. Becher (1989) has drawn attention to the strength and grouping of academic disciplines. However, it is also valuable to explore the nature of the divide between industry and academia. Comparisons can be made at various levels and from different perspectives. Examples extend from approaches to organizational strategy, in collective versus individual development, in approaches to entrepreneurism, to diversity, to infrastructure and to intellectual property. Some of the strengths and weaknesses of the two sectors are compared in Table 7.1.

Table 7.1 A comparison of academic and industrial cultures

Academia	Industry
Accommodates diverse individual strategies	Corporate strategy predominates
Emphasis on individual/group movement	Focus on collective movement of organization
Facilitates individual entrepreneurism	Eschews individual activity
Infrastructure development resources limited	Adequate resources available for infrastructure use
Tolerates diversity	Aims to eliminate diversity
Concern for developing intellectual property only recent	Great emphasis on intellectual property

While it is essential for engineers in their professional development to acquire an appreciation of their professional responsibilities, which for example may entail an appreciation of financial, managerial, ethical, legal and environmental issues, this must be built on a sound initial appreciation of engineering. The pressures of an increasing knowledge base with a wider perspective can only be resolved by ensuring that CPD is seen as an essential part of engineering practice. This has not only to be recognized by those involved, but implemented.

If it is recognized that there are sufficient differences between industry and academia to justify the use of the phrase 'Two Cultures' to describe them, then are we doing enough to bridge the gap between them? With little hesitation, I come to the conclusions that (a) there are in places real cultural gaps between industry and academia, (b) these may be larger than many realize or would care to admit and (c) it will become increasingly important to bridge these gaps effectively, not as a luxury, but as an imperative, to ensure appropriate economic survival in the twenty-first century. At the areas where the cultures meet we must be attuned to these issues, such as in research collaborations and contracts, in technology transfer and in CPD.

If organizational success is to be forthcoming as we move progressively into what has become known as 'the Learning Society', industrial organizations will find it necessary to recognize and absorb key aspects of academic practice. In a similar way, in the future academic institutions will need to recognize and adopt aspects of corporate practice to optimize their activities and to maintain and extend their freedoms and flexibility. No organization can be complacent that tomorrow will be as it is today, or that the practices that in the past have served it well will in the future be equally effective and will continue to be relevant.

Some of the foregoing remarks might appear to be obvious, and yet if that is the case, then the lessons have not been learnt. The forums where academia and industry meet are limited, levels of uncertainty exist within both cultures about the nature, the effectiveness and the external constraints affecting the other, and it cannot be stressed too strongly how important it is that we learn to understand, to develop and to bridge these gaps or schisms of uncertainty if we are not to waste resources and maintain competitiveness.

The entrepreneurial challenge

By common agreement, the concept of entrepreneurship is that of undertaking a business-like activity, with the chance of profit or loss. In the accepted or historic model of a university such ideas have been alien. Universities have been institutions for scholarship, for research and for advanced levels of teaching. None of these activities, however challenging they might be – intellectually, creatively or conceptually – can be considered to be entrepreneurial. In the present century there have been many academics who, at one stage or another, have become entrepreneurs. There are many examples of electronic engineers, biochemists and other technologists who have had ideas, made discoveries and then beyond the confines of the institution have been entrepreneurial in commercially exploiting that idea, some with obvious success, others to fail. The individual has been entrepreneurial, not the university. However, today universities are changing as many aspects that we associate with business cultures are beginning to become more apparent in academia. Financial accountability, business plans and deficit activities, concepts that once might have been considered totally alien, now are much more familiar within institutions, and accepted by most as an inherent part of professional life, as once they might never have been.

If for a moment the university is viewed as a business, then any assessment or audit of its value – as is undertaken of companies – would need to include not only its property and assets but also an estimate of its intellectual capital, because in business terms this is an institution's greatest asset and strength. How does – and indeed should – a university have a responsibility for maximizing the return its makes on these assets – or is an institution just a collection of individual spirits that conveniently have gathered together? There are significant cultural gaps in approach between academic institutions and industry (Jones 1997), yet despite the long history of many universities, they cannot afford to be any less entrepreneurial than businesses. Interesting approaches are beginning to be taken to develop entrepreneurial skills in students as shown by Frade (1998, 2002).

In his review of the entrepreneurial developments that emerged from MIT and the associated growth of 'Route 128' companies, Roberts (1991) has drawn attention to some of the contributing factors. Not unexpectedly, these have included high calibre staff and access to venture capital through appropriate contacts in the financial community, but more interestingly structures within the institution that were conducive to entrepreneurs – even to the extent of encouraging the successful to leave the institution. Of course, a large number of high-technology spin-off companies located within the vicinity of the institution is mutually advantageous, but is not something that is easy to reproduce everywhere. However, this is an example of an institution itself providing incentives, both negative and positive, to encourage entrepreneurial activity.

Hampden Turner (1990) identified three dilemmas in the industry–academia relationship, namely (a) the enhancement of the university's basic mission to teach and develop pure knowledge versus the need to apply its knowledge so as to help the whole nation compete economically, (b) the disciplinary base of the university versus the inter-disciplinary base of most creative solutions, and (c) the university as a force for improving the techniques and practices of wealth creation versus the university as a moral and critical force within society, questioning its goals, priorities and practices. Two areas in which an institution itself takes a more active role in entrepreneurial activity are technology transfer and consultancy (with a principal focus on the commercial developments associated with the exploitation of research knowledge) and CPD (with a greater focus on advanced teaching that is informed by research knowledge).

Technology transfer and consultancy

The exploitation of intellectual property is more straightforward in a commercial organization than in a university. In the former case the role of intellectual property is important both to protect interests in existing activities and markets where the company is present and to establish for the company a strong and broad footing in those areas where it is envisaged that it might need to be active in the future. For an academic institution, the protection of intellectual property is no less important, but the reason for this is somewhat different and broader. It is likely that the exploitable material is of a longer range nature than in industry and the institution is not involved in conventional manufacturing, but its staff are the progenitors of ideas that have resulted from their researches and can be applicable across a wide and diverse range of fields – some of which may not at the time even have been established. The ultimate exploitation of intellectual property could be through many routes. It might be by those involved in the original research establishing a company for exploitation, whilst still being members of the university, or it could be that intellectual property is made available to existing organizations on a commercial basis, perhaps involving a significant level of technology transfer. By whatever route, it will be one of the aims of the institution to ensure that an adequate return is obtained for both the institution and the individual(s) concerned – the relationship between the individual and the organization being significantly more complex in an academic establishment than in a commercial one.

In both intellectual property exploitation and external consultancy the university has the opportunity to – indeed must – establish an entrepreneurial culture, which facilitates the effective development of this activity. Whilst for effectiveness and reputation, matching – or even approaching – the performance of MIT is a formidable challenge, increasing numbers of institutions recognize the importance of this activity and have given greater prominence to it in the development of the institution. The important realization that has happened to academic institutions is the recognition that intellectual property, consultancy and technology transfer are all integral parts of the broad mission of higher education and need to be encouraged and supported.

Continuing Professional Development (CPD)

A second example of where an institution might be entrepreneurial is centred on its approach to CPD. At the more advanced levels, participants themselves can be very knowledgeable. There are many 'stakeholders' with a diversity of interests and their focus and aims are not as coherently well-aligned as they might be to make activities effective (see Jones 1996). In soundly structured foundation education, significant thought is given to devising educational programmes, which (1) reflect the paradigms of the subject, (2) employ a diversity of learning strategies, (3) attempt to match the learning process to the desired outcomes, (4) test the effectiveness of the process in a variety of ways and (5) provide important feedback to both student and teacher. Naturally such statements are easier to make than to implement (Goodlad 1995), but clearly they should form a basis for the educational formation of most scientists and engineers. In contrast, a much lower level of attention has been given to applying these criteria to CPD. For the future, as the importance of CPD – especially for science, engineering and medicine – continues to grow, it will be increasingly necessary to reflect on these shortcomings and put in place mechanisms for improvement.

CPD requires an entrepreneurial approach and, in contrast to undergraduate teaching, where often the debate about resources and responsibilities is conducted separately from the one on educational structures and paradigms, it is far more customer driven. Historically institutions may not have given sufficient thought to the learning, as opposed to the teaching needs of students, but even less thought has been given to the learning needs of professionals and the institutional approaches to meeting these. This is brought into sharp relief when considering the role that new media and IT might play in the evolution of CPD against a changing background of professional practice and pressures.

While from a provider perspective the focus of CPD might seem to be primarily teaching, it is certainly the case with such activities at Imperial College that the presenters must be at the leading edge of their fields if they are to be effective within the College's programmes. In these activities, the scope for the institution itself to be entrepreneurial is manifest. The market is far less captive and more dynamic than undergraduate or postgraduate teaching and the participants more demanding. As such, it is an activity that requires high-quality teachers who both know and are up to date with their subjects and are effective in communicating them to professionals, who may be very knowledgeable in their own right and who will have little sympathy with any aspect that is second rate. It was not very long ago when the very existence of these activities, let alone their importance, would have been questioned and seen as a distraction from the principal purposes of the existence of a university. Unfortunately, however, such views are still not as obsolete as they ought to be.

The driving forces, outlined above, clearly demonstrate the need for effective CPD, but while this is well established and widely recognized, the activity has yet to find an appropriately formalized place in professional life. Its role is often not considered by those concerned with the development of mainstream engineering education, however much this is changing (see Midwinter 1999). I would argue that *inter alia* this is because so far we do not have appropriate mechanisms with which to recognize this and make it an integrated reality. Amongst the questions this poses is how an institution embraces these changes, while still maintaining its inherent and valued culture. At a time when society is becoming increasingly qualification and quality driven, appropriate mechanisms have yet to be developed that can address the issues of lifelong learning.

One way in which these paradigms can be bridged is by giving greater prominence to the role that CPD can and must play and by an increased effort to integrate it with initial education. We must begin to see initial education as laying the essential foundations on which CPD activities will build later. CPD must become a recognized and integrated part of professional practice, with the emphasis on continuing and not remedial, on professional (that is aimed at an appropriate style and level) and on development from a recognized base. It should be emphasized that there can be no compromise to the position that an initial professional education must be of the highest standard and must establish secure foundations in essential disciplines. For example, an engineer without an adequate grasp of mathematics would be a commodity of highly questionable value. Without such foundations, CPD cannot be what it should be.

An example may be drawn from the area of analog circuit design. Today most graduating electrical engineers have acquired a useful and applicable knowledge of design skills in digital electronics. In addition, there are advanced design and support tools, extending from requirements capture through to design, simulation and testing. In contrast, the level of engineering knowledge, expertise and support tools for analog electronics is not nearly as advanced, yet analog designs are key elements in many circuits and systems, for example for mobile phones and medical electronics. At Imperial College intensive courses for professionals (usually over 3–5 days) are regularly scheduled to help develop analog design skills. These courses are presented by international experts from the UK, United States and mainland Europe. The attendance at these courses is high. The qualifications of the engineers attending can be that of a first degree through to a PhD. There is no assessment and no qualification is awarded, with attendance usually being driven by the needs of companies to maintain a competitive edge in a dynamic field and by the engineers to help them both solve immediate problems and enhance their own marketability.

The term CPD embraces a broad range of important but differing activities which extend from formal qualifications through to mentoring. However, by taking a wide variety of forms, its interpretation can give rise to confusion. For example, in the UK, professional engineering institutions have begun to give increasing attention to encouraging and recording the participation of their members in CPD activities; but much work remains to be done. Significantly more changes will have to be made to the nature, quality and formalization of this activity, if it is to be successful in realizing the important changes that will be needed, both for lifelong learning and meeting the needs of professionals, organizations and society.

This brings into focus key concerns regarding the role of initial education and CPD in areas of dynamic change. Before too long, we will need to grasp firmly the nettle of a more integrated approach to the education of professionals – especially those involved in science, engineering and medicine. We will need to give due recognition to the fact that we cannot educate tomorrow's professionals to the level we would wish within the period of initial education, and increased emphasis will need to be placed on a formalized role for CPD. If we move to a broader initial education, then it is all too easy to run the risk of being one that lacks the necessary depth in its essential parts and not forming a useful and coherent body of knowledge. The challenges of CPD for these groups must be addressed as a matter of necessity for effective competitive survival, although unfortunately the resources for such activities can be transitory and the political message frequently somewhat diffuse.

It is part of the responsibility of those who would claim to champion the importance of the role that education should play in developing future economic and industrial prosperity to ensure that an appropriate framework is in place for its development. This framework needs to be flexible enough to embrace diverse inputs, and yet at the same time be able both to reflect high-quality standards in its operation and achieve levels of acceptability, locally and globally. Regrettably, however, there is always a tension between political and educational timescales and, as we discuss movements towards lifetime education, this tension becomes even more pronounced.

Of the trends currently affecting CPD, which are brought about by diverse influences, the foremost being the globalization of economies, international product standards, the move towards a single business language, the information era and educational technology, there are probably three critical themes. Some of these we can influence and make effective. These are that:

- the increasing overlap between business success and education of professionals must be highlighted;

- the increasing importance of technology as a valuable tool in the educational process must be understood and fully harnessed, yet not overstated; and
- any response to the growing emphasis on flexibility and responsiveness within the educational system must be made without sacrificing any level of excellence.

The challenge will be to respond to these themes whilst (importantly) maintaining the established virtues of cohesiveness, continuity and quality. It will be essential to ensure that professionals have a sound initial education, and that throughout a working career CPD is embedded sufficiently in professional practice and is used effectively to reflect the cultural needs of society. The acquisition of the necessary language skills, of managerial and financial abilities, an awareness of environmental, legal and ethical concerns and the placing of these within a broader social context are all topics that can form part of a necessary – and perhaps mandatory – professional development activity.

CPD and the learning society

The changing educational paradigms and the need to match the requirements of the individual, employer and the community are very challenging. Although understandable in comparison with the thought and debate that accompany issues associated with first- or second-cycle education, too little consideration is given currently to these issues within a professional context. A workforce that is constantly being re-educated will be crucial to future economic competitiveness. This does not make it easy either to achieve or to ensure that it receives the necessary resources to make it a reality. Lee and Messerschmitt (1999) paint a future scenario of groups in contact and obtaining education at appropriate stages in their career to meet their needs.

A highly simplified comparison of the role that education plays today, and how it might need to change to meet the future needs of society, is shown in Figure 7.1. The upper part illustrates how today a career follows education, while the lower part indicates several differences Lee and Messerschmitt envisaged changing in the future (they were envisaging a scenario for the year 2049). Although this is a simplified representation, it should be clear that the relationship between career and education is far more intimate and the reasons for this differ little from those that today drive the need for CPD, namely the increasing role that education plays in our society and its linkage to economic competitiveness.

We may still be a long way from this model, and although it might be argued that from where we are today significant changes are suggested, it is surely highlighting the direction in which we need to move. At the same time, if a structure of this nature is more important, and indeed more

Figure 7.1   An evolving role for education

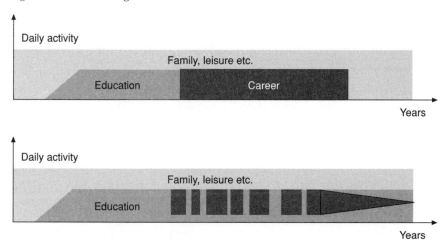

Source: After Lee and Messerschmitt (©1999 IEEE)

prevalent, for the professional of tomorrow, then there are several key questions that need to be addressed. A train of reasoning very similar to that surrounding CPD emerges.

If economic success and business viability are linked to the educational levels of the workforce, which for several reasons need to be refreshed constantly, it will be necessary to move away from some of our current structures. In a society which has become inexorably more qualification conscious and oriented, it will be necessary to identify ways in which CPD activities can be given formal levels of credit, recognizing that these same professionals will be wrestling with a competing range of other company or individual pressures. We are a changing society and it will be vital to reflect this in our education.

As in many other academic institutions, Imperial College departments offer full-time MSc degrees in a wide range of topics and in addition to its 12-month full-time MBA, the Management School offers an executive education programme lasting 24 months that also lead to an MBA – a programme that although expensive is popular and leads to a qualification which is recognized globally. In the CPD programme, the bulk of activities last 1–5 days, although there are exceptions to this with non-credit pro-grammes in petroleum geology and engineering lasting 3 months, but not leading to a qualification. Interestingly, these are truly international, being undertaken jointly with the Institut Français du Pétrol (Jones 2000). If we are to be successful in developing future CPD programmes that meet the needs of society, conform to a Lee and Messerschmitt type model and also meet society's need for qualification recognition, then we will need to bridge this gap and develop qualification-related CPD programmes of a new type.

These will need to be suited to the needs of professionals who will have a first degree, and which, while serving their focused professional requirements, will need to be flexible. They will need to take into account the greater mobility and fluidity in the labour market, but most importantly, not compromise academic rigour. Clearly, these are challenging objectives that will need to be faced.

New paradigms, new cultures, new challenges

A century ago, the establishment of a basic telephony network started a process that has had a profound influence on communication patterns and henceforth on all other aspects of life. Today, the growing penetration of wide-band telecommunication networks and personal computing, accompanied by the increasingly sophisticated software, which can be supported on current hardware, is beginning to have a similarly significant impact on information access, global communication, business practice and education. It could have a significant influence on the future role of educational institutions, as currently recognized, and raises deep questions concerning appropriate ways by which to realize effective educational development in the future. There is the potential to deliver education wherever and whenever required and such opportunities will have an impact not only in countries that happen to be large, scattered or have challenging terrain, but also even in the dense populations of Western Europe. This impact should not be underestimated or misconstrued.

What will be the educational impact of the IT/telecommunications revolution. Will it complement the established order or compete with it? How is it to be understood and 'managed'? In some respects, the borderlines between education and entertainment may become blurred. (Compare how museums are changing in the way they display their collections.) Such a transition – which in part results from technological developments – may not be bad, but if it results in any retreat from the highest standards, however achieved, this will be unacceptable. The aspiration for excellence cannot afford to be compromised. The issue in industry, in academia and in education is to strive to provide honest answers to fundamental questions. Good education is a challenge, a complex interplay of acquiring background facts, of developing lines of thought processes and problem-solving skills, of questioning and of self-realization. The 'best' educators and institutions are the ones that, by whatever methods, are most effective in developing these skills. Perhaps it will be that by the utilization of technology, by whatever means is most appropriate, we can open the best to a wider audience and that is an important key to success. We must harness the best – a mediocre lecture does not help the student and neither will mediocre distance education. At whatever level, the best in education challenges. We have to ensure that this is maintained, otherwise we will not be truly successful. When technology changes, a company cannot be sure that its market share will be maintained, and failure to recognize this may lead to business failure. In a similar way, education will have to be assessed by what is effective in specific circumstances. So while it is inappropriate to identify a single purpose, effectiveness in meeting specific measurable outcomes will become increasingly important; an indicator that education is becoming more tightly coupled with economic strength.

8

Corporate Universities: between Higher Education and the Workplace

Rob Paton and Scott Taylor

Introduction

For their staff, universities are becoming more like commercial work organizations. In the UK, the spectre of the 'McUniversity' (Parker and Jary 1995) is held up as a consequence of opening up higher education to the language and practice of commercial corporations. The arrival of managerial and entrepreneurial discourses in universities is held to be a key development in the provision of higher education and the conduct of research,[1] as 'faculty operatives' become subject to the demands of professional managers and generic managerial systems (Birecree 1988). The ability of the 'iconoclasts and ideologues' traditionally employed in universities (Buchbinder 1993) to keep politics and commerce at a distance is eroded (Marginson and Considine 2000).

Simultaneously, work organizations exist in a new 'knowledge economy', in which capital, machinery and even tangible products become less important as companies are differentiated through the 'knowledge capital' they possess (Scarbrough et al. 1999). In this context, commercial companies produce and manage knowledge to increase shareholder value and serve customers more effectively. As universities absorb the language and practice of corporations, so multinationals become 'epistemological holding companies' (Barnett 1997: 125). The production and legitimation of knowledge moves off-campus into contexts of application: work organizations become primary locales for the generation of new knowledge. This Mode 2 knowledge production institutionally dispersed and socially dependent, contrasts with the Mode 1 knowledge production of traditional universities (Gibbons et al. 1994). The university is no longer the only house of knowledge; indeed, there may even be a village springing up (Spink 2001).

However, the interplay between universities and work organizations goes beyond these dynamics. Many of the largest corporations in Europe and the

United States have gone one step further in expanding into knowledge production and education, setting up their own educational institutions. Skills training and vocational qualifications are now routinely offered by institutions such as the Disney Institute, Hamburger U, and Motorola U in the United States, while in Europe, corporations such as Unipart (owner of the 'fourth university in Oxford', Unipart U), Shell and British Aerospace have invested heavily in either bricks and mortar or virtual learning spaces which are termed universities, colleges or academies. There are a growing number of manuals with advice on how to found and run a corporate university (CU), and a series of CU learning groups facilitated by management development organizations are currently running.[2]

However, analysis of this phenomenon is largely absent from both educational and organizational research. There are only occasional mentions in the *Times Higher Education Supplement* and the *Financial Times*, and academic analyses note primarily the threat to independent scholarship from these barbarians attacking university territory (for example Craig et al. 1999). This lack of interest may be a result of perceptions of CUs as ephemeral, as little more than corporate training facilities – perhaps even resistance to the notion that a company can legitimately use educational terms or pursue educational aims. Such presumptions may be understandable, given the frequency of hyperbole and fads in management, but they are not *a priori* justified. This chapter examines these issues in more detail and makes a preliminary assessment of the significance of the CU phenomenon.

Delineating the phenomenon

Corporate initiatives in training, education or knowledge management may be pursued under a wide variety of labels. Due to legal restrictions on the use of the term 'university' in the UK, British-based CUs tend *not* to be called universities, but use closely related terminology, such as 'U', *universitas*, institute, academy or college. Notwithstanding, the CU, whatever the precise term in use, may be located as an aspect of the many strategic learning initiatives seen recently. Whether, to what extent, and in what ways these initiatives differ from (or alternatively, reproduce) the sorts of training schools that have long been a feature of the corporate landscape is an empirical question considered in the course of the chapter.

Based on a preliminary taxonomy (Taylor et al. 2001), we would suggest that there are two primary definitional strands that differentiate CUs from other educational institutions. First, it must be recognized that while we are dealing with an evolving phenomenon, CUs are essentially part of commercial work organizations.[3] Most activity reported has been in the private sector, although initiatives are underway in the public sector (such as the Air University of the US Airforce, or the NHS University in the UK). Thus, a central aspect of the CU phenomenon is the status of the umbrella organizations: commercial, with missions not driven by teaching or research.

Second and relatedly, CUs draw their clientele exclusively from those currently employed in work organizations, most often the work organization funding the initiative, a supplier or a customer. This restricted clientele and focus means the student body and course content of CUs are often severely limited. Taken together, these aspects of CUs differentiate them clearly from existing modes of educational provision.

The emergence of corporate universities

The first formalized 'corporation schools' appeared during the nineteenth century, taking training in-house and making contacts with educational institutions (Eurich 1985). Corporations such as DuPont and Edison began to provide technical and liberal arts education for current and prospective employees. Filling a gap in state provision, these institutions are the precursors of CUs. However, the medieval split between mental and manual knowledge and learning ensured that work-oriented learning and management education remained outside the academy. Corporations continued to train employees on this basis well into the twentieth century, expanding early initiatives to include the nascent profession of management, bringing more and more employees to the classroom in the expectation that investment in the individual's education would result in a happier, more productive employee, better able to perform job tasks. Personal enrichment and enhanced productivity thus come together happily in a deal with benefits for the individual and the organization.

The structure of corporate education was changed radically, however, by technical colleges and universities willing to deal with business and management. The first schools of commerce in the UK, in Birmingham and Manchester in the 1920s, were early indicators of the potential for higher education in dealing with work organizations. Business and management courses today are the single most popular subject in UK universities; over 20 per cent of undergraduate courses contain a component relating to this area. Business schools are now found in most British universities, and are often financially supportive through delivery of high-margin, 'cash-cow' courses such as MBAs (Burrell 1997). However, attitudes to industry and management within universities are suggested still to be broadly negative, with the result that 'less formal, privately funded' institutions such as Ashridge and Henley are created specifically to service the corporate community (Linklater 1987).

This brings us to the question of how CUs become part of the organizational landscape, and where they fit into this complex interplay between higher education and work organizations. An early analysis of a CU is provided by Wiggenhorn (1990), relating the development of education (as opposed to training) within Motorola to the implementation of new working practices that required a more autonomous worker. In the (then) new corporate world of individual responsibility and understanding, rather than hierarchical abdication and unthinking production, Motorola decided to re-shape employees. However, managers rapidly became aware that many of those employees they wished to introduce to advanced skills and methods of working were functionally illiterate and non-numerate, or unable to follow instructions in English. This resulted in two key innovations. First, managers began to assess employees on a wide range of key skills that would normally have been taken for granted. Second, managers began to talk to local educational suppliers and to make demands as to course content and delivery.

This scenario has been played out across the United States since then, as managers in large corporations flex their financial muscles in relation to educational supply. The dynamics of CU–university interaction and the business drivers for implementing a CU initiative are outlined in detail by Meister in her distillation of CU practice (1998). More than anyone else, she has articulated and influenced the practice of CUs in the United States and Europe, through publications and consulting services.[4] She begins by setting out external conditions that demand the inception of a CU structure. Here we find familiar claims about a shift from bureaucratic to post-Fordist organization of work, the emergence of the knowledge economy in which mental rather than manual skill defines the successful employee, and the replacement of lifetime employment in organizations with the provision of employability for temporary corporate members. Meister asserts that a common overarching goal of corporations with CUs is to 'sustain competitive advantage by inspiring lifelong learning and exceptional performance' (1998: 19). In addition, corporations with CUs will be working to the ideal of individual and organizational learning, rather than simply providing skills training for individuals. More practically, key aspects of the CU include the commitment of senior management to the initiative, forming learning alliances with existing educational providers, the increased use of technology to deliver learning experiences, and the operation of the CU as a separate cost centre.

Meister's work emphasizes the centrality of learning to commercial organizations throughout. Since the early 1990s, the notion of the learning organization (Senge 1993, Marquardt and Reynolds 1994) has entered corporate discourse as an ideal and an aspiration. Operationalizing and even defining this notion is notoriously difficult (Easterby-Smith 1997). Meister purports to offer a clear path to becoming a learning organization, through CU initiatives. However, her treatment of the issues involved are peculiarly American, and recommend that the ultimate goal of any CU initiative should be an independent profit centre, offering learning services to the wider community in competition with established providers. This over-riding concern with commercial viability does not fit well with either developing a learning organization or the aims of education and knowledge production.

Finally, the period that has seen the emergence of CUs is also a time of rapid change in higher education in the UK. Key developments can be summarized in terms of 'massification', further vocationalism and the widespread acceptance of part-time and non-campus-based models of higher education achieved through forms of open and distance learning. All of these developments, at policy level, in work organizations and in British state universities form part of the operating environment that CUs are in.

Framing the research questions

In this section, we pose a number of questions that we consider to be central to understanding CU initiatives in the British and European contexts.

Superficial or substantive changes?

The industrial changes and challenges to which CUs are, according to Meister (1998), a response, have been offered as justifications for many new organizational practices, not all of which have endured. At the same time, she is open about the rationale for using an educational label for this initiative. She argues that re-designating training departments as universities, academies or colleges will 'conjure up the sort of expectations that match their [senior managers'] objectives' (1998: 34), and that such a label acts as a 'metaphor to provide the image for the grand intent . . . [lending] a certain cachet to the corporate training effort that is attractive to employees' (1998: 35). Hence, although Meister claims that CUs are new and important, it is possible that the new elements are not particularly important and that the important elements are not particularly new. For us, therefore, a primary research question is how far and in what ways CUs differ from conventional training schools, and whether any differences seem likely to persist (particularly if they are seen to reflect economic and technological drivers). Alternatively, if the projection of a favourable corporate image is the major concern underpinning CU practice, it would be less surprising if in due course the CU were to drop down the corporate agenda.

University-like or a misuse of language?

Meister's outline of the uses of a CU for managers, employees and the sponsoring corporation emphasizes cost, utility and image above all else. By contrast, many of the themes of higher education and higher learning centre around distinctive values – on notions of democracy, pluralism, the ideal of social justice and a love of the life of the intellect (Calas and Smircich 2001). However, given the diversity of higher education today, the idea of a university is more than ever a problematic and contested concept (Barnett 1997). An idealized or essentialist definition is therefore inappropriate, and instead it seems better to think in terms of a range of characteristics and of 'family resemblances' among institutions. For the purposes of this analysis, we would propose the following characteristics as among the more significant dimensions of 'university-ness':

- a concern for higher learning in terms of intellectually demanding subjects and levels of study, but also concerning the transmission of values or a tradition;
- valuing knowledge in terms of its creation (research) and its preservation;
- a discrete social space, semi-detached from mainstream activity, with distinct social norms (such as collegiality and valuing critical thinking, for example);
- the award of qualifications and a concern for standards in higher learning; and
- pedagogies based on communities of learners and a degree of personalized learning.

Whether and to what extent such characteristics are becoming discernible in CUs thus offers a way of assessing use of the 'U' word – is it a far-fetched metaphor or an increasingly plausible usage, albeit in an unfamiliar context?

Separate or interacting?

As Eurich (1985) emphasized almost two decades ago, corporate-sponsored classrooms are usually seen by managers as complementary to existing educational provision, and historically, they have developed separately from state-sponsored higher education. However, Eurich also foresaw that the developing corporate educational market and activities might become an 'unintended challenge' (1985: 124) to business schools and universities. In any event, corporate demand for education and training services is huge, both in the United States and in Europe, and public educational institutions are far from being the only suppliers – a dynamic that disturbs many in the educational world (Buchbinder 1993). Hence, the possible impacts the emergence of CUs will have on the wider field of higher education are another way in which the significance of the CU phenomenon can be analysed. This can be explored partly through considering the strategies CUs are adopting towards their education and training providers, and partly through considering whether they are changing the patterns of university–industry relations.

Methodology and the case organizations

We begin from the basis that the strategic intent and meaning systems surrounding CUs are first constructed by those leading the initiatives within corporations. This is not to suggest that managerial meanings are the only ones which attach to CUs – indeed, the perceptions of learners, clients and other stakeholders are central in shaping CU practice as it evolves. However, senior managers' discourse provides a fundamental reference point. Exploration of these meaning systems implies the use of interpretative, qualitative methods. To this end, we have begun our investigations into the CU phenomenon with a series of in-depth interviews with CU directors and staff. Each interview lasted between 1 and 2 hours, and covered topics such as the micro-political and operational issues involved in setting up a CU, the educational aims and methods, and the relation of the CU to existing education and training providers. We analysed the resulting data using a combination of qualitative data analysis software and manual coding, in order to begin to identify themes rapidly and reliably, and retain closeness to the data. Four of the companies concerned and their CUs are described in the following paragraphs.

ElectroCo, a French multinational employing more than 70,000 people around the world, set up a CU in the late 1980s, in part as a result of having an empty building on the outskirts of Paris. Initially, ElectroCo created courses focusing on the technological needs of employees, and employed consultants to deliver the courses. These courses then developed into degrees accredited through a partnership with a local state university, and senior management began to lecture regularly at the new 'university'. The CU is now located in the UK after ElectroCo merged with a British multinational, and is presented as a means of fostering a 'learning organization' culture. The university is also the central locus for the transfer of knowledge between employees and business units. Senior managers are encouraged to come to lecture at the university, courses are adopted according to current organizational strategy and the company values are emphasized throughout.

TransportCo is a British company employing more than 40,000 people and is the owner of one of the oldest CUs in the UK. The CU is exclusively internal, offering learning and knowledge management services only to company employees and business units. Initial planning for the CU involved assessing practice in the United States, but managers decided that initiatives there tended to be a 'rebadging' of existing training departments with a focus on cost-cutting and income generation. TransportCo's CU was more concerned with reproducing and extending the higher-level expertise essential for the longer-term success of the business – its champion hoped the CU would provide 'the capacity of an MIT within the company'. It was organized into three faculties, and a small core of faculty leaders were recruited internally. For the great majority of senior professionals and managers, membership of a faculty introduced (or recognized) a dimension additional to their existing roles.

OilCo is a European multinational, employing more than 100,000 people around the world. Senior managers have launched a CU initiative that combines existing face-to-face training and development with electronically delivered and supported distance learning. The OilCo CU is operating to similar business drivers as those of many other companies; electronically delivered and supported learning is seen as a means of reducing the cost of much basic training (such as health and safety), and also of maintaining standards among employees working in isolated locations. To enable the development of 'continuous learning cultures' throughout its operating environment, OilCo is actively pursuing the expansion of its CU as a service for suppliers and customers, so that they are trained to the same standards as OilCo employees. Courses are designed to be sensitive to local cultures while emphasizing the transferability of professional standards. OilCo sees its CU as a way of providing developing countries with a means of raising the skill levels of local employees.

ElectronicsCo is a British multinational that employs more than 100,000 people. The company is in the process of setting up a CU strongly defined by recent technological advances. ElectronicsCo's CU is less exalted in its aims than the other examples outlined above. All of the courses on offer are work-related, as senior managers perceive that line managers would not grant time to employees to pursue 'pottery classes or flower arranging'. The structure of the CU is designed with hi-tech organizations in mind, with little of the hierarchy and rhetoric associated with public universities in evidence, as a deliberate statement to employees not to expect a 'university-style' organization or values.

Findings

Our understanding to date is that CUs tend to differ from more familiar training establishments in four main ways. First, the emphasis on e-learning and virtual campuses, often for compelling reasons of cost, timeliness and accessibility (this was particularly marked at OilCo and ElectronicsCo). Second, the role of training and development not just in skills development but as a 'cultural glue' to assist in holding together large and highly differentiated and dispersed work organizations (highlighted at ElectroCo, OilCo and TransportCo). Third, the intention to integrate a wider range of training and development (not just operational, but also managerial and professional) within a strategic company-wide framework (OilCo and TransportCo in particular). Fourth, a concern not just for courses to convey pre-determined skills and knowledge to employees, but to foster access to and flow of relevant company-specific experience and expertise among employees and between business units, as and when they face unfamiliar challenges (as expressed often through reference to knowledge management and the learning organization, for example at ElectroCo, OilCo and TransportCo). These four themes, although given varying emphases by the interviewees, all have clear resonance in the practitioner literature.

Of course, it is hard to be sure whether these will all continue to be important features of corporate training and education policies as pursued under the CU banner. A concern with public image and 'brand' was apparent in several of the cases, most notably ElectronicsCo, where a senior manager said:

> It was pitched as much for the external image of ElectronicsCo as the internal, with a very high profile launch. So it was as much about 'this is what ElectronicsCo can do for you, member of the public or prospective employee' – here is ElectronicsCo as a forward looking company, establishing a corporate university, particularly for things like the graduate milk-round activity . . . as well as saying, 'here is a company which is active in e-business, e-commerce, and an illustration of the way we do business on the training and development front'.

On the other hand, two of the initiatives (ElectroCo and TransportCo) had already lasted 12 and 6 years respectively, surviving major corporate re-organizations and the departure of their original sponsors and champions. In addition, considerable sums have been invested in the newer initiatives; for example, at ElectronicsCo 30,000 employees were provided with laptops, and large numbers of additional workstations installed, so that all the main categories of staff could readily access the intranet-based training materials.

All the suggested characteristics of 'university-ness' were discernible in the practices and intentions of the CUs described by our interviewees:

- university-level study and discussion of technological and business issues are a feature of three of the CUs, and, as previously noted, the transmission of a common culture was often emphasized;
- evidence for the valuing of knowledge is seen in repeated references to its importance for the longer-term success and survival of the company, and to the use of knowledge management techniques (for example the use of intelligent software to create accessible collections of knowledge-rich documents, and to build communities of practice within which expertise could be pooled);
- recognition that learning had to be separated from mainstream activity even if it was closely related to it, and conducted under different social norms is shown in two of the CUs, notably at ElectroCo, where it was emphasized that the CU should be seen as a 'free space' in which students can speak with complete protection from hierarchical sanction – all managerial, social and national 'tribes' become one, according to the director; and
- professional standards were a particular issue at OilCo, and ElectroCo was able to award degrees for programmes it had developed in partnership with a state university.

On the other hand, only the longest-standing CU (ElectroCo) seemed to possess all of these characteristics of a university, and obviously the limitations of the data mean it remains unclear how significant a part of the CU operations these features are in practice.

There were clear signs that the creation of a CU could change relationships with higher education. For example, at TransportCo, prior to the formation of the CU, relations with universities were driven by many individuals across a wide range of business units. Managers estimated that they had contracts with more than 50 separate universities and business schools, for research and training purposes. The result was, as a senior manager in TransportCo emphasized, that the company simply did not know what was going on at a local level, or whether business needs were being addressed. An important initial aim of the CU thus became the rationalization of these many relationships, to deliver more focus, better value for money and 'additionality' for the company. This concern is echoed in the practitioner literature as supply-chain principles are introduced to sourcing learning services. Such developments could have a far-reaching impact on higher education, although at this stage it is unclear whether they will be sufficiently successful in their own terms to be sustained, as such centralizing initiatives are difficult to operate and often temporary.

Discussion

It appears that CUs are falling into one of two camps at the moment. First, there are initiatives like ElectronicsCo, driven by technology and focusing on providing learning opportunities through corporate intranets and the Internet to very large numbers of staff – a mass approach. Second, there is a more elite model in which senior managers retreat to a country house or corporate centre to examine real business problems and become accustomed to the norms, values and expectations of the work organization – the corporate 'boot camp' (Tichy 2001). The latter design is closer to the idea(l) of the university that is sketched by, for example Craig et al. (1999). Spatially separate, housing an elite community, designed to focus closely on key issues and supportive of a form of critical thinking, such CUs embody some of the ideals of the classic university model.

However, this is likely to seem a generous image to many. Such CUs remain an integral part of multinational corporations. Thus, students will remain enmeshed in the asymmetric power relations of the organization, despite the best intentions of CU directors and staff to create a 'free' space for critique and radical thought. Further, learning and thinking in such institutions is determined by business need, resulting in the generation of knowledge with a market orientation rather than social responsibility (Buchbinder 1993). It might also be argued that suggesting that a CU can encourage students to question work practices and simultaneously become compliant, self-disciplining organizational subjects (Hoskin 1990) is inherently contradictory. Employees encouraged to learn the roles crucial to success in large work organizations (Hirschorn et al. 1989) may not be best placed to imagine the innovative alternatives emphasized so strongly in corporate rhetoric. While employers may emphasize the need for innovation and creativity in work today, they continue to seek control and individual 'fit' with corporate values and practices (Brown and Scase 1997).

While such issues are important, it is useful to be wary of polarized thinking. The sociologies of science and of university life have demonstrated that universities have regularly fallen well short of their espoused ideals. Equally, studies of the modern corporation suggest they can often be pluralistic environments. Further exploration of the issue of labelling may be less rewarding than assessing the organizational impact of CUs in contemporary society. If, increasingly, major corporations want to encompass higher learning, debate, creativity and knowledge creation, how are they seeking to achieve it? Can the creation of a distinctive social space that seems to favour such processes be protected within corporate environments that generally have very different value profiles and time horizons? Accommodating such tensions may be one of the aims of the CU.

A second issue that is put into sharp focus by these preliminary findings concerns the rapid development of and prospects for e-learning. Eurich (1985) presciently noted that computers were the *deus ex machina* of (corporate) education, and it may be that CUs reflect in part increased ease of access to distance learning. Large, well-established business schools in the United States have been relatively conservative in their approach to 'techno-MBAs' and management education using information technology (Vernon 1999). The ubiquity of personal computers and the concomitant abilities to bring information or learning to the manager or employee has driven the development of more flexible, less structurally dependent learning processes. The development of the virtual campus, defined as supplying distance education through the World Wide Web, is dealt with in detail by Stallings (2001). Noting that function is no longer defined by location, it is argued that corporate training will come to be the comparator for traditional university and college courses. The virtual university is approaching legitimation through accreditation, state support and educational foundation endorsement. It is further suggested that this is evidence of it entering the educational mainstream in the United States and becoming a permanent feature of education, rather than a trend in delivery methods. However, Stallings' analysis places prime importance on the communication of information through the World Wide Web, and makes little mention of delivery through corporate intranets, central to many CUs. As we have seen, the resources available for these developments in CUs, and the potential for integrating them in the workplace, either face-to-face or virtually, with other pedagogic elements – peer learning, project work and coaching – are considerable. Hence, it may be that if genuinely new and technologically enabled forms of learning are developing, they will become apparent first in CUs.

Finally, if the CU does become an established feature of both corporations and the higher-education landscape, we would suggest that they are likely to contribute to the re-shaping of the wider institutional field (Powell and Owen-Smith 1998). Table 8.1 provides an outline of how university education and workplace training might begin to form an institutional field. However, it does not explore the scope for movement, dynamic interplay

Table 8.1 The corporate university as part of an institutional field

	Collegial university	Mass university	Corporate university	Company training school
Knowledge creation	Disciplinary, Mode 1	Mix of Mode 1 and applied research	Largely Mode 2	Little or none
Knowledge transmitted	Abstract, primarily non-vocational	Abstract, but often vocationally oriented	Including abstract principles, but strongly contextualized	Strictly practical, highly contextualized
Primary value system/culture of the university	Collegial	Technocratic	Functional, commercial	Compliance
Organization of the university	Collegial, academic/professional dominated	Managerial/professional hybrid	Network; mix of virtual and temporary face-to-face elements	Hierarchy
External links	With other universities or to elites in professions, government, business	With other universities and local employers	With suppliers of learning (or research) services, possibly universities	Few
Student entry and selection	Elite, with exceptions	Mass, meritocratic	Usually staff at many levels; possibly also suppliers and customers	Employees at lower levels
What is provided and transmitted	Disciplinary knowledge; the liberal arts tradition; societal high culture	Preparation for employment	Know-how and a particular corporate culture	Skills, requisite information
Time horizon	Long term	Medium term	Medium term	Short-term
Pedagogy and methods	Person-centred (tutorials) with traditional resource base (lectures, libraries)	Various, including distance learning and non-traditional systems and resources	Varied. Active and problem-centred learning	Instruction/didacticism
Intended outcomes for learners	Personal intellectual development, liberal values and knowledge base for a professional career	Transferable intellectual skills for career in a modern economy	Continuing employability and cultural fit	Improved performance on the job

and blurring among these forms, in part evidenced by individual movement between state education and CUs.

Conclusions

> Neither in its medieval nor in its modern form has the university disposed freely of its own absolute autonomy and of the rigorous conditions of its own unity. During more than eight centuries, 'university' has been the name given by society to a sort of supplementary body that at one and the same time it wanted to project outside itself and to keep jealously to itself, to emancipate and to control.
>
> (Derrida 1983: 19)

This chapter began with the proposition that CU initiatives have not been subject to serious examination either by educational or organizational researchers. We would not claim that CUs must now be taken as a permanent and significant feature of the corporate and educational landscape. This might well prove to be the case, but it is by no means certain – not least because CUs are disparate and in most cases still too recent to have secure niches in the ecology of corporate structures and processes. Rather, we would suggest that the data and analysis presented here support a modest claim: that for a variety of reasons CUs are potentially very significant and, therefore, warrant serious scrutiny by researchers.

In addition, we have argued that if they do prove significant, it is likely to be for two reasons. First, because their emergence reflects underlying economic and technological drivers that make learning – at higher cognitive levels and with dimensions of values and culture – a strategically important concern of large organizations. Second, because, in practice, to encourage such learning among key employees requires in some measure certain of the values, pedagogies and attributes that have characterized higher education.

To the extent that these developments are occurring, they are likely to be important for higher education for two reasons. First, if there are to be new technologically enabled modes of learning, they may well be discerned first in CUs. Second, if higher learning continues to be afforded greater significance by corporations, then their relationship to conventional higher education is likely to change. They may become more direct, more important and more demanding customers for universities and business schools.

Notes

1. The potential for tension in corporation–university research relationships has generated a large number of analyses: see especially Aronowitz (2000), Barnett (1997), Tight (1988) and Craig et al. (1999). This chapter, however, focuses on the interplay of commercial organizations and universities at the educational level.

2. Notable British publications include Fulmer and Gibbs (1998), Sandelands (1998) and particularly Dealtry (2000). Learning groups are currently being run by the European Foundation for Management Development and the Association of MBAs.
3. This is not to suggest that CUs always remain in this institutional position. In the United States, a significant number have been spun off to take their chances as independent, for-profit, educational providers in the wider market.
4. It is not unusual for one book to become hugely influential in the dissemination of management initiatives. However, it is more rare for there only to be one, as a bandwagon tends to develop in which ideas are replicated and refined. So far, however, Meister's books remain the only such publication on the market which is dedicated to CUs.

9

Corporate and Conventional Universities: Competition or Collaboration?

Eddie Blass

The idea of a corporate university

Jarvis (2001: 111) defines the corporate university (CU) as a strategic umbrella concept for the institutions created for developing and educating employees and the company's constituents in order to meet the corporation's purposes; they are systems of teaching and learning rather than universities in the traditional sense.

Arguably, this could also be the description of a training and development department, so what is it that makes a CU more than this? Wild and Carnell (2000: 5) believe it is the alignment of the corporation's training and development strategy and business strategy that is the defining factor and they list various characteristics that corporate universities should display.

Meister (1998) takes the view that CUs should be set against the public provision as they developed out of dissatisfaction with post-secondary education combined with a need for lifelong learning. However, if you ask CUs about their origins, few will admit to such dissatisfaction as being a key driver. Most of them expound the benefits of working with public universities rather than being in isolation.

Perhaps it is better not to try to define a CU too carefully, but to identify a set of continua along which most definitions sit. While each CU has its own peculiarities, there are some elements of common ground which can be summarized in comparison to the UK traditional public sector university as shown in Table 9.1.

Kerr (1995: 31) introduces the idea of the 'multiversity', being 'a city of infinite variety'. Essentially the university has multiple stakeholders, all of which require different outcomes, and as such he recommends that a certain amount of confusion exists 'for the sake of the preservation of the whole uneasy balance' (1995: 14). Table 9.2 demonstrates this stakeholder complexity for a British university.

Table 9.1   Comparative analysis of the public and corporate models of 'university'

	Conventional university sector	*Corporate university*
Title	Originated from scholarly community development into corporations named *universitas*	Title conveys culture and community of learning developed in-house
Historical account	Medieval/classical roots; development of old uni sector nineteenth–twentieth century, new uni sector late-twentieth century	Late-twentieth century; developed from earlier in-house training and education departments; offering new services, creativity, research and development
Aims	To provide liberal and/or professional education at a 'higher' level to individuals	Expand the knowledge base of their companies, adding to competitiveness, acting as catalyst for change
Outcomes	Qualifications (degrees, professional qualifications) and research	Raised horizons on what can be achieved, conveys the ethics, values and history of company
Level of education	Undergraduate, postgraduate and doctoral	Any from low-level functional training to postgraduate study through partnerships with traditional universities
Size and diversity of student body	Anybody who fulfils the entry requirements	Every employee in the organization, some guarantee a minimum amount of training per year
Knowledge generation	Mode 1 production of knowledge; some Mode 2 through industry partnership arrangements; published for public consumption, peer reviewed	Mode 2 production of knowledge; research shared with partner organizations, in-house publication; not publicly published
Ownership and control	Regulated and mostly funded by the state; reports publicly and is accountable to state organizations; 'control' is loose due to concept of academic freedom	Owned by the company, control varies according to the decentralized nature of in-house buying; always has to be some business justification
Links with other universities	Primarily collaboration exists in research projects	Links regarding delivery of accredited courses and some research

Source: Blass (2001: 168)

Table 9.2   Stakeholder analysis for a conventional university

Stakeholder group	Input	Output
Central government	Money	Services (chiefly graduates)
Employees	Labour	Money
Industry/employers/ shareholders	Research contracts, sponsorship	Research findings, employees
Local government	Money	Services
Professional institutes	Advice, money	Members, courses
Research councils	Money	Research findings
Students	Money, effort	Education
Suppliers	Goods/services	Money

Source: Allen (1988: 27)

Table 9.3   Stakeholder analysis for a corporate university

Stakeholder group	Input	Output
Central government	None	Better-educated labour force
Employees	Labour	Money
Industry/employers/ shareholders	Investment	Profit (through increased output)
Local government	None	None
Professional institutes	None	None
Research councils	None	None
Students	Effort	Education, training
Suppliers (including conventional universities)	Goods/services	Money

Source: Adapted from: Allen (1988: 27)

Clearly, there are numerous stakeholders with differing inputs, all requiring different outputs.

A stakeholder analysis of a CU would tell a different story, as shown in Table 9.3. Now the reflection of their ownership is clear. When CUs and conventional universities are working together, their stakeholder requirements may be competing.

Currently, there are four key ways in which conventional universities are responding to the development of CUs and the increasing interest of industry in the university sector: 'entrepreneurial' universities; corporate university partners; 'corporatization' model; and collaborations for common goals.

The 'entrepreneurial' universities

This is the model of the university operating as a corporation itself. While the funding basis may be considered the same for all universities, the reality is it is not. Some, although considered to be very much public and conventional, are to a large extent private with regard to their funding sources. The University of Warwick, for example, earns a considerable amount of its revenues from industry collaborations. It took a pro-industry stance along with its belief in 'academic excellence' and established various collaborative bodies such as the Warwick Manufacturing Group (a members-only research and development club), the Warwick Conference Centre, Science Park and Business School (Clark 1998). Strathclyde University is another that has considerable amounts of funding from the private sector. In particular, Strathclyde has considerable returns from intellectual property rights resulting from pharmaceutical research, and their Institute for Drug Research continues to operate in this manner. Here the institutional belief is one of 'useful learning' (Clark 1998) which necessarily aligns the university with industry as it is industry that makes use of the learning.

Clark (1998) in his analysis of 'entrepreneurial universities' identifies five elements that transform a conventional university into an 'entrepreneurial' one. A 'steering core', both managerial and academic is fundamental. This implies the introduction of a private-sector mentality regarding customers and profit in a sector steeped in traditions of students, collegiality and research for the expansion of knowledge. Second, Clark identifies links with outside organizations and groups; there is an imperative to link with industry. Third comes the concept of a diversified funding base. Entrepreneurial universities are not dependent on a single source of funding, entrepreneurial universities have multiple sources of funds and this increases their autonomy by reducing their dependency on a single financial source. Clark's fourth and fifth elements are the development of entrepreneurial units, that is profit-making elements attached to the university, and the integration of an entrepreneurial culture. Profit is not a dirty word for such universities. They face closure if they operate at a loss.

The Corporate University partners

There are a number of conventional universities that have partnership arrangements with CUs in order to accredit the corporate programmes within the conventional university qualifications framework.

Concern surrounding the practice of CUs establishing such partnerships with conventional universities centres around issues of ownership and control, and the resultant loss of academic freedom.

> Academic freedom means the freedom of student and teacher to do research in their own way and teach as they see fit. As for actual subject matter, that the state leave to each individual. This defines the freedom which it guarantees against all interference, including its own . . . It does not mean the right to say what one pleases.
>
> (Jaspers 1960: 142)

In the CU this kind of academic freedom does not exist as the private corporation sets the academic agenda. In CU–conventional university partnerships academic freedom is limited as the corporate agenda influences the university's operation. Wild suggests that the role of conventional universities in these partnerships is to bring 'academic substance, quality, transferability and standing to what otherwise might be a particular company training initiative' (1999: vii). British Aerospace (1999) claims it achieves a 'balance' between the academic content brought by their partnership organizations with the unique requirements of the company. They have developed a bespoke engineering degree with Loughborough University to meet a specific need of their business (Midgley, 1999: vi). GEC is similarly developing an MSc in International Technology Management which will be delivered and awarded by three different universities in three different countries with Warwick University being responsible for overseeing the quality of the programme (Davies 1999).

The 'corporatization' model

One step further on from the partnership model stated above is the 'corporatization' model where a firm requires a corporate classroom within one or more conventional universities (see, for example, Macfarlane 2000). The corporate students are taught and assessed within the conventional university framework but the curriculum is largely set by the organization. The conventional university exerts little influence over the corporate programme, it merely delivers to the corporate design.

At the present time, there is no central national degree awarding authority in the UK. Since the disbanding of the CNAA, all universities have conferred their own degrees and only universities are allowed to do so. The system of external examinerships, and the regulatory frameworks of the QAA and HEFCE have provided some form of comparability between institutions, but essentially a university governs its own degree-awarding process. As such, if a CU wishes to award formal qualifications to its students, it currently needs to do so in partnership with a conventional university. This is the key to the BAe Virtual University. It works in partnership with universities to provide qualifications, usually at professional and postgraduate level, which are focused on the needs of the corporate body but are provided and accredited by the public body.

One interesting question is what would happen if a central degree-awarding power were reinstated. How many of the CUs would apply for the status to award a degree for their in-house education provisions? Some, in fact the majority, including Unipart and British Aerospace, deny any desire to go down this route. They feel they have more to gain from working in partnership with conventional universities. Others, however, do not share the same view. Motorola have suggested that they would by-pass the middle man, that is the conventional university, and provide everything themselves.

They espouse a great deal of confidence in their ability to provide better education than the conventional university sector. Indeed, they even have the Motorola University Press.

If the conventional universities lost their monopoly in degree-awarding powers, the marketplace would change rapidly, and new areas of competition would need to be addressed. No longer would conventional universities be competing only with each another, but they would be competing with industrial providers who would be offering qualifications and paid work at the same time – a concept that is attractive to many students.

Collaborations for common goals

Many articles have tried to establish the respective benefits to industry and universities from partnership activities (see, for example, Kells 1989, Barden 1993, Marceau 1996, Gregory 1997). While they highlight the benefits and some of the stumbling blocks that partnerships have to resolve, the implications for the future in terms of how these benefits reshape education are largely ignored. Drawing on their evidence, it is possible to summarize the situation as shown in Table 9.4.

The implications derived from this analysis of current collaborative enterprises show a clear path for future collaborations.

Research inputs

The nature of research funding is changing as funding for projects with indeterminable outcomes is disappearing. Mode 1 production of knowledge (Gibbons et al. 1994) is fast disappearing, and research for the sake of discovery is a luxury that universities cannot afford to support.

The shift to Mode 2 knowledge production (Gibbons et al. 1994) will essentially change the nature of university research. There will be the need for a foreseeable outcome from research from which a benefit can be derived either in terms of intellectual property rights for the university, or an industrial use for the partner organizations.

Research outputs

The publication of research findings is also changing. In collaborative projects, industrial partners benefit from the early access to the findings, and they aim to exploit these for maximum profit – that is the fundamental aim of corporate research. Academics, on the other hand, benefit from publishing their work, and the international recognition and esteem that publication affords them. Universities also benefit in terms of the research

Table 9.4 The benefits of partnership and their associated implications for the future of education

Partnership activity	Benefits to university	Benefits to industry	Implications for the future of universities
Research inputs	Access to real world problems and long-term research projects	Access to company specific research	Changing nature of research, knowledge production is primarily Mode 2
Research outputs	Secure funding by putting research output to work, that is possibilities of IPR	Early awareness of discoveries, exploitation of results	Conflict of university: desire to publish discoveries and industry desire for privacy for competitive advantage
Sponsorship	Additional specific funding for chairs, lectureships etc.	Good PR and additional impetus for research focus	Question of what the expectations are if you are funding the professorship
Continuing education	Secure funding by provision of in-house qualifications	Alliances increase provision of continuing education	Industrial influence on continuing education curriculum by buying in provisions for in-house cohorts
Placement students	Secure sources of placements	Recruitment mechanism re talent spotting	Industrial influence on undergraduate curriculum by feeding back to universities what it is they are looking for

assessment exercise. This situation is already changing. Corporate research projects were recognized in the most recent research assessment exercise, even if their results were not published for public consumption.

Sponsorship

The provision of sponsorship of a chair or lectureship raises questions around ownership. While there are substantial public relations benefits to be gained from sponsoring academia, the greater gains for industry are to be achieved through the work of the sponsored employee. It is another reason why there are pressures to focus research not on publishing the results but on exploiting the discovery instead, thus ensuring that only 'useful' research is undertaken.

Continuing education and placement students

The influence of industry on the curriculum can be direct or indirect. If a company employs a university to provide an in-house bespoke course resulting in a qualification specific to its organization, then the corporate influence on the curriculum will be large. The university will be left with the challenge of adapting the corporate curriculum to meet the level required by the qualification framework. Other areas of influence on the curriculum are more subtle. The companies that employ placement students, for example, require students with certain skills. It is up to the university to ensure that these are developed prior to the students applying. Graduate recruiters have a similar influence, as one of the ways in which universities are measured in the league tables is on the ability of their students to find employment on completion. Not meeting the expectations of industry is a costly exercise for universities.

It is easy to draw conclusions that this situation is undesirable; that it is the exploitation of education for industry; that it is moving the conventional university away from its liberal roots to a commercial, utility framework. This is not necessarily the case. The changing funding base of higher education in Britain has meant that universities have had to adapt to survive. There always has been and always will be an economic imperative to education, and the move towards collaboration between industry and universities could be an indicator of improvement in addressing the economic imperative.

The danger lies in the corporate influence being exerted to an excessive degree. If all research were company driven, if all teaching were company specific, if students stated their desired employer when enrolling and their education were tailored to that employer's needs throughout their studies, then the scales may tip too far in favour of industry. Universities need to watch these developments very carefully.

A model for the future

The emergent model of how the corporate and conventional universities co-exist could be interpreted as competitive rather than collaborative. Taking a critical evaluative stance, the focus on Mode 2 production of knowledge where results are largely unpublished but exploited for corporate profit could lead to the CU gaining at the expense of the wider public, and the introduction of sponsored roles coupled with the corporatization of the curriculum allows the CU to exert a large degree of influence over the conventional university. Funding is the key driver here. Conventional universities increasingly need the funding that the CU partnerships offer. However, alternative models to those currently emerging could be developed, redressing power and benefit inequality, and mutually satisfying the needs of both university sectors

Tripartite subsidiary companies

Perhaps the biggest area of contention, because it potentially yields the greatest financial benefits, is the area of research. Who owns the intellectual property rights of collaborative research projects? The exploitation of the knowledge produced does not have to mean the exploitation of the knowledge producers. Some universities are quick to ensure that they own the intellectual property rights, for example Strathclyde University (Clark 1998). Other universities are seeing the growth of small on-campus enterprises set up between academics and the university, for example the CEM centre at the University of Durham (the curriculum education and management centre). The future will probably see these enterprises being tripartite – that is their ownership will lie with the academics, the university and industrial partners. Essentially, they will be joint ownership subsidiary companies, and they will hold the intellectual property rights derived from their investments in research.

The return of Mode 1 production of knowledge

There will also be a move back towards some Mode 1 production of knowledge. As research becomes more and more focused on trying to meet specific outcomes, there is a risk that tunnels of knowledge will exist in voids. Exploration of tangent areas will emerge as necessary to complete the whole picture, and the value of research for discovery and innovation will emerge once again. Tapscott (1996) paints a picture of a future where change is happening so quickly that jobs will reinvent themselves every 12 months. Keeping pace with this change requires continuous learning, but when all the learning is focused on the future and none is focused on checking the present, gaps emerge and crises occur, such as the British beef crisis or the hole in the ozone layer. More Mode 1 knowledge production could have prevented some of these crises. Not taking the time to bridge the gaps will become increasingly expensive for industry, especially with the move towards recognition of 'corporate manslaughter'. Asking the unaskable and finding the answers will reappear on the corporate research agenda, and this can but benefit universities in partnership with them.

Cooperative undergraduate education

Undergraduate education is another area where the future will see yet more change. Already an undergraduate degree is seen by many students as a necessary condition to secure gainful employment. As degrees become more commonplace, employers also want work experience. While some courses offer placement years, the majority do not. Waterloo University in Canada offers cooperative education in the form of a 5-year degree, in which some of the studies take place 'on campus' and others take place in 'industry'. This model of provision requires good collaboration between the university and its partner organizations to ensure that each is providing a meaningful experience of use to the other and to the students. This model of provision is a collaborative model for the future, and one which will help a country to remain competitive in the global education market.

Institutes of applied academic disciplines

The cooperative education model will not be applicable to all disciplines. Not every discipline has a direct application to partner organizations, and this does not necessarily detract from the value of education in that discipline. It simply means that it is 'different', not more or less difficult, not more or less worthy, not harder, nor easier – simply different.

The differences between the applied academic disciplines and the 'pure' academic disciplines will become greater as time progresses. The applied nature of some will require greater collaboration, and the pure nature of others will ensure they are distant from collaborative partners. Models of collaboration already exist. University medical schools collaborate with hospitals. University veterinary schools collaborate with veterinary practices. Teaching colleges collaborate with schools. These collaborative arrangements will expand in the future and engineering, business schools, applied sciences and so forth will align themselves more closely with their application than with their pure academic foundations. If they don't, the corporate universities will, and the students will move away from the conventional universities for their applied studies.

This difference between the 'pure' and 'applied' academic disciplines will result in very different ways of operating, different value sets and different priorities. The two will ultimately conflict with each other as a common operating system will not be feasible. The applied disciplines will need to change continuously and will not survive the restrictions of current university bureaucracy. As such, the two institutions will split, and while they may be mutually supporting regarding inputs such as sharing funding, resources, staffing links and continuous development, they will need to operate as autonomous units in terms of their outputs. Neither will be 'better' than the other, they will simply be 'different'.

Conclusions

From its historical roots, the university has taken giant steps in moving towards collaboration with industry, but more steps need to be taken and more quickly if universities are to survive in their current forms. As these steps are taken, the realization that the current form is hindering the progress will lead to the splitting off of the applied disciplines from the pure disciplines in the operations of the university structure. Collaboration will result in cooperative degrees, tripartite subsidiary companies and a wealth of Mode 2 knowledge production resulting in Mode 1 production on the side. The opportunities are vast for both the universities and their industrial partners, but, as with all collaborations, care needs to be taken that both parties continually gain, rather than one gaining at the expense of the other.

According to Rooney and Hearn (2000), there are three future scenarios for conventional universities:

- the do-nothing scenario – let the momentum of history and the uncertainty of the future determine their strategy (largely the 'ostrich' approach);
- the commodified university – use technology that is available to move more toward a commodity model of knowledge distribution (largely the 'corporatization' approach); and
- the online learning community – using technology to connect and increase the diversity of knowledge through networks (developing a partnership approach).

In attempting to achieve the last of these, it would be easy to see how universities could slip into the commodity model. In trying to establish networks, modules could be produced which in reality could result in education becoming a commodity rather than a community. While an online community may become the standard model, the transition and development required to move to this may be very unattractive to many academics. The future academic in the future CU will be a very different being from the current academic.

Part 3

Enterprise in Universities and Colleges

Introduction

How are individuals and groups in universities and colleges reacting to the resource dependency pressures outlined in Part 1 and the organizational changes discussed in Part 2? Clark wrote of a stimulated academic heartland, suggesting that the pressures of resource dependency when resources are constrained invigorate the teaching and research of those who are working in the areas of conventional academic strength. This is very much the picture painted by Slee and Hayter who describe the work of a powerful group of support units in their university whose function is to raise large-scale resources that underpin the teaching and research of the university. Their conclusion is that the best enterprise support teams focus on major projects for big-picture ideas in areas that have the critical mass in top-quality staff, teaching and research. They need to take advantage of existing strengths and provide strategic support for the institution's long-term future. This is very much a view of enterprise as a collective strategic activity by the university in which the success of the enterprise units enables the academics to get on with what they are best at, namely research and teaching.

The other chapters in this section take a rather different view of enterprise: it is seen as a characteristic that needs to be exhibited by all or many members of the university or college. Hay, Butt and Kirby report on the psychological attributes of entrepreneurs and conclude that some of the items on which entrepreneurs score highly are similar to those on which academic staff of universities do well, but there are some differences. Generally, levels of task orientation were high and levels of creativity were moderate. However, the demand for autonomy and the level of calculated risk-taking were lower amongst the academics than shown in earlier studies. They speculate that this may reflect long-term cultural acceptance of a more managerial approach to higher education in the last decade.

Johnson's small sample of middle-level academic staff with marketing responsibilities suggests a more amateurish approach to the problems than that described by Slee and Hayter. Her small sample suggests that some academics at least are continuing to conceptualize their occupational role in terms that reflect the nature of the higher education sector *before* the recent structural changes. She speculates that this can be seen as an expression of vested interests or as the expression of the values of a group of professionals determined to retain their own 'moral and conceptual frameworks'.

10

Integrated Income Generation: the Durham Model

Peter Slee and Scott Hayter

In this chapter, we explain how, as members of the University Support Services, we have tried to improve service to 'enterprising academics' through the development of 'joined-up support'. We call this the Durham Integrated Income Generation (DIIG) Model. We explain the rationale for creating such a model and then set out the 'golden rule' for its smooth working. Finally, we illustrate how the DIIG Model works in practice via two case studies, and offer a brief summary of 'best practice'.

Rationale

There are two distinct 'drivers' which underpin our model. The first is strategic. The second is structural. The strategic driver is based on changes to patterns of state funding to UK universities.

In common with all European countries, higher education in the UK is highly dependent on state funding. Across Europe, the average of total university funding provided by the state is 75 per cent; in the UK, it is 72 per cent. Changes to state funding, therefore, have a critical impact on universities. Over the last 15 years its pattern has changed in three important ways. First, core funds for teaching and research have been disaggregated, and their allocation predicated on the achievement of stipulated targets, that is contracted student numbers and agreed standards in research. Disaggregation makes universities focus on markets. The outcome is that most universities have established specialist 'schools liaison' or 'recruitment' offices to help ensure they fill their specified quotas with students of the 'right sort' and 'research offices' which coordinate research policy.

The second major change is linked to the first. Following disaggregation comes deregulation of funding. Core funding is squeezed and greater sums are made available at the margins through open competition. The competition for these funds is intense. Their circumscribed nature means that competition is a zero sum game. There are winners and losers. The winners increase the scale of the losers' deficits. This trend has led to the increased specialization of support service provision. The good all-rounder will lose out in most cases to the highly trained market specialist.

The third funding change is the year-on-year reduction in 'the unit of resource'. Depending on one's point of view, this has either been the catalyst for productivity revolution in higher education (student numbers have doubled since 1989, while the unit of resource has fallen by almost 40 per cent, the proportion of top-quality rated research has also more than doubled over the same period) or it has contributed to a reduction in standards. Either way, there is no doubt that it also forced universities to think about diversifying their income streams and to look for new sources of funding. Over the last decade, British universities have chased EU and regional funds, developed their short course, consulting and intellectual property portfolios, and taken up systematic fundraising in the long-established US manner. In every case, they have had to seek advice and, over time, develop specialist support to do so.

The outcome of these significant shifts in the pattern of funding has been threefold. First, it has created a more market-led, but still under-funded system. Overall, a recent report estimates that in order to maintain current standards of teaching and research an extra £5 billion is required (*THES*, no. 1512, 9 November 2001: 1). The government has made it clear that this money will not be forthcoming from public revenues. Therefore, successful universities in the future will be those that become better at raising money from non-governmental sources. Durham University today gets less than 40 per cent of its income for core functions from state allocations. The rest – another £80 million annually – has to be earned in the marketplace.

Second, the funding pressures have changed the nature of academic leadership. Deans of faculties and heads of departments are now managers of what are, in effect, small or even medium-sized businesses. The vice-chancellor or principal is now the chief executive officer of a highly complex conglomerate comprising these micro-businesses. To a large extent, the success of the conglomerate depends on the success of the micro-businesses, each of which operates in its own complex market. To succeed, these businesses must provide demonstrably top-class education and/or groundbreaking research. To do that, however, they must be able to attract students to educate and money to fund research projects. Deregulation means competition for these resources is more intense. So academics can easily be drawn into spending more time chasing money, and correspondingly less time professing their discipline.

This leads to the third element underpinning the DIIG Model. The relatively recent pressure on academics to generate the resources they need to conduct their business has led to the development within UK universities of business support services, such as development offices. But in almost every UK university these services face a dilemma. On the one hand, following funding 'deregulation', university or 'corporate' income generation is an illusion, in as much as universities, *per se*, do not generate income. Rather, *academic departments* generate income from the delivery of specific services or initiatives. However, on the other hand, the combined financial needs of over 100 such units are often greater than any development office or income generation team can hope to meet in parallel.

The DIIG Model aims to address these three issues. First, it has to ensure that the university is able to meet its own strategic goals. Second, to do so it must provide effective support to a wide proportion of the academic constituency. Third, this must be achieved on limited resources, so making the money stretch is a critical issue.

The golden rule

Put simply, integrated income generation means the coordination of resource generation in support of strategic institutional goals. The golden rule of integrated income generation is synergy. This synergy needs to operate at three levels:

1. strategic integration;
2. structural synergy; and
3. shared objectives.

Strategic integration

Strategic integration of resource generation is absolutely vital. Using a business analogy, this means two things: first, clear integration between institutional or 'corporate' and departmental or 'service' strategies; second, a clear relationship between corporate strategic priorities and the operational plans for the services that will deliver them.

Durham has three corporate strategic goals established for the years up to 2007:

* to offer world-class learning and research;
* to create a closer 'fit' between our learning and research and the needs of twenty-first-century society; and
* to ensure we create a world-class infrastructure for our staff, students and other clients who deliver and use our services (University of Durham, University Strategy Document 1999–2007, 1999: 1).

These strategic goals shape the planning process in every academic department, which must then decide what they need to change and develop to deliver relevant world-class services to their clients. These needs in turn shape the agenda of the business support services.

The income generation objectives are clear. Departments need to:

- attract additional world-class academic leaders;
- develop an endowment to ensure that we continue to attract the best students, rather than those who can simply afford to pay; and
- increase investment in buildings and IT infrastructure.

In short, integrated income generation bridges the strategic and operational levels, tailoring operational plans directly to strategic goals. It makes clear to everyone what the specific priorities are, what will be done to achieve them, and – by definition – what will not be a priority and so cannot or will not be done.

Structural synergy

The integrated income generation structure aims to address the perennial practical problems of an imbalance between supply and demand. Currently, 98 per cent of Durham University income comes from three main income streams:

- human resource development activities (teaching and training);
- intellectual property activities (research and consulting); and
- exploitation of physical resources (accommodation, meals and conferences).

Given the 'deregulation' of UK higher-education funding, every one of these income streams is competitive and requires specialized support. This support is generally of three types:

- market intelligence;
- promotion and selling; and
- networking and fundraising.

In some cases, even within an income stream, universities may find that different academic disciplines require highly specialized, dedicated input. Nevertheless, many higher-education institutions have found it difficult to release enough core resources to invest significantly in broad-based specialist services, such as schools liaison or fundraising. This shortfall has limited their strategic impact.

As an example, to run a 'Rolls Royce' (perhaps Cadillac?) fundraising service, a university needs professional staff to address:

- research (which gathers and collects information about funding prospects);
- alumni relations (which builds long-term relationships with the largest grouping of potential supporters and donors);
- an annual fund (which generates small regular gifts from a large cross-section of donors);
- major gifts (which focuses on generating single gifts of over £20,000);
- fulfilment, donor recognition and donor relations (making sure gifts are acknowledged, thanked, registered and spent in accordance with the donor's wishes, and that regular reports to donors are made); and
- events management, finance, PR and IT (managing office infrastructure).

Servicing these tasks could easily require a staff of 25, with an investment of around £1 million. Outside Oxbridge, this level of investment has not been made. Europe is not yet a mature philanthropic market. In 1998, universities in the United States generated twice as much income in philanthropic donations as the whole of the UK charitable sector combined. Most established UK universities generate only 1 per cent of their turnover from donations. Yet these universities will generate some 30 per cent of their turnover from winning highly competitive research funding from the government. This gives any university senior management group food for thought. Pound for pound, investment in winning mainstream research funding is much less speculative than a comparable investment in traditional fundraising activities. After all, the funding sources are clearly defined and universities have a clear indication of their own research strengths.

Here is the cleft stick. UK higher-education fundraising does not yet sufficiently command the market to justify high investment in staff. However, without that investment, it cannot create that market. The result is a hugely under-funded and generally weak profession, where the overall level of expertise is low and success limited.

Shared objectives

A coordinated strategy for income generation related to clear strategic priorities and backed up by an integrated support structure can begin to overcome this blockage. In an integrated structure, philanthropic fundraising can punch above its weight. Its role is not to carry the burden of being a major income stream in and of itself, but rather to leverage income from donors to attract matching funding generated by the major income streams, namely human resources, intellectual property and physical resources.

In Durham, this income generation strategy is applied at the project level. As such, each project is clearly defined and clearly related to the corporate strategy. Each project is also carefully planned, and involves funding specialists from research, regional, European and student recruitment teams. There follow two examples of the process at work.

Case study 1: Ogden Centre for Fundamental Physics

Strategic integration

This project was generated by Durham University's strategic vision to create a series of world leading research teams. The Department of Physics had already established significant global networks in particle physics phenomenology and computational cosmology that aim to unlock the secrets of the universe. To develop a genuinely big-hitting centre of excellence with a critical mass unmatched in Europe, the Department required the sophisticated infrastructure necessary to attract new staff and additional funding for research and equipment. Accordingly, Physics developed a case for support that generated full departmental and institutional backing.

Structural synergy

The Development Office worked with colleagues in Research and Economic Support Services (REDSS) and the Physics Department to develop an integrated funding strategy. Potential funding bodies included the Particle Physics and Astronomy Research Council (PPARC) and two other government challenge-based funding opportunities: the Joint Infrastructure Fund (JIF) and the Joint Research Equipment Initiative (JREI).

Shared objectives

A communications plan including proposals, presentations, events and internal/external communications was developed by Corporate Communications. This was instrumental in the success of the proposals submitted to PPARC, JIF and the JREI. The Director of Development led the team, ensuring everyone was singing from the same hymn sheet. He took the vision to a prospective private donor who had been well stewarded over several years since making a significant major gift previously. The ability to demonstrate university strategic and financial commitment was a crucial issue to him, indicating that this was a major project with the full backing of the institution.

Proposals were submitted to potential funders. Timing was critical, in particular for the JIF bid, as it required a firm pledge from the private donor before making a commitment. In turn, the JIF commitment led to commitments from other funders. Thus, the private donation, in effect, became the lever that opened the door to the other funding pots. In November 2000, the University of Durham was able to announce the establishment of the Ogden Centre for Fundamental Physics which included a £5.5-million four-storey building, an Institute for Particle Physics Phenomenology (IPPP), an Institute for Computational Cosmology (ICC) and Ogden Chair in Fundamental Physics, a Centre for Nano-Technology and a Condensed Matter Laboratory.

All told, the integrated income generated for this project came from the sources shown in Table 10.1.

Table 10.1 Sources of income for the Ogden Centre for Fundamental Physics

Source	Purpose	Amount (£ millions)
Private donor	Leadership gift – ICC	2
JIF	Building	2.9
PPARC	IPPP	10
PPARC	ICC	1.3
European Community/Royal Society	ICC	0.3
JREI	Supercomputer	0.7
SUN Microsystems	Matching JREI	0.7
Anonymous private donation	Nano-Technology	2.2
	TOTAL FUNDS RAISED:	**20.1**
University own funds	Building and staff	5
	TOTAL PROJECT COST:	**25.1**

Case study 2: Wolfson Research Institute

Strategic integration

This project began with Durham University's strategic vision to develop a world-class research capability in health and medicine that would meet the healthcare needs of one of the UK's most economically deprived regions. The project's starting point was to establish a research institute at its newly founded Stockton campus, which would bring together an interdisciplinary research team drawn from existing high-quality departments. Once in place, this Institute would then provide the basic infrastructure to underpin a submission to the Higher Education Funding Council for England for the establishment of a new pre-clinical medical school. The school's first phase would involve a pre-clinical medical programme for 100 medical students. The combined programme therefore would sustain and enhance research and teaching in health, medicine and the environment within the University, while providing a critical service to the region.

Structural synergy

The challenge lay in the simultaneous presentation in the case for support of both infrastructure (building, equipment and new programmes) and staff and students. The initial problem was that the potential funders all wanted agreement from the others before making their own commitment. The approach we adopted to address this problem was to try to win a substantial leadership gift that would demonstrate enough support to lever out funds from the other prospective funding bodies. Toward this end, cultivation began in 1999, with the Wolfson Foundation as the prime prospect. The foundation had a long and supportive history with the University, but had never made a significant major gift.

Shared objectives

Again, the University Development Office worked with REDSS to identify other potential funders based on the high potential of both research outcomes and the regional economic impact. The scope of the initiative was such that we determined that regional funding opportunities (including One North East, which is the Regional Development Agency, a government agency responsible for inward investment in the North East of England, and Stockton Borough Council, which is the local city council) and the European Regional Development Fund (ERDF) were the best prospects to match the leadership gift. Advice on gaining the support of local and regional partners was crucial to the success of this project. REDSS staff played a key role in this regard working very closely with the senior leadership team at the Stockton campus. The Corporate Communications team developed a communications plan (media, press releases and proposals and events). The student recruitment team developed a recruitment plan for the Higher Education Funding Council for England bid to secure 100 funded medical student places. Proposals were then submitted to the various potential funders.

On 30 December 1999, the Vice-Chancellor secured a lead gift from the Wolfson Foundation for the building, and on 31 December (the deadline for ERDF funds) an additional significant gift was secured from the ERDF. In January 2000, the University of Durham was able to announce the establishment of the Wolfson Research Institute. The project included a £9.4-million research building at Stockton campus, a Faculty of Health, Medicine and Environment, a Pre-clinical Medical School, an International Centre for Regional Regeneration and Development, a Laboratory for Geo-Information, a Centre for Health and Environment and a Centre for Pollution, Hazard and Risk.

The integrated income generated for this project came from the sources shown in Table 10.2.

Table 10.2   Sources of income for the Wolfson Research Institute

Source	Purpose	Amount (£ million)
The Wolfson Foundation	Leadership gift	4
ERDF		3.5
Stockton Borough Council	Land	0.5
One North East	Land reclamation	0.5
	TOTAL FUNDS RAISED:	**8.5**
University's own funds	Building contribution	0.9
	TOTAL PROJECT COSTS:	**9.4**

Lessons for best practice

With regard to strategy, the whole institution needs a clear vision and strategic objectives to which everyone subscribes. The support services must establish what needs to be achieved to deliver the strategy, and then win institutional consensus. With regard to structure, a major gift as a leadership gift to leverage funds from other well-researched sources is extremely useful. With regard to synergy, it is essential to work as a team. All of the specialists involved – development, research grants, industrial liaison, corporate relations, public relations, communications, regional affairs and student recruitment – must avoid parochialism. The critical mass gained from close collaboration provides the expertise and knowledge essential to optimize the institution's chance of success in income generation.

In summary, the best enterprise support teams will focus on major projects for big-picture ideas in areas that have the critical mass in top-quality staff, teaching and research. Large wins for priority investment areas take advantage of existing strengths and provide strategic support for the institution's long-term future. For the most part, prospective major funders will only support a vision if it is unique, will make a difference and is of very high quality.

11

Academics as Entrepreneurs in a UK University

David B. Hay, Faith Butt and David A. Kirby

The enterprise agenda

Burrows (1991) claims that entrepreneurship became recognized as a main-stream social activity only as recently as 1979. Until then, entrepreneurship was the province of exceptional and often obsessive individuals. It is now, however, one of the dominant paradigms of British business and there is widespread belief that enterprise (or more specifically, entrepreneurship) is the key to unlocking future economic potential. The higher-education sector has not been spared; indeed, it is enterprise at the boundary of interactions between university-led research and business that is most commonly seen as the necessary spur to British economic development, especially in what is frequently referred to as a knowledge economy.

The UK's overall record of business funding of industrial research is poor. In 1997 only Canada and Italy of all G7 nations invested less in research as a percentage of GDP. Nevertheless, government considers the quality of British research activity to be consistently high and the House of Lords Select Committee report of 1997, for example, cites the OST reports of comparative national publication rates (OST 1997) as evidence of the pre-eminence of British research science. However the rate of successful patent application in the UK is far below that of the United States and many parts of Europe, such as Germany. It appears that Britain lacks the entrepreneurial culture and the support of enterprise that is necessary to convert technology into profit. 'The UK has an excellent science base but is widely perceived as having a relatively poor record of technological innovation' (Lissenburgh and Harding 2000: i). Higher-education institutions and other public-sector research organizations have an important role to play in improving this situation. This chapter argues for changes in the culture, organization and attitudes to universities so that they have 'the capacity and incentives to commercialise research and engage with business in making the journey from discovery to innovation and in improving existing products, services and processes' (Lissenburgh and Harding 2000: i).

The fact that business and entrepreneurial development is now listed as one of four strategic goals for British universities (Universities UK 2000) is evidence of just how seriously the enterprise agenda is taken in higher education in the UK. Some (such as Armstrong 2001) continue to dissent and argue simply that under-funding and poor resourcing is a far more parsimonious explanation for the relatively poor economic yields of British research than the lack of enterprise among researchers and business people. Nevertheless, the infusion and development of enterprise is now firmly established as a central policy agenda for British universities, and it is likely to remain so.

There are three principal ways in which universities can contribute to enterprise development: spin-out companies, enterprise development in students and consultancy.

First, the support and encouragement of spin-out enterprises is the direct conversion of research into wealth creation. Numerous recent papers have examined the strengths and weaknesses of various spin-out strategies (for example Hague and Oakley 2000, Brooksbank and Thomas 2001). In some cases, the commercialization of research-generated intellectual property rights is pioneered by the academic researcher, in others it is handed on to business champions with enterprise experience and merely facilitated by the university itself. In either case, the risk to the individual (researcher or business champion) is usually low, since only successful initiatives actually reach the stage of spin-out, and then relationships with customers, suppliers and others are already established. Thus, Armstrong argues that 'If the present processes of science-based company formation are maintained, there are no grounds for believing that its volume will be expanded through the encouragement of a risk-taking mentality in the course of education in entrepreneurship. Indeed, it may be inhibited' (2001: 549).

Some 'spontaneous spin-out' does occur in British universities, usually where individuals become so frustrated at the failure of their organizations to capitalize on industrial potential that they do it themselves (Steflensen et al. 2000). It may be that the individuals who take such initiatives have the loosely defined character traits of the entrepreneur – low tolerance of bureaucracy and high tolerance of risk and opportunism – but whether these tendencies can be inculcated is highly questionable, especially when they are most commonly expressed as a reaction against the *status quo*. Thus, Franklin et al. (2001) conclude that universities must employ enterprise development strategies that comprise both the entrepreneurial development of academic staff and the support of academics through 'surrogate entrepreneurship' by others. Where spontaneous enterprise emerges, it should be enabled, not hindered. Efforts to promote an enterprise culture within the university should make academics aware, for example, of support and help to facilitate the patent-application process, of potential economic markets for their discoveries, and of the rewards and prestige associated with enterprise over academic publication as well as the physical provision of services, resources and advice.

The second aspect of enterprise culture in universities includes the development of undergraduates and postgraduates for self-employment and entrepreneurship. Efforts have been made to do this since the early 1980s (Kirby 1992), but see the December 1999 issue of *Industry and Higher Education* for a collection of papers on entrepreneurial education in British universities.

Third, many universities are involved in both direct and indirect support for small businesses and enterprise through consultancy and other outreach services, such as educational and consultancy support for local firms. Watkins and Stone (1999), for example, report that 86 of the 172 degree-awarding institutions that responded to their survey claimed to be active in community-based entrepreneurship education and small and medium enterprise (SME) development. Overall, these authors concluded that the results of their survey showed entrepreneurship and SME education to be one of the fastest growing aspects of business education across the UK. According to Watkins and Stone, the main weakness in the UK remains the fact that most entrepreneurship development programmes seek the direct amelioration of unemployment, a legacy of their great expansion in the 1970s as part of the 're-employment programme'. This means that unlike in the United States, British support for SMEs is often coloured by a 'social agenda'.

The traits of the entrepreneur

Defining the 'entrepreneur' is a difficult task. This is one of Armstrong's most pertinent criticisms of the 'entrepreneurship literature', as without a robust definition of the subject, meaningful tests of its validity are hard to come by. Despite considerable criticism of the psychometric literature, and no consensus on the actual psychological traits of the entrepreneur, Chell et al. (1991) have loosely described the entrepreneurial personality as follows:

- a propensity to create business organizations;
- a tendency to pro-actively seek or create business environments for new opportunities;
- a creative and innovative approach to the solutions of problems and opportunities;
- an enthusiasm for autonomous and strategic roles in the conversion of opportunities to goods or services;
- a vigorous striving to achieve profit with business growth; and
- a willingness to bear the risks associated with these behaviours.

Of these attributes, much has been made of the last – risk-taking. Often it is held that it is the propensity to take risks that distinguishes the entrepreneur from the rest of the population. However, while this may be rather talked-up by entrepreneurs who have survived to become financially stable, the research on risk suggests that entrepreneurs are moderate, not high, risk-takers – they try to minimize the risk involved. As Armstrong has observed:

> First, an association between entrepreneurship and risk tolerance can be demonstrated within psychometric research only by the manipulation of samples so that it becomes true by definition. Second, surveys and case studies of small business owners show that the vast majority of them are not risk-takers. Third, research on the formation of science-based new ventures frequently tells a story of the transfer or avoidance of risk, rather than engagement with it.
>
> (Armstrong 2001: 527)

Entrepreneurs are, therefore, moderate risk-takers, who are able to cope with ambiguity and the uncertainty of doing something new.

Baron (2000) argues that successful entrepreneurs think differently from other people and, in particular, are less likely to engage in counter-factual thinking and more likely to show confidence in their own judgements. He also claims that successful entrepreneurs have better than average social perception and adapt to new social situations more readily.

Some researchers, Gibb (1987) for example, have suggested that entrepreneurs possess attributes such as initiative, flexibility and creativity, but have gone on to point out that these are common to a variety of people in different circumstances and are not the exclusive province of business founders who have established successful ventures. Comparisons have been made between managers of well-established firms and managers who left stable employment to create their own business. 'Intrapreneurs' (who work internally within existing business frameworks) are thought to need political insight and the skills to accomplish change within existing organizational structures, whereas entrepreneurs choose ends, define missions and maximize profits (Fulop 1991). Allinson et al. (2000) suggest that entrepreneurs can be distinguished from company executives and managers by their reliance on intuition.

A variety of psychodynamic tests have been used to test these assertions and to diagnose specific entrepreneurial traits (see reviews by Cromie 2000, Hisrich 2000). They have given conflicting results and investigations of backgrounds, environments and education factors, as well as studies of the personality of entrepreneurs, have led to few robust conclusions. Jennings and Lietham (1983) reported strong associations between the entrepreneurs' intentions, their career success and their internality.[1] Despite this, however, many researchers have criticized the psychometric approach for ignoring economic and social activities in their wider context (for example Hisrich 2000). Similarly, Chell (2000) argues that although there have been some significant advances in our understanding of entrepreneurship in the last 30 years, it is only a combination of the social constructivist viewpoint and the psychometric method that will really explain entrepreneurial behaviour. In particular, Chell (2000) points out that:

- business founders (with whom most studies of entrepreneurship have been done) are not necessarily entrepreneurs;
- entrepreneurs are anything but a homogeneous group; and
- analysis of individuals in isolation from the context of their social interaction process can be misleading and sometimes highly misrepresentative since evidence of exactly who did what and why is missing.

Entrepreneurship among university staff: aims and methodology

Caird (1991) is one of the few researchers to have carried out psychometric tests of entrepreneurial behaviours among a variety of occupational groups. Her approach is based on the psychometric methods of Johnson and Caird (1988) and is generally well regarded among researchers of entrepreneurship.[2] The test measures calculated risk-taking, creative tendency, the need for autonomy, the need for achievement and the internal locus of control. These are all traits previously found as strong personality attributes among business founders and company owner-managers. Caird's work suggests that business owner-managers have higher enterprising tendency scores (in all areas) than other occupational groups. This is not surprising since the test itself was first designed to produce maximum scores from this group. More interesting for the present chapter, however, Caird (1991) also found that the overall scores from lecturers and trainers were not significantly lower than those of the business owner-managers, and, indeed, the scores for autonomy, creativity and calculated risk-taking were all comparable. Only the need for achievement score and the internal locus of control significantly differentiated owner-managers from lecturers and trainers, although all other occupational groups were clearly different and separable statistically by their lower total scores.

The new research reported in this chapter uses the Durham University Business School General Enterprise Tendency (GET) test which was developed by Johnson and Caird (1988) to examine the entrepreneurial tendencies of the academic staff at the University of Surrey. The test comprises 54 items (or statements) that require 'agree' or 'disagree' responses. Responses are 'forced' and must be one or the other. 'Correct' responses are positive and negative in equal proportions and correct responses score 1 point (to a maximum possible score of 54).

All academic staff at the University of Surrey (circa 500) were sent an email with an electronic attachment comprising the GET test and were asked to complete and return it. Forty-nine staff did so within 3 weeks.

Table 11.1   Results of the GET test on academic staff at the University of Surrey, England

(a) Data from this study: Mean scores ± standard deviation

Need for achievement (max. = 12)	Autonomy (max. = 6)	Creativity (max. = 12)	Calculated risk-taking (max. = 12)	Locus of control (max. = 12)	Total [GET] (max. = 54)
8.8 (± 2.1)	3.3 (± 1.5)	7.9 (± 2.3)	7.4 (± 2.3)	8.6 (± 2.1)	36.1 (± 6.9)

(b) Data from Caird (1991): Mean scores ± standard deviation

Need for achievement (max. = 12)	Autonomy (max. = 6)	Creativity (max. = 12)	Calculated risk-taking (max. = 12)	Locus of control (max. = 12)	Total [GET] (max. = 54)
Business owners/managers (n = 73)					
9.98 (± 1.6)	4.1 (± 1.4)	8.7 (± 1.9)	8.7 (± 2.0)	9.5 (± 1.7)	41.0 (± 5.4)
Nurses (n = 33)					
8.5 (± 1.5)	2.8 (± 1.3)	8.0 (± 1.8)	6.6 (± 1.9)	7.7 (± 2.1)	33.3 (± 4.5)
Lecturers and trainers (n = 24)					
8.9 (± 1.8)	4.1 (± 1.3)	8.5 (± 2.4)	8.6 (± 2.1)	8.2 (± 2.1)	38.3 (± 7.6)

Entrepreneurship amongst university staff: results

The means (and standard deviations) resulting from the survey of the academic staff of the University of Surrey are shown in Table 11.1.

The average GET score (the total measure of the generalized entrepreneurial tendency) was relatively high (mean + sd = 36.1 + 6.9) in comparison to other occupational groups (33.3 + 4.5 for nurses, 29.4 + 7.2 for clerical trainees, 33.5 + 7.2 among civil servants). Interestingly, it was somewhat lower than previously reported among lecturers and trainers (Caird 1991).

Furthermore, the distribution of data, although close to normal, showed elongated tails in both directions, that is some of the staff had much higher than average scores and others much lower than average. The mean scores for all parts of the GET test are shown in Table 11.1, but in general, the results showed that the sample population comprised highly independent people with considerable belief in their own abilities. They had high tendencies to equate results with effort and tended to believe in fate or luck much less than is common among business owners.

Discussion

Generally, levels of task orientation were high and levels of creativity were moderate. The demand for autonomy and the level of calculated risk-taking was low. The high levels of self-confidence common to most lecturing staff were found to be largely the result of belief in independent effort and rewards for hard work, rather than creative venturesomeness or serendipity.

In brief, the academics in the Surrey sample proved themselves to be creative people with strong beliefs in the need for independent efforts and the rewards of hard work. The need for autonomy, however, was considerably lower than that previously reported by Caird (1991) and may reflect either long-term cultural acceptance of a more managerial approach to higher education in the last decade, or the specific and idiosyncratic nature of staff at the University of Surrey, possibly both. Kinman (1998: 20) reports that 'a high proportion of academic staff and academic-related staff feel that traditional educational values have been marginalized, and that the academic ethos has been transformed from collegiality and co-operation to corporation and competition'.

In Lyons' (1998) study of university lecturers, autonomy was commonly described as the predominant motive for the choice of an academic career. A decrease in autonomy and increasing levels of accountability without the possibility of active participation in important decision-making was one of the most commonly expressed dissatisfactions with the job. Similarly, Gray (1992) reports that autonomy, independence of centralized authority and employment flexibility (especially where flexibility allows the freedom to pursue non-business goals) are the most common motivations for self-employment.

Lyons also reports that despite increasing managerialism and apparent wholesale belief in the role of individual profit as the main motivator for work in general, university lecturers remain largely indifferent to monetary considerations and are motivated largely by commitment to the professional ethos, collegiality and the perceived autonomy of academic work. Even the prospects of promotion are largely neglected by academics when talking about their work. Lecturers' aspirations are rarely focused on what Burch describes as the 'instrumental benefits of work', but more commonly on the personal, social, societal and professional. There are grounds for likening university staff to the owners and managers of small independent firms because of their need for autonomy and flexibility, but the similarity is fully valid only for those 'lifestyle companies' that do not place profit as the primary reason for existing. Indeed, running a small research group in a university has many similarities with the running of a small 'lifestyle' firm. Burch (1986: 6) defines the entrepreneur as 'the person who undertakes a venture, organises it, raises capital to finance it, and assumes all or a major portion of the risk'. In all but the assumption of personal financial risk, this is common to university research leaders. Other definitions of entrepreneurship also support this contention. Schumpeter's (1983) description of the entrepreneur, for example, emphasizes the innovatory aspect of entrepreneurship as its distinguishing feature.

However, risk (or risk-taking tendencies) alone cannot be taken to distinguish academics from successful business founders. Castells' report of successful start-ups in Europe and the United States dispels the belief that founding businesses is necessarily risky (Castells 1996) and Armstrong (2001) concludes that contrary to much popular wisdom, successful spin-out companies are usually soft-starts and involve a minimum of risk to the individuals who start them. Perhaps, as Chell (2000) claims, entrepreneurial activity is not the unencumbered result of specific personality traits and behavioural propensities. Rather, it is a series of expressed behaviours resulting from life and business interaction with others and with other systems of organization and control. If this is so, it is important to look to the environment that surrounds the academics to explain the entrepreneurial behaviour (or often the lack of it) of academic staff, at least as much as their innate tendencies and motivations.

Middlehurst claims that the three predominant views of the university are the collegiate, the professional and the bureaucratic. Writing of the collegiality of the university system she says:

> The collegial image, historically the oldest description of Universities, has exerted a powerful influence on the culture and functioning of academia even though many of its significant features are now more symbolic than real. Central to the vision of a community is the idea of a group of scholars who work together to their mutual advantage within a self-governing collective. The image carries other associations: of consensus decision-making and academic autonomy, of democracy and cohesion based on a limited hierarchy of seniority and expertise, a common heritage and shared ideals. The chief organ of government in a collegial institution is the committee system.
>
> (Middlehurst 1993: 49)

The other views of the university, the professional and the bureaucratic, present different, but equally burdensome, barriers to the development of an entrepreneurial culture in higher education.

Conclusion

The UK government continues to look at the university sector as a principal source of wealth-creating research, arguing that much economic benefit still remains 'locked up' in universities. The fact that the United States, for example, appears to be much better at converting research to economic activity does suggest that there is room for improvement of university participation in the process of entrepreneurship in the UK. However, whether or not this can be achieved solely through initiatives to promote entrepreneurial behaviour in the university sector and to engender a more entrepreneurial culture in higher education is debatable. Armstrong (2001: 524) suggests that current policy is an act of faith and its 'reliance on enterprise is less a solution to the economic needs of Britain than a hope that one will spontaneously appear'.

This survey of academic staff of the University of Surrey confirms Caird's (1991) finding that academics are quite enterprising. For some, this might be a surprising finding. Possibly, it is a reflection of those who completed the questionnaire – those most interested in the topic – but it has probably always been the case. Certainly, the motives for an academic lifestyle (the opportunity to be creative, the need for autonomy, the need for achievement and the internal locus of control) are similar to those of entrepreneurs, even if academics commonly lack the profit motive frequently associated with entrepreneurship. However, it is established that entrepreneurs are not driven solely by money, which is seen by them mainly as an indicator of their success. Academic staff are, therefore, probably very similar to the traditional entrepreneur.

This would suggest that if British universities are to promote the creation of spin-outs and start-ups, they must be helped by government to develop a culture that is more supportive of enterprise. To achieve this it would be necessary to:

- stop the erosion of autonomy and flexibility amongst academic staff as they are the attributes of the job most likely to attract entrepreneurial people to the sector;
- reduce the number of performance-monitoring programmes, especially those with onerous audit trail obligations, as these are likely to be associated with bureaucratic and managerial overburdening and to discourage entrepreneurial staff;
- change the reward system so that entrepreneurial staff are recognized and shown to be clearly valued (while economic rewards are seldom, if ever, dominant motivators in the academic workplace, professional and peer group recognition are likely to be levers that inculcate entrepreneurial behaviour); and
- support applied research and not just the research that contributes most to the ratings in the Research Assessment Exercise (British universities, collectively, ought to be lobbying government to ensure the Assessment Exercise meets more clearly its objectives with respect to enterprise and the transfer of knowledge to the business community).

This study is tentative. While the findings corroborate those from earlier investigations, they are based on a small sample in one university. This is a topic that is important not just to universities, but to the whole fabric of society. Universities have always had an important role to play in economic and social development, but in a knowledge-based economy and society access to knowledge is as important to social and economic development as access to raw materials was in the nineteenth century. As business entrepreneurs were the catalyst for social and economic development in the nineteenth century, intellectual entrepreneurs will become the catalyst in the twenty-first century. Therefore, it is important to understand them and the factors that contribute to their development.

One of the more fruitful of the new directions for broad-based entrepreneurial research is the study of how entrepreneurs identify and pursue opportunities (Chell 2000). Within the context of academic entrepreneurship, attention should be focused on:

- the motivations of academic staff for seeking out opportunities;
- the processes by which opportunities are found and turned into action; and
- the methods by which individuals evaluate their own abilities to exploit opportunities.

Whilst entrepreneurship is, itself, a relatively recent phenomenon, academic entrepreneurship is a focus that, to date, has not received the attention it requires if academics are to play the role expected of them in a modern, highly competitive knowledge economy.

Notes

1. Usually referred to as the internal locus of control and described loosely as the control that an individual feels he or she has over life.
2. See, for example, the variety of papers presented in the special edition of the European Journal of Work and Organisational Psychology, Vol. 9, Part 1, which focuses entirely on entrepreneurship.

12

The Marketing Orientation in Higher Education: the Perspectives of Academics about its Impact on their Role

Helen Johnson

The quasi-market

Higher-education institutions are no longer virtually guaranteed an existence through governmental income streams. As funding now follows students, higher-education institutions must literally be *attractive*; hence, the importance of marketing.

From the late 1970s onwards, successive British governments withdrew from direct participation or reformulated their manner of operating in the public arena. The device used to replace such a governmental presence was the quasi-market (LeGrand and Bartlett 1993). Its rationale was to replace bureaucratic and monopolistic state providers by competitive, independent providers, who would respond to customer demands.

Implicit in this is the view that the paternalism of public-sector bureaucracies and the control of the definition of needs by professional elites should be replaced by market mechanisms. These are driven by customer wants and customer behaviour. The relationship between the provider of the service and its recipient is supposedly equal, and contractual or quasi-contractual in form. In this 'contractual' relationship, that is often more rhetorical than legal, the 'generalized public' is replaced by a specific individual and the actual relationship 'narrowed' to become two or more specified parties. A concern about equity and justice is, if not totally absent, not the focus of such a mechanism (Ball 1994).

Understanding the quasi-market's impact on organizational structures

Until the early 1980s, it was possible, according to Becher and Kogan 'to view the whole structure of [higher education] in Britain, at least, as reasonably autonomous'. Accompanying such autonomy was the institutional variety in terms of different histories and origins, aspirations, targets and goals for the future (Scott 1995). Different interpretations of them as organizational structures can also be offered.

Less than 13 years ago, Allen (1988) could report that the defining purpose of most universities was 'habitually avoided'. Today, vice-chancellors are adding 'chief executive' to their job titles and strategic plans, as required by the Higher Education Funding Council for England, are published. As early as the beginning of the 1990s, Williams explored the behavioural consequences of such action: 'It would be fair to say that financial success is the main way in which institutional heads are being judged, that likely success in *promoting the institution externally* and in attracting funds has become a major criterion in the appointment of institutional heads' (1992: 18, emphasis added).

Strategic management in higher education is now required by government departments and their supporting quangos, such as the Higher Education Funding Council for England. This is to enable each higher-education institution to determine, design and establish its own presence, portfolio of activities and image in an increasingly varied, complex and competitive post-compulsory education sector. 'Mission', 'objectives' and 'goals' are intended to give the institution signposts through a turbulent environment. The institution is no longer a community or professional organization, where the important objectives belong to individual staff members. It is expected to be a formal organization, with, in Middlehurst's terms (1993), 'an entrepreneurial image', engaged in securing its own survival and future direction.

However, the university is no simple organization with a homogeneous staff. The academic staff belong to different 'disciplinary cultures' or 'tribes' (Becher 1989). Most of the respondents in Rowland's (1996) study of the cultures of higher-education institutions were convinced that they or their departments were in some way 'special'. A culture presupposes shared values, some form of social cohesion and some sense of and desire for belonging. That desire, however, can be strong in some organizational actors and weaker in others. Peters (1997), in vivid fashion, has written of a 'corporate skunk', who works at the fringes of the organization, using its facilities, but not belonging to it in any meaningful way. It could perhaps be said, on an anecdotal basis, that some academics have long been working and operating in this manner. In more neutral tones, Gouldner (1957) classified such actors in his duality as 'cosmopolitans' and 'locals'. The former are committed to their work and to their field, and so are likely to identify strongly to similar specialists in *other* organizations. 'Locals' identify more closely with their *own* organizations and see their career trajectory in terms of the organization to which they belong. Again, it is possible to see different kinds of academics in these terms.

The changing nature and interpretation of professional culture

Much change has occurred in higher-education institutions and this has impacted on occupational roles. Halsey (1992) has described the 'decline of donnish dominion', and Nixon (1996) has discussed the 'crisis of professional identity'. This identity crisis, if one exists, could be in terms of the possible symbiotic/dichotomized relationship between teaching and research. It is also possible to focus on the arguments that have revolved around the definition of the term 'professional' in respect of the status and work of academics, in an attempt to distinguish it from the term 'managerial'.

Within this formulation, the relationship between the professional and his or her client is unequal. Lawton notes:

> . . . asymmetric information can exist . . . and professional relations are often characterised by . . . inequalities in information. The problem is where one side uses the power that can emerge out of unequal dependencies. This is where trust comes in; we have the right to trust professionals because we do not have the expertise to judge the rightness or wrongness of their judgements.
>
> (1998: 21)

Whatever the long-term outcomes of the changes brought about by the market reforms – some of which can be expected to make a profound impact on 'unequal relationships' and 'trust' – within higher-education institutions, a 'professional' culture is likely to remain. This can be described as the basic norms or values, which direct the behaviour, attitudes, symbols and self-perceptions of academics. (Having said this, it has to be noted that there can be a tendency to overlook the 'discrepancies' between how things are believed to be and how they really are.)

Using role in an organizational context

More recently, it is possible to see the public role of the professional solely in terms of achieving the 'goals of the organisation' (Jones 1984). In this view, the professional's own individual goals are simply an expression of those of the organization as a whole, rather than those of the professional grouping to which he or she belongs. These organizational goals or expectations can be interpreted by individual employees in a manner that goes beyond the performance requirements of the individual description of a particular job role. Organ (1990) calls this 'organisational citizenship behaviour', which is displayed in 'co-operation . . . enhancing the reputation of the work unit . . . suggesting improvements'; and perhaps, most importantly of all, 'abstaining from negative behaviours' (Nord and Fox 1996: 155).

Becher (1989) has shown that in many cases 'the academic tribes' acquire their culturalization from their experiences as undergraduates. In this way, it can be that their expectations of their role could be acquired 15, 20 or even 30 years before they reach a senior management post. Given the changes in structures and processes in higher-education institutions that have been discussed earlier, the potential is self-evident for conflict or the rejection of new organizational expectations about the role of academics. This is especially likely in instances where professional behaviour, with its emphasis on trust and disinterest, has crossed or is moving into areas of values and activities that can be described as managerial, commercial, entrepreneurial and business-like.

Marketization of the organization and the marketing orientation

With the marketization of higher education, higher-education institutions are becoming increasingly aware of the need to seek out and compete for customers. Leavitt (1960) has said that the focal point of all activities of any organization should be the wants and needs of its customers. This is the *marketing orientation*, that is the matching between the institution's human, financial and physical resources and the demands of its customers. It is accepted in the specialized marketing discourse that this matching takes place in a dynamic and competitive environment, one that is never stable. Anecdotal evidence suggests that sometimes academics equate marketing with selling. However, on the most practical level, a marketing approach could be seen as appropriate for any institution that has services to offer and that wishes to identify and respond to the demands and interests of those who may use those services. Twenty years ago, Peters and Waterman (1982) in a highly influential phrase, called this awareness 'the need to be close to the customer'. Such 'closeness' can be seen as part of the new relationships, encouraged by policies to enforce quality standards of successive British governments since 1979. In this way, through the need to take the market services of the highest quality, higher-education institutions are made conscious of their customers' behaviour – and, very importantly, their own.

Resistance to the marketing orientation

Change of any kind can be resisted. Accompanying sometimes very real practical issues, such opposition tends to be drawn from personal factors, where the proposed changes introduce something new (and sometimes, unknown) and so existing value systems and attitudes are challenged (Kanter 1983).

Specifically, the change brought about by the difficulties in introducing the market orientation into an organization has also been the subject of research (Deshpande 1999), in both the public and private sectors. Resistance to a market orientation could be expected in public-sector organizations; however, similar resistance has also been found in private-sector businesses that are driven by a customer-led perspective.

Slater and Narver (1999) emphasize the need for a conscious organization plan to develop a 'culture and climate' that has a marketing orientation, with 'superior customer value'. So, an overall change in the culture of any organization may be an important element of successful implementation of such an orientation. This is supported by Ruekert (1992), who has argued that the *principal* barrier to a market orientation can be a corporate or organizational culture that contains 'traditional' thinking and practices and the self-interest of staff within their own departments.

Thus, important as organizational intent is in the successful implementation of change, the values, beliefs and vested interests of the staff cannot be ignored. An important part of those attitudes will be the manner in which marketing as a practice is characterized or interpreted.

Marketing as a practice

If the marketing orientation is essentially a perspective, marketing itself is a managerial function comprising various techniques and approaches. Morgan looks beyond the practicalities of marketing to see it as 'being best understood as a set of practices and discourses, which help constitute social relations in modern western societies' (1992: 137). Three sub-discourses have been identified in the marketing discourse (Johnson 2001) as:

- a set of neutral, 'common-sense' practices, which regards itself as such;
- a controlling/reinforcing device, which seeks to see the power relationships within it; and
- a means of overcoming tradition and introducing new ideas, products and services, in which marketing is regarded as a change agent.

Thus, as the identification of these three sub-discourses shows, marketing is more than it might appear to be at first glance. Clearly, there is room for movement, or at least discussion, in the attitudes of academics towards the practice.

The wider political issues aside, whether or not profit is the paramount consideration, it is the transaction – the exchange relationship – that underpins all marketing. In such a relationship, a quid is exchanged for a quo, thus establishing mutual dependencies through negotiation. The term 'negotiation' carries with it, if not necessarily a total equality, some sense that discussion is possible until a mutually satisfying agreement is reached. (This is in contrast, as was seen earlier, to the declared 'asymmetrical' nature of the relationship between professionals and their clients.)

Reaching the customer with what?

Given the importance of the marketing orientation, with its focus on the customer, it is clear that the higher-education institution (or any organization) cannot function effectively as a closed system. In this perspective, there is an expectation that the institution must enter into connections, transactions and exchanges with the 'world out there', specifically, with its environment and market. For this to happen effectively, it is necessary for there to be within the institution itself an organizational culture that recognizes, encourages and supports such transactions.

It is possible for the higher-education institution to identify certain services, for example BEd. or MA programmes, to be marketed in terms of the much-used marketing mix of the four Ps – the four important factors to be taken into account in most marketing strategies, namely product, price, place and promotion (Kotler and Fox 1995). The last is given prominence in most HEI marketing and comprises the various activities an organization undertakes to communicate the merits of its products or services (Kotler and Fox 1995). The desired outcome of this activity is that targeted customers are persuaded to buy or enrol. Examples of promotional activities in a higher-education institution can be listed as videos, flyers, websites, entries in compendia, advertising, public relations and what remains, even in the era of the website (Strauss and Frost 1999), the most influential of all, the institution's prospectus (Roberts and Higgins 1992).

However, it is possible to go beyond the specific product or service to consider something wider and more complex. Increasingly, contemporary marketers are looking to relationship marketing (Christopher et al. 1994). In this approach, the need to go beyond the single, finite transaction to something less tangible, but emotionally more plangent is emphasized. Thus, what is to be marketed is more than the diploma and the degree. In the higher-education context, it is the institution itself, its functioning and its culture – and its people. Those who come into direct contact with students and other customers are especially important. Thus, the educational role of the academic as a teacher and tutor, interacting with students, can be seen also to have a marketing significance.

Additionally, as higher education takes on a 'lifelong' learning perspective, relationship marketing is increasingly relevant. The relationship with the student is most likely to start with an undergraduate programme. That, in turn, may lead to postgraduate study, and then to subsequent and regular professional updates. So the relationship with the higher-education institution is lengthened, across a student's potential adult lifetime. It could be expected that such a relationship is to be predicated on a positive and coherent, although not necessarily uniform, organizational culture, in which all members of the institution are involved. Therefore, this culture may have to be managed in a planned, and so self-aware, manner. As a consequence of this, it is clear that the job descriptions and wider organizational role of all institution staff, including academics, may have to be redefined and enhanced.

The marketing orientation and academics: their perceptions of its impact on their role

How do academics themselves perceive their own role in marketing activity? As part of a series of lengthy interviews with academics and marketers in a variety of British higher-education institutions, six were carried out with academics working in institutions that were perceived as having to attract students. The selection of the subjects was on a case-by-case basis identified by the insights that they could be expected to contribute to the study. A summary of those interviews is reported here (the opinions expressed are consistent with the other academics interviewed). They are presented as a case study of academics drawn from a particular part of the higher-education system.

Steve, Ingrid, Clare, Eddie, Maggie and Una were in higher-education institutions that did not have the financial capacity to ignore the market. However, the institutions were drawn from both the 'old' and 'new' university sectors, and one, although openly 'upwardly mobile', at the time of the interview remained on the 'wrong' side of the binary line. All the academics, except one, who was also in an applied field, were in faculties of education (hence, the high representation of women).

Academics as managers

The role of the senior academic comprises many strands. It is likely that he or she is engaged in research, teaching, and administration and management. Clare, Una and Steve were deans; Ingrid was a head of a division and Eddie was a head of a department. Whatever the breadth and concentration of their duties, they are no longer playing an 'individual' role, but have moved into a position as a significant organizational actor within the institution and in the outside world. All except for Maggie had formal input at a strategic level. Ingrid was typical: 'I'm middle management in a way. I'm on the University Research Committee. I'm on the University's Equal Opportunities Committee . . . I'm on the University Academic Standards Committee, which is elected. I represent the Faculty . . . I'm interested in those.'

Steve described his own role almost entirely in terms of his relationships with government agencies and departments: 'I'm on lots of internal committees. I spend my life going to meetings. And lots of meetings outside and the quangos, the TTA, of course . . . and there's Ofsted and can't forget the DfEE.'

Ingrid, despite her senior position as a head of a division, seemed almost detached from the responsibility for the way things were at her institution: 'I think the other thing about [this higher-education institution] and I don't know how it is in other new universities, is that the organization is so bad . . . the systems don't work here, you know.'

A direct role in marketing?

Five of the interviewees were involved in strategic management. They addressed this role with a 'broad sweep' approach, and spent a considerable amount of time at meetings. What did those meetings about university strategy decide? Was marketing discussed?

Ingrid was not part of how her higher-education institution marketed itself and marketing was seen as the responsibility of the functional specialists: 'No, there's Marketing Division, but I do have input into the prospectus.' In the course of the interview with Ingrid, it was found that her MA course was missing from the prospectus: 'I wondered why it wasn't recruiting well . . . well, obviously, the person [dealing with the prospectus] had thought the course had gone out or had disappeared . . . the other thing is that there has been a shrinking administration.'

Una had ideas for a public relations strategy: 'We could put this stuff in the [local newspaper] every week about education in the Faculty.' But Una's higher-education institution did not do so, and it can be inferred that she did not regard it as her responsibility. In contrast to both Ingrid and Una, Eddie recognized the importance of marketing and thought that 'students will be increasingly influenced by marketing functions. How does the campus seem, how good is the teaching, what kind of literature would be best and so, marketing, effective marketing by the new universities will increasingly appeal to students.' From an institutional perspective, he identified marketing as important for the 'new' universities – as these are the ones that will 'have to persuade students to come to them'. In his own institution (an 'old' university), marketing seemed to be unplanned, reactive and on an ad hoc basis:

> I mean we've got an information office that does publicity and every now and again, they push us to do a bit more and every now and again I'll push them to do a bit more, especially with new courses. We design our departmental literature, our own leaflets and brochures, which are not very slick. I'm sure that [this higher-education institution] will be the last on the Internet.

Steve saw marketing in terms of the activities of others to attract students. From his perspective, in teacher training, much of teacher recruitment was determined and encouraged by the Teacher Training Agency, and in that way was essentially 'beyond his control'.

Clare talked in terms of her institution's competitors and those institutions with whom it did not compete. She clearly had a strong sense of the nature of its market: 'Students . . . why do they come here and one of the answers is it is local . . . and the excellence of certain departments attracts overseas students.' The strategic issues were addressed in this way: 'We get round it in some ways by having a limited mission . . . to the arts and the humanities and so on . . . and this makes it rather easier to market yourself.' Clare's higher-education institution has no marketing department: 'We've got an information secretariat . . . one of their jobs is external relations marketing, producing the prospectuses, and marketing the college generally.'

Given her political perspective that 'marketing reinforces the market ideology' and with it the 'class structure of society', it is perhaps significant that Clare, alone among these six academics, commented on the importance of how students were informed about this new mass market in higher education:

> . . . if you've got a mass market . . . you need much more careful guidance systems for actually explaining to students what goes on . . . and many students haven't got access to the kind of information that middle class students or private school students or students whose parents have been to university . . . so you do need strategies for disseminating information which could be called marketing . . .

Only Ingrid talked of her higher-education institution doing market research (in the past) to find out what students actually wanted. The three deans (Clare, Una and Steve) did find themselves involved, in what they termed a peripheral way, in decisions about prospectuses. It is interesting to note that five of the six interviewees had little formal knowledge of marketing, its techniques and practices. (The exception was Eddie, who was a professor in a department of management.) All viewed it as a functional specialism that was essentially carried out at an operational level either by a discrete marketing department, with which they had little direct contact, or by administrators in their own departments, who designed leaflets to publicize courses and inform students. None had any awareness of relationship marketing.

Again, with five of the six holding senior management positions, the academics had not 'merged' with their higher-education institutions, or identified with them, even as a professional pose. Steve, for example, always spoke in terms of institutions, but used 'I' rather than 'we'. The academics spoke openly and freely, making many critical remarks about their institutions, their peers, their staff and seemingly virtually everybody of whom they spoke. They were clearly not making any attempt to 'sell' the benefits of their institution to the researcher (and in this way, did not display any organizational citizenship behaviours).

Promoting yourself: a cosmopolitan or corporate skunk?

The interview with Maggie, a prominent academic, who held no senior management post, was very different from the other five. She had no formal input into the strategic management and marketing of her higher-education institution. However, she did outline a comprehensive strategy for self-promotion. This was based not so much on the substance of actual performance (although, of course, this should not be overlooked), but as a 'conscious strategy' to 'build a public profile'. She felt this could be 'orchestrated'.

Maggie suggested 'self-advertising' through 'subliminal editorial advertising', and to network at conferences and other 'strategic events'. In her own field of education, it was necessary to be a 'popular practitioner' as well as an academic. Such popularity would assist in becoming a 'media guru' as that status would result in an individual being quoted or appearing regularly on television. This, of course, would be a self-perpetuating cycle. To assist in this strategy, it was necessary to be 'articulate', 'presentable' and 'available'. It would be sensible to live 'near a television centre' or other media. 'A mobile phone would be useful.'

An important part of Maggie's strategy was a lack of attachment to her higher-education institution. Heavy teaching, administrative and management loads were to be avoided, as they interfered with the 'real work'.

Conclusion

Marketing is a cultural practice, as, in organizational and managerial terms, it is a planned, conscious activity that has organization-wide implications. At its narrowest, it is about the promotion of products and services; at its widest, it is concerned with an orientation to the customer that is the focal point of all organizational goals and objectives. Such an orientation impacts on the roles of all organizational actors in higher-education institutions, be they administrators, managers or academics.

It is clear that the importance of 'role' in the organization cannot be underestimated. The job description held by each individual member of staff sets out the specific requirements of an organizational position and post. However, role theory in the form of organizational citizenship behaviour can take those requirements much further. This could be in the form of a wider and perhaps more meaningful performance that incorporates cooperation and collaboration within the organization, be it a higher-education institution or any other. The essence of such organizational citizenship behaviour would seem to be an awareness of 'other people being there', in terms of work colleagues, students, other customers and stakeholders. It also includes the recognition that the organization in which the job or work is housed does have a purpose and focused existence. This purpose, at its widest, is expressed in the mission statement; and at its narrowest, is simply the desire to survive. Whatever its form, it can be shared and supported by all organizational actors, whatever their specific job description and role.

The academics interviewed did not 'promote' their higher-education institutions. They were not reluctant to criticize their institutions and others – sometimes in great length and detail. This is perhaps not surprising, as it can be expected that academics will adopt a critical stance to whatever happens in society and in their own institutions. After all, 'critiquing is what they do' (Barnett 1997).

Therefore, not unexpectedly, they saw much in abstract terms. They discussed, at length, the political and social consequences of the marketization of higher education and the higher-education institution. They did not spend long on any discussion of the market mechanism's impact on the survival and thriving of their own (and others') institutions, in the short and long term. From the interviews (and this was also reflected in the other interviews with other academics), it was evident that the task of ensuring survival was not theirs.

None had any meaningful involvement in marketing, and had little awareness of its as an area of specialized knowledge. The strategic implications of marketing had not registered, for example, in the managerial, academic and educational consequences that result from the positioning of a higher-education institution in a particular segment of the higher-education market. (Such positioning decisions will impact directly on the nature of the student intake and the courses students wish to follow.)

The academics interviewed had an attachment to the higher-education institution that was pragmatic, and in the case of Maggie, that was tenuous. When they spoke, references made to their institutions were de-personalized: it was 'the university' or 'the institution', and there was little identification with the organization through the use of 'we'. Their perceptions of the academics' role was implicit in their behaviour, in terms of what they did and did not do. Becher's (1989) remark about how 'the academic tribes' acquire as undergraduates and *retain* their culturalization seems especially relevant. (All those interviewed were approximately the same age; and so it is possible there is a generational issue present, that is that all had been socialized as undergraduates in higher education before the reforms of 1988 and 1992.)

Thus, it can be said that some academics are continuing to conceptualize their occupational role in terms that reflect the nature of the higher education sector *before* the recent structural changes. (This in itself is important; it becomes even more significant if this remains the model of the academic that is passed down and used by subsequent generations.) Such a continuance can be seen as an expression of vested interests. On the other hand, it can be seen as the expression of the values of a group of professionals, who despite government pressure, are determined to retain their own 'moral and conceptual frameworks' (Becher and Kogan 1993: 3).

Such a stand-off between two value systems could have direct and detrimental organizational consequences. There could be an organizational battle between competing groups, in terms that Baldridge et al. (1978) would expect. Such warfare could be disruptive and costly. However, there is a way forward that allows what is relevant from the past to be retained while the realities of today and tomorrow are fully explored – and perhaps even enjoyed. Some form of synthesis – the 'localization' of the cosmopolitan (Gouldner 1957) – could be attempted and in this way, a new professional culture for academics developed (Trowler 1998). Nicholls (2001: 79) notes that as a 'consequence of changing conditions' a new professionalism in academia is emerging.

Nicholls follows this point through by arguing that a dialogue between academics and their publics would produce a 'learning profession': 'whose sense of professional identity is derived from their capacity to listen, learn from and move forward with the communities they serve' (2001: 80–1).

The development of a new professional identity has focused primarily on the need for academics to be able to teach effectively (Ramsden 1992; Nicholls 2001). However, this 'expanding' identity could be taken further by a particular form of organizational development approach by higher-education institutions themselves: the inculcation of organizational citizenship behaviours, at the very least, in terms of some sense of belonging and contributing to the institution. This learning process would be based on the participants' own experience and take cognisance of their values. In any such formal training intervention, staff members could be given a positive sense of the institution in terms of its values, needs and priorities and how that impacts and shapes the job role of individuals and teams. A next step would be for the higher-education institution to offer some linked awareness training in the marketing orientation, basic marketing practices and relationship marketing. Thus, the educational and market priorities can become entwined, with a resulting synthesis, which can underpin the strategic direction taken by the higher-education institution.

Are such interventions more 'shoulds' than 'musts'? They are, in fact, essential. However much more acceptable or palatable it is to present the market orientation as simply 'interaction' with the communities served by the higher-education institutions, certain realities remain. These are financial and entrepreneurial. Decisions about the activities and direction of the higher-education institution will have to be made – and, sometimes, not simply on academic terms. So, while Nicholls (2001) writes of a new professionalism that revolves around researching and teaching, it is also necessary for academics in the future to have some form of organizational awareness, market orientation and, perhaps, entrepreneurial expertise. If they do not have such attitudes, knowledge and skills, they are unlikely to contribute influentially to the strategic decision-making processes in the restructured higher-education sector. How will the higher-education institution survive and thrive, and on whose terms, if managerial and marketing realities and possibilities are not understood and addressed by academics themselves?

Part 4

Enterprise in the Curriculum

Introduction

The idea of enterprise can have two separate meanings in higher education. One is the development of entrepreneurialism as a university management style inspired in part by financial stringency but mainly by the ideological changes about the provision of public services which emerged in the 1980s and which found explicit expression for higher education in this country with the passage of the 1988 and 1992 Acts. The other is the exhortation by government and some employers over recent years that in order to support a rapidly changing economy 'enterprise' should become an explicit part of the higher-education curriculum. This forms part of the 'employability agenda' which became very prominent in much of the higher-education debate during the 1990s.

In many ways this is an inevitable consequence of mass higher education. As enrolments increase, it is inevitable that smaller proportions of graduates are entering the professions and public service. A growing percentage is taking up types of employment and going into occupations in which a capacity to be enterprising may be an important quality. The growth of student interest in areas of study in which this is superficially likely is shown by the massive expansion of enrolments in subjects such as business studies and management since 1990. The debate about the introduction of key employment skills into the curriculum through teamworking, work experience and oral presentations also exemplifies the growing interest in the learning of enterprise-related skills.

Unfortunately, few of the papers presented to the SRHE conference on which this book is based dealt with this issue. Brenda Little reports preliminary findings from a study of the relevance of work experience to graduates entering employment. Her findings are cautious. Although most graduates today have some work experience as part of their courses, the research evidence is uncertain about the extent to which this is really useful to them in their early years of employment. More significantly from the viewpoint of the present book, there is evidence that employers are more concerned that graduates learn teamworking skills than the more individualistic qualities associated with enterprise.

Finally, Gilbert Frade reports briefly on one successful experiment in the Ecole des Mines in France in which the very able students who enter this Grande Ecole are required to undertake an act of enterprise as an integral part of their course. He claims to have shown that it is possible for anyone to be innovative even when he is convinced of the contrary. It is possible for anyone to start an enterprise project and to achieve it. When you have done it once, you are confident for future innovation and you dare to create more easily. Contrary to some earlier evidence, the enterprise acts show that women are not less entrepreneurial than men.

13

Undergraduates' Work Experience and Equitable Access to the Labour Market

Brenda Little[1]

Introduction

In the UK, there is considerable interest in the nature and extent of undergraduates' work experience. Government has been pressing higher education to make greater linkages with the world of work, and employers, for their part, have continued to be critical about the lack of work-related skills that new graduates possess. Higher-education institutions' responses to such pressures have been many and varied in terms of specific curriculum developments: for example, some have sought to build elements of work experience into the taught curriculum, others have sought to make more explicit particular skills development within existing curricula. Furthermore, as the system of student financing has changed, so has the extent to which students may need to boost their income through employment. Recent survey findings within the UK indicate that the majority of undergraduates now work during vacation time, and some institutional surveys have found that more than half of all full-time undergraduates are regularly working during term-time.

But is this drive towards work experience for undergraduates enhancing or damaging students' access to the labour market? In this chapter I will look at the question from two perspectives. First, the extent to which (employer-desirable) skills might be developed through work experience, and second from the perspective of graduate employment data, and the extent to which work experience during a students' undergraduate career eases transition in to the labour market and impacts on longer-term employment prospects.

The curriculum of work experience

Much has been written in the last decade in the UK about the nature of the undergraduate curriculum and the drives to make it more overtly geared towards developing in all students skills and attributes that are needed to be effective in a changing work environment. Such developments have not necessarily been welcomed whole-heartedly. Many questions have been raised, including what motives lie behind such developments (see, for example, Brown and Scase 1994, Fulton et al. 1999). There are also questions about whether an undergraduate curriculum is necessarily the best place for developments linked to employability skills to take place, particularly given continuing debates about the extent to which skills developed in one context are easily transferred into another context (see, for example, Atkins 1999).

Notwithstanding such questions, in certain disciplinary areas, work-based elements have long been designed 'into' the formal curriculum. Very many programmes of study now include generic work-based learning units, which are based around curricular devices designed to help students articulate and reflect on learning derived from their experiences of work. Earlier government-funded initiatives in this area were aimed towards the 'planned curriculum' and work-based learning as part of that planned curriculum, but more recent institutional initiatives (some again funded by government) have focused on providing similar curricular devices but this time aimed towards students' part-time, *ad hoc* work, which has not been planned as part of their undergraduate curriculum. Rather it is undertaken term-time, alongside the students' studies, or during vacations.

Emerging findings about the significance of informal learning in the workplace which arises naturally out of the challenges of problem-solving at work and out of social interactions with colleagues, customers or clients (Eraut et al. 1999) strengthens the case for such devices. These curricular devices place primary emphasis on guiding the student through a process of reflection (for example on situations encountered in the workplace, actions taken, activities achieved and particular skills developed) such that ultimately the student is in a sense 'learning how to learn' from non-formal learning situations – in this case their place of part-time work. Depending on the institutional scheme in operation, evidence of the learning derived from such work experiences may be formally acknowledged in the form of academic credit, which then takes its place alongside academic credit gained through formally taught units within the programme.

Without a comprehensive survey of undergraduate curricula across the UK it is difficult to know just how many institutions now offer such a facility for recognizing learning gained through *ad hoc* experiences of work, and thus just how widespread is undergraduates' access to such devices. Yet even where such a facility is available, it seems that the proportion of students working part-time who actually make use of the facility is probably fairly low (Department for Education and Skills forthcoming). Yet, it may be that it is the student's ability to articulate to a future employer just what they have learned and what processes they have used to think about what they have learned (for example, about their own skills and attributes in dealing with certain workplace situations; about the way an organization works) that carries more weight than the fact that they have had some work experience. The quotation below from an employer, taken from a study that the Open University's Centre for Higher Education Research and Information (CHERI) is conducting on processes of transition from higher education into the labour market illustrates this point:

> . . . it's amazing how many people [interviewees] when you ask them about team working situations will talk about themselves . . . don't talk about team work . . . what you're looking for is people who understand what it is to work in a team, to work with different types of people . . . and make a team effective . . . whereas quite often people will give you a situation where they've achieved something over other people, rather than working in a team situation.' (Graduate recruiter, large computer software company)

Work experience and the labour market

Work experience may serve a number of purposes – one function being that of smoothing the transition from study into work, both for school pupils, and for those who have continued beyond compulsory education. A particular emphasis on work experience during higher education was emphasized by the Dearing Committee. In analysing evidence presented to the Committee by a range of stakeholders, the high value placed by employers on new recruits having had work experience was noted. The Committee concluded that 'those with higher education qualifications should be familiar with the outside world and be able to reflect constructively on issues related to work, such as how they have managed situations or learned from work experiences' (National Committee of Inquiry into Higher Education 1997: 136).

But what do we really know about the impact of work experience on access to the labour market? Employers may claim to place high value on work experience, and in some circumstances are prepared to pay a premium to graduates with relevant work experience (Association of Graduate Recruiters 1998). But, in practice, does having work experience really make a difference to graduates' access to the labour market and, if so, how?

Where the work experience is part of a planned programme of study, a year-long (or equivalent) work placement within a sandwich degree programme, then we are able to say something. One analysis of first destination statistics (relating to graduates' situations 6 months after graduation) found a higher proportion of graduates from sandwich courses were in employment than graduates from full-time courses, but the extent of the labour-market advantage was dependent on subject area. For example, pure science and languages 'sandwich' graduates did not enjoy a significant advantage, whereas most built environment, business/finance and management, engineering and social science 'sandwich' graduates did (Bowes and Harvey 2000). In some ways, it would be surprising if those who had completed a sandwich programme (with its year-long period of planned work experience) did not enjoy some advantage immediately after graduation in terms of employ-ment status. In the first place, by their very nature, sandwich programmes are more vocationally oriented than other programmes, and one could assume that those who opt to follow a sandwich programme are more interested in exploiting the direct linkages between their undergraduate programme and immediate employment prospects than might otherwise be the case. Moreover, contacts made and experiences gained during their period of 'placement' could well stand students in good stead on gradu-ation, and significantly ease the period of transition into employment.

However, sandwich courses currently account for less than 10 per cent of the undergraduate student population in the UK. Although it is known that many full-time undergraduate programmes also include planned elements of work experience (see, for example, National Centre for Work Experi-ence 2000), mapping student cohorts on such programmes in any consist-ent manner (and hence subjecting them to similar first destinations statistics analyses) has proved difficult (Little et al. forthcoming).

Alongside planned periods of work experience during undergraduate programmes, higher-education students regularly gain work experience outside their studies. In the UK, it has long been the case that the majority of undergraduates tend to undertake temporary employment during vaca-tions. Are we able to say anything about the subsequent employment experi-ences of those who have gained such work experiences? Analysis of UK data collected as part of a Europe-wide study of higher education and employment (see Brennan et al. 2001) is starting to shed some light on this. Emerging findings indicate that such work experience can improve the labour-market situation of graduates to some extent, particularly for those who have studied non-vocational subjects (Blasko et al. forthcoming).

In the last few years, and particularly since the introduction of changes to the system of financing student support (whereby the previously means-tested student maintenance grants were replaced with student loans and tuition fees), attention has been drawn to the increasing incidence of term-time working. Many UK universities now regularly undertake surveys of their own undergraduates to ascertain (amongst other things) the incid-ence of paid employment during term-time. A number of findings from these institutionally based surveys and others undertaken across a range of institutions have emerged:

- the proportion of full-time undergraduates working part-time during term-time varies greatly between institutions. One recent study involving four contrasting UK universities found the proportion ranged from a low of 27 per cent to a high of 60 per cent (Metcalfe 2001).
- those who are working during term-time work an average of 11 or 12 hours per week (Callender and Kemp 2000, Metcalfe 2001).
- there is some evidence that students from lower socio-economic back-grounds, and those living at home with their parents tend to work more than other student groups (Barke et al. 2000, Callender and Kemp 2000).

Interest in the incidence of undergraduate term-time work is not unique to the UK. A national study of Australian university students (commissioned by the Australian Vice-Chancellors Committee) recently highlighted the extent to which many students are in paid work as a matter of necessity, and reported that the proportion of full-time students in paid employment during semesters had increased in the last two decades, from 5 in 10 students (in 1984) to 7 in 10 (in the year 2000) (Long and Hayden 2001). Reports from the American Council on Education (quoted in McInnis 2001) indicate that approximately four-fifths of US undergraduates, were working whilst studying. Working whilst studying is now part and parcel of the undergraduate experience for significant numbers of full-time students in many wealthy countries.

Immediate access to the labour market

An undergraduate's access to the labour market during term-time may vary according to any number of factors, including the availability of 'suitable' work in the locality of their higher-education institution, the individual's 'need' to work during term-time and the relative ease with which jobs might be found. In fact, very many UK higher-education institutions now operate (increasingly web-based) employment services for their students, and it is estimated that over 90 university 'job shops' are currently in operation. Such job shops may be based in the institution's careers service, or the students' union, or in personnel, student services or education support offices. Job shops are often a part of a wider range of services linking a university to industries in the locality (and some operate on a wider, regional basis such that a web-based employment matching service is provided for all higher-education providers and employers in the region). So for the majority of UK undergraduates, it seems that ways of finding term-time employment are readily accessible through services provided by the universities themselves. University authorities are not necessarily averse to their students' term-time working *per se*, but many may try to set a limit on the extent of term-time work by setting regulations stating students should not work outside their studies for more than 15 hours per week. There is probably little that any one university could do to enforce such a regulation, but for some, its very existence signals to students that they will be unable to use their weekly 'job' as a possible excuse for poor performance in their course units.

What about the question of 'needing' to work during term-time? Do different types of students have different needs? At one level, undergraduates may 'need' to work during term-time just to survive, to pay the rent, to pay for food and to pay their tuition fees; others may feel they 'need' to work to fund a particular lifestyle. Some may see it as a way of keeping the size of their student loan within reasonable bounds, and others might work in term-time because it is what they have become accustomed to – having already been working prior to becoming a full-time undergraduate. The following quotations, taken from a series of interviews with UK graduates as part of the CHERI study (referred to earlier) illustrate some contrasting approaches to working during term-time:

> . . . all through university I continued to work in the local paper shop, Sunday mornings and Monday evenings [at the job I'd had while at school] . . . it was nice to get a bit of a break from studies. (Young female graduate who lived at home whilst at university)

> I did part-time work during term-time . . . pub work and waitressing, mainly at weekends . . . doing about 12 hours per week . . . but sometimes weekday evenings as well . . . it was to supplement my student grant . . . but for someone who'd worked for 10 years [before going on to higher education] it seemed very alien for me to just bury myself in books . . . and do nothing with my people skills . . . I like being with people, so I felt I had to carry-on [working] . . . obviously the money was very useful but I just didn't envisage not working at all for the 3 years of my course. (Mature female graduate)

> I worked over each of the summer holidays to have money as a top-up . . . just in the local supermarket, filling shelves, things like that . . . if I'd been living away from home then that [term-time work] would have been the thing to do . . . didn't work at Christmas or Easter . . . there wasn't enough time really . . . I was just focusing on me studying, revision or whatever. (Young male graduate who lived at home whilst at university)

Impact of term-time working on studies

As well as investigating the incidence and extent of term-time working amongst undergraduates, many surveys have also sought students' views on the impact of that work. A balance sheet of pros and cons can be constructed from some recent reports of student surveys and is shown in Table 13.1.

Many of the positive impacts listed in Table 13.1 mirror those mentioned in studies of younger students in the UK. For example, studies of full-time 16–19-year-old students' involvement with part-time work found that students were using part-time work to earn money and to 'sharpen their ability to get organised, manage time and develop social skills' (Hodgson and Spours 2001: 382). However, undergraduates are more likely to report negative impacts. Although undergraduates might perceive term-time working as having primarily negative effects on their studies, employers may also view the very fact that an undergraduate has worked to provide an additional source of finance in a positive light. They may consider that the individual student has responded to their situation in a pro-active and financially responsible manner, and, as such, has been enterprising in

Table 13.1 Full-time students' perceptions of impact of working whilst studying

Positive impact	Negative impact
Gain skills and experience	Quality of academic work suffers/ reduced time for studying
Improve time management	Missed taught sessions
Gain opportunities to develop communication and organization skills	Difficulties participating in group work and accessing the library and computing facilities
Meet people from outside the university	Less time for leisure
	Less time for family

Sources: University of Central Lancashire, spring 1999 survey; 1999 survey of hospitality and non-hospitality students in eight universities (HAVE Report); University of Central England in Birmingham, February 2000, Time and Funding Survey. These are all referred to in Little et al. forthcoming; spring 2000 survey in four universities (Metcalfe 2001)

reducing potential problems brought about by levels of expenditure exceeding levels of income.

Although students' perceptions of impact have been sought, little work has been done on measuring the impact on objective measures of academic performance, that is assessment outcomes. Of course, trying to isolate the impact of 'one' factor (in this case term-time working) on an individual's academic performance is difficult. One such study by the University of Northumbria found that for second-year students, the mean percentage grade for students who had worked during term-time was 1.7 percentage points below that of non-working students, and the effect was stronger for males than females (Barke et al. 2000). However, that study did not try to link the analysis of impact on performance to why the students were doing part-time work during term-time. Some might argue that negative impacts (when found) might be as much to do with aspects of certain students' lifestyles, which might be financed through term-time work, as the work itself. Moreover, this same study reported that similar effects were not found in the third year, even though students' propensity to work was similar in both years. The researchers suggested that one reason for this 'lack' in the final year could be that after the survey (and before final examinations) the students actually left their jobs in the run-up to their final examinations (Barke et al. 2000: 47).

The impact of term-time working on transition into the labour market

Although there are some data on the impact of work experience when it is a planned part of the curriculum, existing data on graduates' transition into the labour market say little about the impact of term-time work during full-time study on later employment outcomes. The CHERI study is starting to provide some indications of impact. This study focuses on graduates 3 years after graduation (a period arguably beyond the initial period of transition into the graduate labour market) and hence provides more meaningful graduate employment data than is provided through first destinations surveys. On the downside, the graduates in this study were in the higher-education system during the early to mid-1990s. Hence they were not subject to the most recent significant changes to the UK student support system (and thus the incidence and extent of term-time working for 'our' undergraduates might have been less than now). Nevertheless, initial regression analyses provide some interesting evidence of the impact of term-time working on later employment outcomes, even when a range of background and educational factors are taken into account. For example, in the case of male graduates who were working for more than 10 hours per week during term-time, the likelihood of having a graduate job three and half years after graduation is reduced by 55 per cent, and these same graduates are almost 45 per cent less likely to say that their current job requires a degree. Even when class of degree and amount of time spent on extra-curricular activities are introduced into the regression model, the disadvantages – although reduced – are still significant. However, as can be seen from Table 13.2, the impact of term-time work affects males and females in different ways.

The analysis is not yet complete, but the balance sheet (in Table 13.2) presents a tantalizing picture of both positive and negative impacts of term-time work on subsequent access to and progression in the labour market. Why, for example, does term-time working seem to lower female graduates' risk of unemployment after graduation, but seems not to bring similar advantage to male graduates? On the contrary, males who had worked on average more than 10 hours per week during term-time seem prone to experience only negative effects (for example less likelihood of a graduate job). Given that part-time work whilst studying now seems to be the 'norm'

Table 13.2   Impact of term-time work on employment situation during the 3–4-year period after graduation

	Positive impact	*Negative impact*
Females who worked 1–10 hours per week	Lower risk of unemployment	Less likely to have graduate job
Females who worked more than 10 hours per week	Lower risk of unemployment	
Males who worked more than 10 hours per week		Less likely to have graduate job, less likely to say job required a degree

Source: Unpublished CHERI internal working paper

for significant numbers of full-time undergraduates, further investigations on the impact of such activities on subsequent employment prospects should be undertaken.

Conclusions

This chapter has presented a number of findings relating to undergraduates' work experience and access to the labour market. The picture is mixed. Where work experience is a planned part of the curriculum, it seems to enhance access to paid employment (at least in the case of sandwich programmes and in the short term). Where work experience is undertaken primarily during vacation times, certain advantages also accrue over the medium term, particularly for those on non-vocational programmes. However, where work experience outside of the curriculum is gained during term-time, then there seems to be some evidence emerging of disadvantages in the labour market in the longer term. Yet for many students it may be that income from this same term-time work experience is the (only?) way that they can afford to be an undergraduate in the first place.

At this time we see the government continuing to 'push' the general work-experience agenda, most recently via the launch of a Higher Education Active Community Fund (amounting to some £14 million), through which it wants to see the creation of some 14,000 new opportunities for student volunteering. Such volunteering is viewed as 'helping both staff and students gain new perspectives and enable them to develop their *employment skills* while enhancing the quality of life in disadvantaged sectors of the community' (Higher Education Funding Council for England 2001: 2, emphasis added).

I suggest that alongside these various 'pushes' to help undergraduates gain work experience, it is now time to take stock and ask whether such 'pushes' are in fact at least as likely to hinder, as to enhance, access to the labour market for some groups of students.

Note

1. I am indebted to Zsuzsa Blasko and colleagues in the Centre for Higher Education Research and Information for sharing with me some of the initial results from their current project 'Access to what? How to convert educational opportunity into employment opportunity for groups from disadvantaged backgrounds' funded by the higher education funding councils, the Careers Services Unit, the Commission for Racial Equality, the Council for Industry and Higher Education, Universities UK, and the Open University.

14

Entrepreneurship: a Mega Trend for Nations, Enterprises and Universities

Gilbert Frade

From creation of knowledge to creation of wealth

At the beginning of the twentieth century, knowledge and know-how were the preserve of universities. An engineering degree was valid for the whole career of the graduate. A company could rely on stable markets and durable products; it was the company that determined what products its customers would buy. The company was a place of expertise and the way it was organized and its own hierarchy were based on a given stock of knowledge. The manager was the man who knew everything and the worker was the man who did not know much. Production was geared to the division of labour, with everyone performing specific tasks.

During the twentieth century know-how developed more and more rapidly and new technologies and new sciences emerged. The way companies were organized began to change, and new products become numerous, were launched and then disappeared at an increasing rate.

The scale of know-how expanded rapidly and the lifespan of products and technologies began to shrink. In the 1950s a degree could ensure some 15 years of respite in a professional life. Emerging automation and information technology were already heralding a new world. Today, the accelerating development of knowledge, the continual emergence of new technologies and new forms of management are among the most striking challenges facing organizations. Many technologies and products are replaced after 3 years or less. The average period of renewal for engineering skills has become as brief as a period of study in an engineering school. Knowledge is no longer the sole preserve of the universities and other academic institutions. It is created at the university, in industry and also, more recently, in consultancy firms.

This has several consequences. In industry and enterprises we find new types of organization:

- fewer hierarchic levels;
- more horizontal structures;
- the development of internal networks;
- the importance of project management and project leaders; and
- the manager is the man who can control the flow of knowledge and bring into contact those who know.

Companies nurture new skills and fashion new careers. As the foundations of industrialized economies have shifted from material resources to intellectual assets, managers have been compelled to examine the knowledge underlying their businesses and how that knowledge is used.

The transmission of knowledge is part of the daily activity of any company. Since the 1990s, senior managers have been talking about knowledge management in parallel with the expansion of continuing education and lifelong learning.

Universities have continued to create know-how without enjoying exclusive rights over it. They have focused increasingly on skills in terms both of initial training and lifelong education. We are witnessing a rapid expansion in the creation of new courses and new forms of training. Current engineering practice is being delocalized. There is a trend towards curricula jointly developed by universities and industry and future curricula will be hybrids.

Another form of organization has become more common in harnessing and creating expertise – consultancy firms. As knowledge is their core asset, management-consultancy firms were among the first businesses to pay attention to management of knowledge. They were also leaders in exploring the use of information technology to capture and disseminate knowledge. The rise of networked computers has made it possible to codify, store and share certain kinds of knowledge more easily and more cheaply than ever before.

The future of society is based on the creation of wealth and on managing knowledge, expertise and skills in a constantly changing world. This will be possible with the help of close partnerships between the main suppliers of knowledge, which are universities, companies and consultancy firms.

Universities, which no longer have a monopoly in creating knowledge, have now to focus on creating wealth and on developing companies. In many countries, there are signs of a development of entrepreneurship and specific training courses, which promote a spirit of enterprise. Most of tomorrow's jobs will be provided by organizations with fewer than 500 people (Sociological Study Ecole des Mines de Paris 1998. Internal report).

Examples from the United States

In the United States, many academic institutions have capitalized on the explosion of the knowledge economy by creating offices that oversee the transfer of technology developed on campus to industry. Schools have created burgeoning business centres filled with experts in intellectual property and corporate negotiation. They recruit venture capitalists, write business plans and take equity in start-up companies.

Universities did not become seedbeds of corporate innovation until the 1980s. Since 1980 roughly 2600 new companies have been formed, based on licences for inventions developed on campus: 280,000 jobs have been created from university spin-off companies, which have contributed approximately $33.5 billion to the economy (*Prism*, January 2000).

Some critics say that universities' quest for dollars – and their partnership with the private sector – runs the risk of harming the basic academic mission, which is to teach and conduct research (*Prism*, January 2000). However, John Hennessy, provost of Stanford, has said:

> It is very easy, sitting in an university, to become too isolated and ivory tower-ish especially in engineering and not realise all the challenges of making these technologies work. When you create a company, it gives you a much greater appreciation for how challenging it is to take an idea and turn it into a successful product.
>
> (*Prism*, January 2000)

Hennessy's entrepreneurial experience has other benefits for Stanford as well:

> ... the majority of our students will work in industry, not faculty members elsewhere. So you are in a much better position to give them advice, to understand what the trade-offs are, to give them some real world experience on the kinds of challenges that they will face in the real world.
>
> (*Prism*, January 2000)

Entrepreneurship in 21 countries

The Global Entrepreneurship Monitor (GEM) was created in 1997 as a joint research initiative by Babson College and London Business School, with support from the Kauffman Centre for Entrepreneurial Leadership (www.babson.org and www.lbs.ac.uk or www.entreworld.org). The central aim was to bring together scholars in entrepreneurship to study the complex relationship between entrepreneurship and economic growth. Ten countries participated in the study in 1999 – the G7 (Canada, France, Germany, Italy, Japan, the UK and the United States), plus Denmark, Finland and Israel. GEM 2000 added 11 countries: Argentina, Australia, Belgium, Brazil, India, Ireland, Korea, Norway, Singapore, Spain and Sweden.

Data were assembled from three principal sources:

- surveys of the adult population;
- in-depth interviews with national experts on entrepreneurship in each country;
- a wide selection of standardized national data.

More than 43,000 individuals were surveyed and nearly 800 were interviewed around the world. The findings lead to the following conclusions:

- the level of entrepreneurial activity differs significantly between countries: in Brazil, 1 in every 8 adults was currently starting a business, compared with 1 in 10 in the United States, 1 in 33 in the UK and 1 in 100 in Ireland, France and Japan;
- entrepreneurship is strongly associated with economic growth: all countries with high levels of entrepreneurial activity have above-average economic growth; only a few high-growth countries have low levels of entrepreneurial activity, among them France;
- most firms are started and operated by men, with peak entrepreneurial activity among those aged 25–44; overall, men are twice as likely as women to be involved in entrepreneurial activity – the ratio of male to female participation varies from 12 to 1 to 2 to 1 in Brazil and Spain;
- financial support is highly associated with the level of entrepreneurial activity: the amount of formal venture capital invested in 1999 ranged from 0.52 per cent of growth domestic product in the United States to 0.02 per cent in Japan; and
- education plays a vital role in entrepreneurship; if the level of participation in post-secondary education were the only factor used to predict entrepreneurial activity, it would account for 40 per cent of the difference between GEM countries.

Providing individuals with quality entrepreneurship education, that is training in the requisite skills for converting a market opportunity into a commercial enterprise, was consistently one of the top priorities identified by the experts interviewed in all 21 countries (Reynolds et al. 2000).

The situation in France

In France, 1 in every 100 adults is currently starting a business (compared to 10 in 100 in the United States). France has the lowest female participation in entrepreneurial activity among the 21 countries observed. The majority of new business ventures are launched by males aged 25–43. The French economy is characterized by a strong intervention of the state, high corporate tax rates and social charges, and a rigid labour market – all of which impede entrepreneurship. While education plays a vital role in entrepreneurship, France shows a good level of educational participation at the post-secondary level. However, the educational system, particularly pre-university, does not promote values compatible with entrepreneurship, such as individual initiative, autonomy, risk-taking and personal responsibility.

This is the exact reverse of what is seen in the United States or in Canada, where the culture of entrepreneurship is deeply rooted, entrepreneurs are celebrated as role models, failure is seen as a learning experience and the entrepreneurial career option is regarded as attractive. Moreover, if we look at the number of enterprises created in France over 10 years, it has been decreasing, although the number of curricula dealing with entrepreneurship in management schools and engineering schools has grown. Thus, there is not a direct correlation between the existing training in entrepreneurship and creation of enterprises.

L'Acte d'Entreprendre

In 1995, I decided to try to change this situation. Students at the Ecole des Mines de Paris, one of the leading engineering schools in France where I am employed, are trained to become high-level professionals in the engineering sciences, technology and management. As key figures in industry and business, they have to handle large-scale project management, to be innovative and to display autonomy and initiative. Several activities are devoted to developing this range of skills, especially in the international field. For example, it is compulsory for the students to have at least one industrial training period abroad, in order to graduate. In our view, however, this was not sufficient, as although the graduate engineers were excellent managers, few of them were real entrepreneurs.

I decided to introduce a new type of pedagogical activity called *L'Acte d'Entreprendre*, based on a simple principle. Just as the only way to learn how to 'play the violin' is to 'play the violin', so the only way to become more enterprising is to try entrepreneurship. We have explained to the students entering the school that, from now on, all of them have to try something based on the idea that 'if we really want to achieve something, we can'.

During the 3 years he or she spends at Ecole des Mines, each student has to draw up a personal innovative project dealing with science, technology, culture, society or humanitarian action, define it in precise terms and submit it to a steering committee. If the project is approved, a tutor is designated who is at the disposal of the student. In addition, the student may seek guidance and advice from any other faculty member as appropriate. Trying is compulsory, but failure is permitted.

The development of the experiment is as follows:

- May 1995: idea of *L'Acte d'Entreprendre* from the Dean;
- academic year 1995–96: experiment with some students of the implementation of the concept, analysis of the results and research on the appropriate methodology;
- academic year 1996–97: large-scale launch on the basis of voluntary participation: 50 per cent of students volunteer, 25 per cent develop interesting projects; discussions with different authorities of the School result in acceptance of the project; creation of a steering committee, registration of the trademark *L'Acte d'Entreprendre* (2 December 1997), capitalization of the experiment, and analysis and evolution of the methods implemented;

- academic year 1997–98: decision to make *L'Acte d'Entreprendre* compulsory for all the students; beginning of the modifications of the curriculum to introduce free time and change the pedagogical activities;
- academic year 1998–99: creation of several start-up companies and increase of follow-up patent registrations; and
- academic year 1999–2000: *L'Acte d'Entreprendre* now compulsory for all students and one of the necessary prerequisites for their engineering degree.

The experiment has now been mobilized throughout the institution. So far 250 projects are in progress with 320 students and 250 tutors from firms and university. The main educational results are new pedagogic methods, the introduction of new courses, the strong introduction of information and communication technologies, and the growth of inductive methods. More generally, there has been a big increase in patent registrations, more than 30 enterprises have been established and the School has won successes in national competitions. It won the trophy for the best pedagogical project among the 250 French Grandes Ecoles in 2000. During the last 5 years, the students and alumni have created more enterprises than during the whole of its previous 213-year history.

Some examples of successful projects are:

- *La Tri-Alpine Guisane Granon* (rafting and mountain bike race) took place on 2 June 2001; it received a FF10,000 grant in the competition for the Grant for Innovating Projects;
- Cultural events for handicapped persons. The project received a FF25,000 grant in the Bouygues Telecom competition;
- The I-nova creation enterprise was awarded a prize by Schneider Electric Foundation (I-nova is an enterprise that develops software and methods for innovation);
- Oxyen research is an enterprise created after end of the scholarship; in 1999 it won the prize for enterprise creation in the field of innovating technologies, organized by the Ministère de l'Education Nationale; and it also won an award as one of the five best start-ups in France (Oxygen Research is a start-up that is specialized in the animation of digitized images); and
- The enterprise from Musarna '98 to Geocarta won a prize in the competition Tremplin, organized by the French Senate (this enterprise develops and commercializes a unique and patented technology of sub-soil cartography).

Other interesting activities include an intelligent alarm clock, participating in the creation of a video games start-up, the 'smart' handbag with chameleon effects, a new type of mountain bike gear, the creation of a student radio broadcast on the Internet, the creation and publication of a role-playing game on the Internet, and the conception and marketing of a silent and folding cello.

Conclusions

The internal resistance of faculty members and student reluctance to commit themselves have totally disappeared. A Professor of Management, who said at the beginning of the project 'your *Acte d'Entreprendre* is ridiculous, pathetic, fashionable', recently said 'Can you propose to us another idea as brilliant as the *Acte d'Entreprendre?*'

We have shown that it is possible for anyone to be innovative even when he is convinced of the contrary. It is possible for anyone to start a project and to achieve it. When you have done it once, you become confident for future innovation and you dare to create more easily. Women are not less entrepreneurial than men.

Entrepreneurship is one necessity for the future of the world. It is impossible for the universities to stay out of the creation of wealth or they cease to exist. Many factors improve entrepreneurship in the education system. Research into new methods of teaching it is essential and I am sure there is not just one way of improving entrepreneurship.

References

Adams, D. (2000) Views of academic work, *Teacher Development*, 4(1): 65–78.

Ade Ajayi, J., Lameck, K., Goma, G. and Johnson, A. (1996) *The African Experience with Higher Education*. Accra: Association of African Universities and James Currie.

Allen, M. (1988) *The Goals of the University*. Buckingham: SRHE/Open University Press.

Allinson, C.W., Chell, E. and Hayes, J. (2000) Intuition and entrepreneurial behaviour, *European Journal of Work and Organisational Psychology*, 9(1): 31–4.

Altbach, P. (ed.) (1999) *Private Prometheus: Private Higher Education and Development in the 21st Century*. Westport: Connecticut/London: Greenwood.

Armstrong, P. (2001) Science, enterprise and profit: ideology in the knowledge driven economy, *Economy and Society*, 30(4): 524–52.

Arnold, M. ([1869] 1983) *Culture and Anarchy*. Cambridge: Cambridge University Press.

Aronowitz, S. (2000) *The Knowledge Factory: Dismantling the Corporate University and Creating True Higher Learning*. Boston: Beacon Press.

Association of Graduate Recruiters (AGR) (1998) *Graduate Salaries and Vacancies 1999 Survey*. Warwick: AGR.

Atkins, M.J. (1999) Oven ready and self-basting: taking stock of employability skills, *Teaching in Higher Education*, 4(2): 267–80.

Australia, Department of Education, Science and Training (2000) Statistics relating to higher education, Canberra, Commonwealth Department of Education, Science and Training. www.deet.gov.au/highered/statinfo (accessed December 2001).

BAe (1999) *Achievement Through Knowledge*. Farnborough: BAe (in-house virtual university prospectus document).

Baldridge, J.V. (ed.) (1971) *Power and Conflict in the University*. New York: Wiley.

Baldridge, J.V., Curtis, D., Ecker, G. and Riley, G.L. (1978) *Policy Making and Effective Leadership*. San Francisco: Jossey-Bass.

Baldwin, R. and Chronister, J. (2001) *Teaching Without Tenure*. Baltimore: Johns Hopkins Press.

Ball, S. (1994) *Education Reform*. Buckingham: SRHE/Open University Press.

Barden, L. (1993) University-business partnerships: effects on regional economic development, *Industry and Higher Education*, 7(4): 220–8.

Barke, M., Braidford, P., Houston, M. et al. (2000) *Students in the Labour Market: Nature, Extent and Implications of Term-time Employment among University of Northumbria*

Undergraduates. London: Research Report RR 215, Department for Education and Employment.

Barnett, R. (1994) *The Limits of Competence: Knowledge, Higher Education and Society*. Buckingham: SRHE/Open University Press.

Barnett, R. (1997) *Higher Education: A Critical Business*. Buckingham: SRHE/Open University Press.

Barnett, R. (2000) *Realizing the University*. Buckingham: SRHE/Open University Press.

Baron, R. (2000) Psychological perspectives on entrepreneurship: cognitive and social factors in entrepreneurs' success, *Current Directions in Psychological Science*, 9(1): 15–18.

Baty, P. (2002) Cambridge dilutes democratic government, *The Times Higher Education Supplement*, no. 1524, 8 February.

Becher, T. (1989) *Academic Tribes and Territories*. Buckingham: SRHE/Open University Press.

Becher, T. and Kogan, M. (1992) *Process and Structure in Higher Education*, 2nd edn. London: Routledge.

Bell, S. and Gordon, J. (1999) Scholarship – the new dimension to equity issues for academic women, *Women's Studies International Forum*, 22(6).

Becher, T. and Kogan, M. (1992) *Process and Structure in Higher Education*. London: Routledge.

Berry, Frank (1999) From Periphery to Core? Foreign Direct Investment, Cost Competitiveness and the Transformation of the Irish Economy. Paper presented to Trade and Industry Policy Secretariat Annual Forum on Growth and Investment.

Berrell, M. (1998) The place of research, scholarship and teaching in newly established universities, *Higher Education Management*, 10(2): 77–93.

Biggs, J. (1999) *Teaching for Quality Learning at University*. Buckingham: SRHE/Open University Press.

Birecree, A. (1988) Academic freedom in the academic factory, *Challenge*, July–August: 53–6.

Birnbaum, R. (1988) *How Colleges Work: the Cybernetics of Academic Organization and Leadership*. San Franciso: Jossey-Bass.

Blasko, Z., Brennan, J. and Shah, T. (forthcoming) Access to What? How to convert educational opportunity into employment opportunity for groups from disadvantaged backgrounds. HEFCE.

Blass, E. (2001) What's in a name? A comparative study of the traditional public university and the corporate university, *Human Resource Development International*, 4(2): 153–73.

Bowes, L. and Harvey, L. (2000) *The Impact of Sandwich Education on the Activities of Graduates Six Months Post-graduation*. London: National Centre for Work Experience. Birmingham: Centre for Research into Quality, University of Central England.

Boyer, E.L. (1990) *Scholarship Reconsidered. Priorities of the Professoriate*. New York: Carnegie Foundation for the Advancement of Teaching.

Brennan, J., Johnston, B., Little, B., Shah, T. and Woodley, A. (2001) *The Employment of UK Graduates: Comparisons with Europe*. Bristol: Higher Education Funding Council for England.

Brew, A. (2001) *The Nature of Research: Inquiry in Academic Contexts*. London: Routledge.

British Aerospace (1999) *Prospectus*. In-house virtual university prospectus. Farnborough: BAe.

Brooksbank, D. and Thomas, B. (2001) An assessment of higher education spin-off enterprises in Wales, *Industry and Higher Education*, 15(2): 415–20.

Brown, R. (2001) Evidence-based policy making or policy-based evidence? The case of quality assurance in higher education. Inaugural professorial lecture, City University, London.

Brown, P. and Scase, R. (1994) *Higher Education and Corporate Realities: Class, Culture and the Decline of Graduate Careers*. London: UCL Press Ltd.

Brown, P. and Scase, R. (1997) Universities and employers: rhetoric and reality, in A. Smith and F. Webster (eds) *The Postmodern University: Contested Visions of Higher Education in Society*. Buckingham: SRHE/Open University Press.

Buchbinder, H. (1993) The market-oriented university and the changing role of knowledge, *Higher Education*, 26: 331–47.

Bunting, I. (1994) *A Legacy of Inequality: Higher Education in South Africa*. Cape Town: University of Cape Town Press.

Burch, C. (1986) *Entrepreneurship*. London: John Wiley.

Burrell, G. (1997) *Pandemonium: Towards a Retro-organization Theory*. London: Sage.

Burrows, R. (1991) Entrepreneurship, petty capitalism and the restructuring of Britain, in R. Burrows (ed.) *Deciphering the Enterprise Culture*. London and New York: Routledge.

Caird, S.P. (1991) The enterprising tendency of occupational groups, *International Small Business Journal*, 9(4): 75–81.

Caird, S.P. (1993) What do psychological tests suggest about entrepreneurs, *Journal of Management Psychology*, 8(6): 11–20.

Calas, M. and Smircich, L. (2001) Introduction: Does the house of knowledge have a future?, *Organization*, 8(2): 147–8.

Callender, C. and Kemp, M. (2000) *Changing Student Finances: income, expenditure and take-up of student loans among full-time and part-time higher education students in 1998/9*. London: Research Report RR 213, Department for Education and Employment.

Castells, M. (1996) The information age: economy, society and culture, *The Rise of the Network Society*, Vol. 1. Oxford: Blackwell.

Castells, M. (2000) *The Rise of the Network Society*. Oxford: Blackwell.

Chell, E. (2000) Towards research on the 'opportunistic entrepreneur': a social constructionist approach and research agenda, *European Journal of Work and Organisational Psychology*, 9(1): 63–80.

Chell, E., Haworth, J.M. and Brearley, S.A. (1991) *The Entrepreneurial Personality: Concepts, Cases and Categories*. London: Routledge.

Christopher, M., Payne, A. and Ballantyne, D. (1994) *Relationship Marketing*. Oxford: Butterworth and Heinemann.

Clark, B.R. (1983) *The Higher Education System: Academic Organisation in Cross-national Perspective*. Berkeley, California: University of California Press.

Clark, B. (1995) *Places of Inquiry. Research and Advanced Education in Modern Universities*. Berkeley, California: University of California Press.

Clark, B. (1996) Diversification of Higher Education: Viability and Change, in V.L. Meek, L. Goedegebuure, O. Kivinen and R. Rinne (eds) *The Mockers and Mocked: Comparative Perspective on Differentiation, Covergence and Diversity in Higher Education*. Oxford: IAU Press/Pergamon.

Clark, B.R. (1998) *Creating Entrepreneurial Universities: Organizational Pathways of Transformation*. Oxford: Pergamon Press.

Cloete, N. and Bunting, I. (2000) *Higher Education Transformation: Assessing Perform-ance in South Africa.* Pretoria: Centre for Higher Education Transformation.

Coaldrake, P. and Stedman, L. (1999) *Academic Work in the Twenty-first Century.* Australia: DETYA.

Coate, K., Court, S., Gillon, E., Morley, L. and Williams, G. (2000) *Academic and Academic Related Staff Involvement in the Local, Regional and National Economy.* London: Association of University Teachers/Institute of Education, University of London.

Coffield, F. (2002) 101 initiatives but no strategy: policy on lifelong learning in England, Open Lecture, Institute of Education, London, 8 January.

Committee of Vice-Chancellors and Principals (CVCP) (1999) *Technology Transfer: the US Experience.* London: CVCP.

Commonwealth Secretariat (1994) *Women Managers in Higher Education,* Summary report of the ACU-CHESS Steering Committee Meeting. London, Common-wealth Secretariat.

Cooper, D. and Subotzky, G. (2001) *The Skewed Revolution: Trends in South African Higher Education 1988–1998.* Cape Town: Education Policy Unit, University of the Western Cape.

Council on Aid to Education (1997) *Breaking the Social Contract: The Fiscal Crisis in Higher Education.* Santa Monica, California: Rand Corporation.

Council on Higher Education (South Africa) (2000) *Towards a New Higher Education Landscape: Meeting the Equity, Quality and Social Development Imperatives of South Africa in the 21st Century.* Pretoria: Council on Higher Education.

Craig, R., Clarke, F. and Amernic, J. (1999) Scholarship in university business schools: Cardinal Newman, creeping corporatism and farewell to the 'disturber of the peace'?, *Accounting Auditing and Accountability Journal,* 12(5): 510–24.

Cromie, S. (2000) Assessing entrepreneurial inclinations: some approaches and empirical evidence, *European Journal of Work and Organisational Psychology,* 9(1): 7–30.

Curran, P.J. (2001) Competition in UK higher education: applying Porter's diamond model to geography departments, *Studies in Higher Education,* 26(2): 223–51.

Dale, A. (1991) Self-employment and entrepreneurship, in R. Burrows (ed.) *Deciphering the Enterprise Culture.* London and New York: Routledge.

David, P.A. (1999) Preface, in A. Geuna, *The Economics of Knowledge Production. Funding and the Structure of University Research.* Cheltenham: UK Edward Elgar.

Davies, J.L. (1987) The entrepreneurial and adaptive university: report of the second US study visit, *International Journal of Institutional Management in Higher Education,* 11(1): 12–104.

Davies, T. (1999) Implementing a Creative Approach to Training and Corpor-ate Degrees, IQPC Conference on the Corporate University, 22–23 June, London.

Dealtry, R. (2000) Strategic directions in the management of the corporate university paradigm, *Journal of Workplace Learning,* 12(4): 171–5.

De Groot, J. (1997) After the ivory tower: gender, commodification and the 'academic', *Feminist Review,* 55 (Spring): 130–42.

Delamont, S. (1996) *A Woman's Place in Education.* Aldershot: Avebury.

De La Rey, C. (2001) *Women and Management in Higher Education in South Africa.* ACU/IoE Seminar on Managing Gendered Change in Selected Commonwealth Universities, Johannesburg, South Africa, February.

Department for Education and Skills (forthcoming) *Work Related Learning.* DFES.

Derrida, J. (1983) The principle of reason: the university in the eyes of its pupils, *Diacritics*, 13(3): 3–21.

DES (1988) *Letter from Secretary of State to the Chairmen of the New Funding Councils*, 31 October. London: DES.

Deshpande, R. (1999) *Developing a Market Orientation.* Thousand Oaks, CA: Sage.

Dill, D.D. and Teixeira, P. (2000) Program diversity in higher education: an economic perspective, *Higher Education Policy*, 13(1): 99–117.

Easterby-Smith, M. (1997) Disciplines of organizational learning: contributions and critiques, *Human Relations*, 50(9): 1085–113.

Education Commission of the States (1998) Survey of nation's governors. Reported in the 19 June, *Chronicle of Higher Education.*

Edwards, R. (1993) *Mature Women Students.* London: Falmer Press.

Eraut, M., Alderton, J., Cole, G. and Senker, P. (1999) The impact of the manager on learning in the workplace, in F. Coffield (ed.) *Speaking Truth to Power; Research and Policy on Lifelong Learning.* Bristol: Policy Press, University of Bristol and the Economic and Social Research Council.

Eurich, N. (1985) *Corporate Classrooms: The Learning Business.* Princeton, NJ: The Carnegie Foundation for the Advancement of Teaching.

Ewell, P. (1997) Organizing for learning: a new imperative, *AAHE Bulletin*, December, 50(4): 3–6.

Fine, B., Lapavistas, C. and Pincus, J. (eds) (2001) *Development Policy in the 21st Century. Beyond the Washington Consensus.* New York: Routledge.

Frade, G. (1998) *L'Acte d'Entreprendre*: how to improve entrepreneurship in engineering education, SEFI Conference Helsinki, 2–4 September, 55–8.

Frade, G. (2002) Entrepreneurship: A Mega Trend for Countries, Enterprises and Universities. Buckingham: SRHE/Open University Press.

Franklin, S.J., Wright, M. and Lockett, A. (2001) Academic and surrogate entrepreneurs in University spin-out companies, *The Journal of Technology Transfer*, 26(1/2): 127–41.

Fraser, N. (1997) Justice Interruptus: Critical Reflections on the 'Postsocialist' Condition. New York and London: Routledge.

Fraser, N. (1998) Social justice in the age of identity politics: redistribution, recognition and participation, in Peterson, G. (ed.) The Tanner Lectures on Human Values, Salt Lake City: University of Utah Press, Vol. 19: 1–67.

Fulmer, R. and Gibbs, P. (1998) Lifelong learning at the corporate university, *Career Development International*, 3(5): 177–84.

Fulop, L. (1991) Middle managers: victims or vanguards of the entrepreneurial movement, *Journal of Management Studies*, 28: 25–44.

Fulton, O., McHugh, G., Machell, J. et al. (1999) *Higher education, the state and the economy.* Paper presented at UK National Workshop, Higher Education and the National Economy Project, 26 April.

Geiger, Roger L. (1993) *Research and Relevant Knowledge. American Research Universities Since World War II.* New York and Oxford: Oxford University Press.

Geuna, A. (1999) *The Economics of Knowledge Production. Funding and the Structure of University Research.* Cheltenham: Edward Elgar.

Gibb, A.A. (1987) Entrepreneurial culture – its meaning and implications for education and training, *Journal of European Industrial Training*, 11: 1–38.

Gibbons, M. (1995) The university as an instrument for the development of science and basic research: the implications of mode 2 science, in D.D. Dill and

B. Sporn (eds) *Emerging Patterns of Social Demand and University Reform: Through a Glass Darkly.* Oxford: IAU Press/Pergamon.

Gibbons, M., Limoges, C., Nowotny, H. et al. (1994) *The New Production of Knowledge: The Dynamics of Science and Research in Contemporary Societies.* London: Sage.

Gill, S.K. (2000) Voices and choices: communicative concerns of Asian women, in S.H. Shahabudin and S.K. Gill (eds) *Asian Women Leaders in Higher Education: Management Challenges for the New Millennium.* Bangi: UNESCO and Centre for Academic Advancement, University Kebangsaan.

Gilliland, N. (1993) Training to win, *Training and Development,* February.

Goodlad, S. (1995) *The Quest for Quality.* Buckingham: SRHE/Open University Press.

Gouldner, A. (1957) Cosmopolitans and locals: towards an analysis of latent social roles – 1, *Administrative Science Quarterly,* 2(3): 281–306.

Government of India (1998) *Higher Education in India. Vision and Action.* Country paper to the UNESCO World Conference on Higher Education in the 21st Century. Available online at http://education.nic.in/htmlweb/unhighedu.htm (accessed December 2001).

Gray, C. (1992) Growth orientation and the small firm, in K. Caley, E. Chell, F. Chitttenden and C. Mason (eds) *Small Enterprise Development: Policy and Practice in Action.* London: Paul Chapman, 59–71.

Gray, H. (ed.) (1999) *Universities and the Creation of Wealth.* Buckingham: SRHE/Open University Press.

Gregory, E.H. (1997) University-industry strategic partnerships, *Industry and Higher Education,* 11(4): 253–4.

Gutiérrez, J. (1996) The 1994 Columbus Seminar on Research Management, in M. Carpenter (ed.) *The Management of Research in Universities.* Paris: Cre-Columbus-UNESCO.

Hague, D. and Oakley, K. (2000) *Spin-offs and Start-ups in UK Universities.* London: Committee of Vice-Chancellors and Principals.

Halsey, A.H. (1992) *The Decline of Donnish Dominion.* Oxford: Oxford University Press.

Hampden Turner, C. (1990) *Charting the Corporate Mind.* Oxford: Basil Blackwell.

Handy, C. (1985) *Understanding Organisations,* 3rd edn. Harmondsworth: Penguin.

Hargreaves, D. (1996) *Teaching as a research-based profession: possibilities and prospects.* London: Teacher Training Agency Annual Lecture.

Hearn, J. (1994) The organization(s) of violence: men, gender relations, organizations and violences, *Human Relations,* 47(6): 731–54.

Henkel, M. (2000) *Academic Identities and Policy Change in Higher Education.* London: Jessica Kingsley.

Higher Education Funding Council for England (HEFCE) (1999a) *RAE 2001: Consultation on Assessment Panels' Criteria and Working Methods* (RAE 4/99). Bristol: HEFCE.

Higher Education Funding Council for England (HEFCE) (1999b) *RAE 2001: Assessment panels' criteria and working methods* (RAE 5/99). Bristol: HEFCE.

Higher Education Funding Council for England (HEFCE) (2001) *Higher Education Active Community Fund: Guidance and Allocations* (01/65). Bristol: HEFCE.

Higher Education Funding Council for England (HEFCE) (2001) *Strategies for Widening Participation in Higher Education: A Guide to Good Practice.* Bristol: HEFCE.

Higher Education Statistics Agency (HESA) (2000) Staff Tables Higher Education Statistics Agency. www.hesa.ac.uk (accessed December 2001).

Hillage, J., Pearson, R., Anderson, A. and Tamkin, P. (1998) *Excellence in Research in Schools*, Research Report 74. London: DfEE.

Hirschorn, L., Gilmore, T. and Newell, T. (1989) Training and learning in a post-industrial world, in H. Leymann and H. Kornbluh (eds) *Socialization and Learning at Work: A New Approach to the Learning Process in the Workplace and Society*. Aldershot: Avebury.

Hisrich, R.D. (2000) Can psychological approaches be used effectively: an overview, *European Journal of Work and Organisational Psychology*, 9(1): 93–6.

Hoare, G.A. (1995) Scales economies in academic excellence: an exploratory analysis of the United Kingdom's 1992 research selectivity exercise, *Higher Education*, 29: 241–60.

Hodgson, A. and Spours, K. (2001) Part-time work and full-time education in the UK: the emergence of a curriculum and policy issue, *Journal of Education and Work*, 14(3): 373–88.

Hogan, J. (2001) 'Old and new: Stockton and Durham', in D. Warner and D. Palfreyman (eds) *The State of UK Higher Education*. Buckingham: SRHE/Open University Press.

Hoskin, K. (1990) 'Foucault under examination: the crypto-educationalist unmasked', in S. Ball (ed.) *Foucault and Education: Disciplines and knowledge*. London: Routledge.

Huisman, J. (1998) Differentiation and diversity in higher education, *Higher Education Handbook of Theory and Research*, Vol. 13. New York: Agathon Press.

Inayatullah, S. (1998) Alternative futures of the university: globalisation, multi-culturalism, virtualisation and politicisation, *Futures*, 30(7): 589–602.

Jansen, J. (2001) Does the national plan effectively address the critical issues facing higher education?, *South African Journal of Higher Education*, 15(3): 5–9.

Jarvis, P. (2000) The changing university: meeting a need and needing to change, *Higher Education Quarterly*, 54(1): 43–67.

Jarvis, P. (2001) *University and Corporate Universities*. London: Kogan Page.

Jaspers, K. (1960) *The Idea of the University*. London: Peter Owen.

Jayaweera, S. (1997) Higher education and the economic and social empowerment of women – the Asian experience, *Compare*, 27(3).

Jennings, D.E. and Lietham, C.P. (1983) Locus of control; a review and directions for entrepreneurial research, in K.H. Chung (ed.) *Proceedings of the 43rd Annual Meeting of the Academy of Management*. Dallas, Texas: Academy of Management.

Johnson, C. and Caird, S. (1988) *The Measurement of General Enterprising Tendency*. Durham: Durham University Business School.

Johnson, H. (2001) Neutral, colluding or subversive: recognizing the political implications of the marketing subdiscourses in English higher education, *Educational Management and Administration*, 29(3): 261–74.

Johnston, R.J., Jones, K. and Gould, M. (1995) Department size and research in English universities: inter-university variations, *Quality in Higher Education*, 1(1): 41–7.

Jones, G. and Lengkeek, N. (1997) Research development: the experience of the new university, *Research and the New Tomorrow*. New Zealand: UNITEC.

Jones, M.E. (1993) Continuing engineering education and global development, Proceedings International Conference on Engineering Education, Singapore: National University of Singapore, 10–12 November: 619–26.

Jones, M.E. (1996) Challenges in changing paradigms for engineering education, Proceedings World Congress of Engineering Educators and Industry Leaders, 2–5 July, Paris: UNESCO, Vol. II: 193–6.

Jones, M.E. (1997) Cultural Schisms: Science and humanities, industry and academia, Proceedings SEFI Conference Cracow, J. Szpytko, Z. Waszczyszyn, F. Maffioli and S. Mitkowski (eds). Krakow: Akademia Gorniczo-Hutnicza.

Jones, M.E. (2000) International continuing professional development for the petroleum industry, Proceedings SEFI Conference Paris, ed. Jean Michel and CD-ROM, 6–8 September, AA Balkema Rotterdam.

Jones, W.T. (1984) Public roles and private roles and differential moral assessment of role, *Ethics*, 94: 603–20.

Kamoruao-Mbuende, O. (1999) Are there barriers preventing women academics reaching high position in academe? Career paths of women academics a comparative perspective Namibia and England. MA dissertation, University of London Institute of Education.

Kanter, R.M. (1983) *The Changemasters*. London: Paladin.

Katjavivi, P. (2000) Empowering African women through higher education, in M.L. Kearney (ed.) *Women, Power and the Academy: From Rhetoric to Reality*. Paris: UNESCO and Berghahn Books: 59–70.

Kells, H.R. (1989) The nature of the university-industry alliance and its limits, *Higher Education Policy*, 2(2): 9–12.

Kerr, C. (1995) *The Uses of the University*, 4th edn. Cambridge, Massachusetts: Harvard University Press. (Based on Godkin lectures at Harvard University, April 1963.)

Kinman, G. (1998) *Pressure Points: A Survey into the Causes and Consequences of Occupational Stress in UK Academic and Related Staff*. London: Association of University Teachers.

Kirby, D.A. (1992) Developing graduate entrepreneurs: the UK graduate enterprise programme, *Entrepreneurship, Innovation and Change*, 1(2): 165–77.

Klug, F. (2000) *Values for a Godless Age*. London: Penguin.

Klus, J.P. (1996) *Learning on Demand: A New Continuing Education Challenge*, IACEE Report no. 7 Highlights of 6th World Conference on Continuing Engineering Education, Brazil (1995): 11–19.

Kotler, P. and Fox, A. (1995) *Strategic Marketing for Educational Institutions*. Englewood Cliffs, NJ: Prentice Hall.

Lamptey, A.S. (1992) Promoting women's participation in teaching research and management in African universities, *Higher Education in Africa: Trends and Challenges for the 21st Century*, Dakar, Dakar Regional Office UNESCO.

Lawton, A. (1998) *Ethical Management for the Public Services*. Buckingham: SRHE/Open University Press.

Leavis, F.R. (1962) Two cultures? The significance of C.P. Snow, *Spectator*, 9 March.

Leavitt, T. (1960) Marketing myopia, *Harvard Business Review*, July–August: 45–6.

Lee, E.A. and Messerschmitt, D.G. (1999) A highest education in the year 2049, Proceedings IEEE, 87(9): 1685–91.

LeGrand, J. and Bartlett, W. (eds) (1993) *Quasi-Markets and Social Policy*. London: Macmillan.

Linklater, P. (1987) Introduction, in P. Linklater (ed.) *Education and the World of Work: Positive Partnerships*. Milton Keynes: SRHE/Open University Press.

Lipset, S.M. (1994) In defense of the research university, in J.R. Cole, E.G. Barber and S.R. Graubard (eds) *The Research University in a Time of Discontent*. Baltimore and London: Johns Hopkins University Press.

Lissenburgh, S. and Harding, R. (2000) *Knowledge Links: Innovation in University-Business Partnerships*. London: The Institute for Public Policy Research (IPPR).

Little, B., Moon, S., Pierce, D., Harvey, L. and Marlow-Hayne, N. (forthcoming) The nature and extent of undergraduates' work experience, Appendix, *Work Related Learning*. Bristol: HEFCE.

Long, M. and Hayden, M. (2001) Paying their way: a survey of Australian undergraduate university student finances, 2000. Australian Vice-Chancellors' Committee, http://www.avcc.edu.au, accessed 9 January.

Lund, H. (1998) *A Single Sex Profession? Female Staff Numbers in Commonwealth Universities.* London: CHEMS.

Lyons, C. (1998) The motives, satisfactions and dissatisfactions of UK higher education lecturers in 1998 – an exploratory qualitative study. Unpublished M.Sc Dissertation, University of Surrey, Guildford.

Mabizela, M. (2001) Towards a contextual analysis of structural patterns of private-public higher education in South Africa. Unpublished MEd dissertation, University of the Western Cape, Cape Town.

McCormick, A.C. (2000) 'Bringing the Carnegie Classification into the 21st century, *Bulletin*, American Association of Higher Education, January.

Macfarlane, B. (2000) Inside the corporate classroom, *Teaching in Higher Education*, 5(1): 51–60.

McInnis, C. (2001) Signs of Disengagement?: responding to the changing work and study patterns of full-time undergraduates in Australian universities. Paper presented at Consortium of Higher Education Researchers Annual Conference, 2–4 September, Dijon.

McNay, I. (1995) From the collegial academy to the corporate enterprise: the changing cultures of universities, in T. Schuller (ed.) *The Changing University?* Buckingham: SRHE/Open University Press.

McNay, I. (1998) *Organisation culture, leadership and the role of the senior management team in universities.* Inaugural professorial lecture, 5 February, University of Greenwich: 3.

McNay, I. (1999) Changing cultures in UK higher education: the state as corporate market bureaucracy and the emergent academic enterprise, in D. Braun and F.-X. Merrien (eds) *Towards a New Model of Governance for Universities: A Comparative View.* London, Jessica Kingsley.

Makhubu, L. (1998) The right to higher education and equal opportunity particularly for women: the major challenge of our time, *Higher Education in Africa: Achievements, Challenges and Prospects.* Dakar, UNESCO Regional Office for Education in Africa.

Manicas, P. (1998) Higher education at risk, *Futures*, 30(7): 651–6.

Manya, M.O. (2000) Equal opportunities policy (gender). A means to increasing the number of female senior managers and decision-makers at the university of Nairobi. MA dissertation, Institute of Education, University of London.

Marceau, J. (1996) University-industry-government relations: a 'complexes' equation, *Industry and Higher Education*, 10(4): 252–60.

Marginson, S. and Considine, M. (2000) *The Enterprise University: Power, Governance and Reinvention in Australia.* Cambridge: Cambridge University Press.

Marquardt, M. and Reynolds, A. (1994) *The Global Learning Organization.* Burr Ridge, Illinois: Irwin.

Marshall, T.H. (1992) *Citizenship and Social Class.* London: Pluto.

Marshall, C. (ed.) (1997) *Feminist Critical Policy Analysis. A Perspective from Post Secondary Education.* London: Falmer.

Mason, G., Williams, G.L. Cranmer, S. and Guile, D. (forthcoming) *How Higher Education Enhances the Employability of Graduates*. Bristol: HEFCE.

Mayberry, M. and Rose, E.C. (1999) *Meeting the Challenge. Innovative Feminist Pedagogies in Action*. New York: Routledge.

Meek, V.L. and O'Neill, A. (1996) Diversity and differentiation in the Australian unified national system of higher education, in V.L. Meek, L. Goedegebuure, O. Kivinen and R. Rinne (eds) *The Mockers and Mocked: Comparative Perspective on Differentiation, Covergence and Diversity in Higher Education*. Oxford: IAU Press/Pergamon.

Meister, J. (1998) *Corporate Universities: Lessons in Building a World-class Work Force*. New York: McGraw-Hill.

Metcalfe, H. (2001) Increasing Inequality in Higher Education: the Role of Term-time Working. London: National Institute for Economic and Social Research.

Middlehurst, R. (1993) *Leading Academics*. Buckingham: SRHE/Open University Press.

Midgley, S. (1999) Up, up and away – almost, *The Guardian Higher Education Supplement*, 2 March: vi–vii.

Midwinter, J.E. (1999) The Challenge of Lifelong Learning, IEE, *Engineering Science and Education Journal*, 8(12): 271–80.

Miller, R. (1992) Double, double, toil and trouble: the problem of student selection, *South African Journal of Higher Education*, 6(1): 98–103.

Ministry of Education (South Africa) (2001) *National Plan for Higher Education*. Pretoria: Department of Education.

Mitter, S. and Rowbotham, S. (eds) (1997) *Women Encounter Technology*: Changing Patterns of Employment in the Third World. London: Routledge.

Mlama, P.M. (1998) Increasing access and equity in higher education: gender issues, *Higher Education in Africa: Achievements, Challenges and Prospects*. Dakar: UNESCO Regional Office.

Modood, T. and Acland, T. (eds) (1998) *Race and Higher Education: Experiences, Challenges and Policy Implications*. London: Policy Studies Institute.

Morgan, G. (1992) Marketing discourse and practice: towards a critical analysis, in M.A. Levesson and H. Wilmott (eds) *Critical Management Studies*. London: Sage.

Morley, L. (1997) Change and equity in higher education, *British Journal of Sociology of Education*, 18(2): 229–40.

Morley, L. (1999) *Organising Feminisms: The Micropolitics of the Academy*. London: Macmillan.

Morley, L. (2000) The micropolitics of gender in the learning society, *Higher Education in Europe*, 25(2): 229–35.

Morphew, C.C. (2000) Institutional diversity, program [sic] acquisition and faculty members: examining academic drift at a new level, Special Issue: Diversity, Differentiation and Markets, *Higher Education Policy*, 13(1): 55–78.

Muller, J., Cloete, N. and Badat, S. (eds) (2001) *Challenges of Globalisation*. South African debates with Manuel Castells. Cape Town: Maskew Miller Longman.

National Center for Educational Statistics, United States Department of Education (1987, 1992 and 1998) *National Study of Postsecondary Faculty*.

National Centre for Work Experience (NCWE) (2000) Results of NCWE's second survey of academically recognised work experience, 1998–99, in *NCWE Work Experience News*. London: NCWE.

National Commission on Higher Education (South Africa) (1996) *A Framework for Transformation*. Cape Town: CTP.

National Commission on the Cost of Higher Education (1998) *Straight Talk about College Costs, Final Report*. Phoenix, AZ: The Oryx Press.

National Committee of Inquiry into Higher Education (NCIHE) (1997) *Higher Education in the Learning Society*. London: NCIHE.

Neave, G. (2000) Research and the making of frames, *Comparative Social Research*, 19: 257–71.

Newman, F. and Scurry, J. (2001) Online technology pushes pedagogy to the forefront, *The Chronicle Review*, 13 July.

Nicholls, G. (2001) *Professional Development in Higher Education*. London: Kogan Page.

Nixon, J. (1996) Professional identity and the restructuring of higher education, *Studies in Higher Education*, 21(910): 5–16.

Nord, W. and Fox, S. (1996) The individual in organizational studies: the great disappearing act?, in S.G. Clegg and C. Hardy (eds) *Studying Organizations: Theory and Method*. London: Sage.

Nwomonoh, J. (1998) *Education and Development in Africa: a Contemporary Study*. San Francisco and London: International Scholars Publications.

O'Malley, E. (1989) *Industry and Economic Development. The Challenge for the Latecomer*. Dublin: Gill and Macmillan.

OECD (1991) *Alternatives to Universities*. Paris: OECD.

OECD (1999) *University Research in Transition*. Paris: OECD.

OECD (2001) *Education at a Glance*. Paris: OECD.

Onsongo, J.K. (2000) Publish or perish? An investigation into academic women's access to research and publication in Kenyan universities. MA Dissertation, London, University of London Institute of Education.

Onsongo, J.K. (2001) *Gender issues in higher education management in Kenya*. ACU/IoE Seminar on Managing Gendered Change in Selected Commonwealth Universities, Johannesburg, South Africa, February.

Organ, D.W. (1990) The motivational basis of organizational citizenship behavior, *Research in Organizational Behavior*, 12: 43–72.

OST (1997) *The Quality of the UK Science Base*. London: OST.

Parker, M. and Jary, D. (1995) The 'McUniversity' – organization, management and academic subjectivity', *Organization*, 2(2): 319–38.

Peters, T. (1997) *The Circle of Innovation*. Glasgow: HarperCollins.

Peters, T. and Waterman, R. (1982) *In Search of Excellence*. New York: Harper and Row.

Pham, B. (2000) Research at regional universities in Australia: visions and realisation, *Higher Education Management*, 12(2): 117–29.

Porter, M.E. (1990) *The Competitive Advantage of Nations*. London: Macmillan.

Powell, W.W. and Owen-Smith, J. (1998) Universities as creators and retailers of intellectual property: Life sciences research and commercial development, in B. Weisbrod (ed.) *To Profit or Not to Profit? The Commercial Transformation of the Non-profit Sector*. Cambridge: Cambridge University Press.

Pratt, J. (1997) *The Polytechnic Experiment: 1965–1992*. Buckingham: SRHE/Open University Press.

Prism: Journal of the American Society of Engineering Education, January 2000.

Quinn, R. (1996) *Deep Change: Discovering the Leader Within*. San Francisco: Jossey-Bass.

Ramsden, P. (1992) *Learning to Teach in Higher Education*. London: Routledge.

Ramsey, E. (2000) Women and leadership in higher education facing international challenges and maximising opportunities. Kuala Lumpur, University Kebangsaan, Malaysia. Unpublished internal report.

Rathberger, E.M. and Adela, E.O. (2000) *Gender and the Information Revolution in Africa*. Ottawa: IDRC.

Rawls, J. (1971) *A Theory of Justice*. Cambridge: Harvard University Press.

Republic of South Africa (1996) The Constitution of the Republic of South Africa (Act no. 108). Pretoria.

Republic of South Africa (1997a) *Education White Paper 3: A Programme for the Transformation of Higher Education*. Pretoria: Government Gazette no. 18207.

Republic of South Africa (1997b) *Higher Education Act*. Pretoria: Government Gazette no. 19842.

Reynolds, P.D., Hay, M. and Camp, S.M. (2000) Global Entrepreneurship Monitor – Executive Report.

Rivlin, C. and Roberts, C. (2001) Degree classification: a matter of equity, paper to SRHE Conference, Cambridge, December.

Roberts, D. and Higgins, T. (1992) *Higher Education: The Student Experience*. Leeds: HEIST.

Roberts, E.B. (1991) An environment for entrepreneurs, in K.R. Manning (ed.) *MIT: Shaping The Future*. Cambridge, Mass: MIT Press.

Rooney, D. and Hearn, G. (2000) Of minds, markets and machines: how universities might transcend the ideology of commodification, in S. Inayatullah and J. Gidley (eds) *The University in Transformation: Global Perspectives on the Futures of the University*. Westport, Connecticut: Bergin and Garvey.

Rowland, S. (1996) Relationships between teaching and research, *Teaching in Higher Education*, 3(2): 133–41.

Rowland, S. (2001) Is the university a place of learning? Compliance and contestation in higher education, Inaugural Lecture, University College London, 15 November.

Rozario, S. (2001) Claiming the campus for female students in Bangladesh, *Women's Studies Intenational Forum*, 24(2): 157–66.

Ruekert, R.W. (1992) Developing a market orientation: an organizational strategy perspective, *International Journal of Research in Marketing*, 9: 225–45.

Rumble, G. (1999) Cost analysis of distance learning, *Performance Improvement Quarterly*, 12(2).

Russell, C. (1993) *Academic Freedom*. London: Routledge.

Sadlak, J. (1998) Globalization and concurrent challenges for higher education, in P. Scott (ed.) *The Globalization of Higher Education*. Buckingham: SRHE/Open University Press.

Sandelands, E. (1998) Developing a robust model of the virtual corporate university, *Journal of Knowledge Management*, 1(3): 181–8.

Scarbrough, H., Swan, J. and Preston, J. (1999) *Knowledge Management: A Literature Review*. London: Institute of Personnel and Development.

Schumpeter, J.A. (1983) *The Theory of Economic Development* (first printed in 1934). London: Transaction Books.

Scott, I. (1995) The interface between higher education and secondary/further education as a key determinant of access to and success in HE. Paper commissioned by the National Commission on Higher Education. http://star.hsrc.ac.za/nche/final/tg5/systems/papers.html

Scott, P. (1995) *The Meanings of Mass Higher Education*. Buckingham: SRHE/Open University Press.

Seager, J. (1997) *The State of Women in the World Atlas*. London: Penguin.

Sen, A. (1999) *Development as Freedom*. Oxford: Oxford University Press.

Senge, P. (1993) *The Fifth Discipline: The Art and Practice of the Learning Organization*. London: Century Business.

Singh, M. (2001) Re-inserting the 'public good' into Higher Education Transformation. Paper presented at the SRHE Conference 'Globalisation and Higher Education: Views from the South', March, Cape Town, South Africa.

Singh, J. and Gill, S.K. (2001) Women in higher education management. The case of Malaysia. ACU/IoE Seminar on Managing Gendered Change in Selected Commonwealth Universities, Johannesburg, South Africa, February.

Skilbeck, M. (2001) *The University Challenged. Review of International Trends and Issues with Particular Reference to Ireland.* Ireland: Higher Education Authority.

Skoie, H. (2000) Faculty involvement in research in mass higher education: current practice and future perspectives in the Scandinavian countries, *Science and Public Policy*, 27(6): 409–19.

Skolnik, M.L. (1998) Higher education in the 21st century: perspectives on an emerging body of literature, *Futures*, 30(7): 635–50.

Slater, S. and Narver, J. (1999) Market orientation, performance, and the moderating influence of competitive influence, in R. Deshpande (ed.) *Developing a Market Orientation.* Thousand Oaks, CA: Sage.

Slaughter, S. and Leslie, L.L. (1997) *Academic Capitalism: Politics, Policies, and the Entrepreneurial University.* Baltimore: Johns Hopkins University Press.

Snow, C.P. (1964) *The Two Cultures.* Cambridge: Cambridge University Press.

Spink, P. (2001) On houses, villages and knowledges, *Organization*, 8(2): 219–26.

Spivak, G. (1999) *A critique of Postcolonial Reason.* London: Harvard University Press.

Sporn, B. (1999) *Adaptive University Structures.* London: Jessica Kingsley.

Stallings, D. (2001) The virtual university: Organizing to survive in the 21st century, *Journal of Academic Librarianship*, 27(1): 3–24.

Steflensen, M., Rogers, E.M. and Speakman, K. (2000) Spin-offs from research centers at a research university, *Journal of Business Venturing*, 15(1): 93–111.

Strauss, J. and Frost, R. (1999) *Marketing on the Internet: Principles of On-Line Marketing.* Upper Saddle River, NJ: Prentice Hall.

Subotzky, G. (2001) *Background Research Report for 2000–2001 Annual Report of the Council on Higher Education,* South Africa. Belville: Education Policy Unit at the University of the Western Cape.

Swainson, N. (1991) Tertiary education and training needs for post apartheid South Africa, in Commonwealth Secretariat *Human Resource Development for Post Apartheid South Africa: A Documentation.* London: Commonwealth Secretariat.

Tapscott, D. (1996) *The Digital Economy: Promise and Peril in the Age of Networked Intelligence.* New York: McGraw-Hill.

Taylor, S., Paton, R. and Chisholm, K. (2001) Mapping the corporate university phenomenon: Issues and frameworks to focus an empirical study. Paper presented to the Knowledge and Learning stream of the British Academy of Management Conference, 5–7 September, Cardiff.

Thomas, D. (1999) The corporate university as a model for organisational and individual learning. Paper presented to the IQPC Conference on the Corporate University, 22–23 June, London.

Tichy, N. (2001) No ordinary boot camp, *Harvard Business Review*, April: 63–70.

Tight, M. (1988) So what is academic freedom?, in M. Tight (ed.) *Academic Freedom and Responsibility.* Milton Keynes: Open University Press.

Tooley, J. and Darby, D. (1998) *Educational Research – an Ofsted Critique.* London: Ofsted.

Trowler, P. (1998) *Academics Responding to Change.* Buckingham: SRHE/Open University Press.

Turpin, T., Garrett-Jones, S., Rankin, N. and Aylward, D. (1996) *Patterns of Research Activity in Australian Universities.* Commissioned Report no. 47, National Board for Employment, Education and Training, Australian Research Council, Australian Government Publishing Service.

Twigg, C. (1996) Is technology a silver bullet?, *EduCom Review,* March/April. www.center.rpi.edu (accessed 30 Nov. 2001).

UNESCO (1995) *Women in Higher Education in Africa.* Dakar: UNESCO Regional Office.

UNESCO (1998) *World Declaration on Higher Education for the Twenty First Century.* Paris: UNESCO on line at www.unesco.org

UNESCO (2001) *World Education Indicators, Gross Enrolment Ratios by Sex: Tertiary.* www.uis.unesco.org/en/stats/stats0.htm (accessed December 2001).

UNIFEM (2000) *Progress of the World's Women 2000.* New York: United Nations Development Fund for Women.

Universities UK (2000) *A Forward Look – Highlights of our Corporate Plan 2001–2004,* Vol. 9. London: Universities UK.

Van Gelderen, M. (2000) Enterprising behaviour of ordinary people, *European Journal of Work and Organisational Psychology,* 9(1): 81–8.

Van Vught, F. (1996) Isomorphism in higher education? Towards a theory of differentiation and diversity in higher education systems, in V.L. Meek, L. Goedegebuure, O. Kivinen and R. Rinne (eds) *The Mockers and Mocked: Comparative Perspective on Differentiation, Convergence and Diversity in Higher Education.* Oxford: IAU Press/Pergamon.

Vernon, T. (1999) The Techno-MBA: One alternative for knowledge workers. Unpublished EdD thesis, University of Pennsylvania.

Walker, M. (1997) Simply not good chaps: unravelling gender equity in a South African university, in C. Marshall (ed.) *Feminist Critical Policy Analysis: A Perspective from Post Secondary Education.* London: Falmer.

Warner, D. and Leonard, C. (1997) *The Income Generation Handbook,* 2nd edn. Buckingham: SRHE/Open University Press.

Watkins, D. and Stone, G. (1999) Entrepreneurship education in UK HEIs, *Industry and Higher Education,* 13(6): 382–9.

Weick, K. (1976) Educational organisations as loosely-coupled systems, *Administrative Science Quarterly,* 21(1).

Whitby, Z. (1992) *Promotional Publications: A Guide to Editors.* Leeds: HEIST.

Wiggenhorn, W. (1990) Motorola U: When training becomes an education, *Harvard Business Review,* July–August: 71–83.

Wild, R. (1999) Is it time to tie the corporate knot?, *The Guardian Higher Education Supplement,* 2 March: vii.

Wild, R. and Carnell, C. (2000) *Corporate Universities: Learning Partnerships for the Future.* Henley: Henley Management College.

Wildman, P. (1998) From the monophonic university to the polyphonic university, *Futures,* 30(7): 625–33.

Williams, G. (1992) *Changing Patterns of Finance in Higher Education.* Buckingham: SRHE/Open University Press.

Williams, P. (1993) *The Alchemy of Race and Rights.* London: Virago.

Wolpe, H., Badat, S. and Barends, Z. (1993) *The Post-secondary Education System: Beyond the Equality vs Development Impasse and Towards Policy Formulation for Equality and Development.* Cape Town: Education Policy Unit, University of the Western Cape.

Yates, C. and Bradley, J. (eds) (2000) *Basic Education at a Distance*. London: Routledge Falmer.

Yuval-Davis, N. (1997) *Gender & Nation*. London: Sage.

Zindi, F. (1998) Sexual harassment in Zimbabwe's institutions of higher education, *Perspectives in education*, 17(2): 39–48.

Zubrick, A., Reid, I. and Rossiter, P. (2001) *Strengthening the Nexus between Teaching and Research*. Australia: Higher Education Division, DETYA.

Index

Page numbers in *italics* refer to tables.

The Society for Research into Higher Education

The Society for Research into Higher Education (SRHE), an international body, exists to stimulate and coordinate research into all aspects of higher education. It aims to improve the quality of higher education through the encouragement of debate and publication on issues of policy, on the organization and management of higher education institutions, and on the curriculum, teaching and learning methods.

The Society is entirely independent and receives no subsidies, although individual events often receive sponsorship from business or industry. The Society is financed through corporate and individual subscriptions and has members from many parts of the world. It is an NGO of UNESCO.

Under the imprint *SRHE & Open University Press*, the Society is a specialist publisher of research, having over 80 titles in print. In addition to *SRHE News*, the Society's newsletter, the Society publishes three journals: *Studies in Higher Education* (three issues a year), *Higher Education Quarterly* and *Research into Higher Education Abstracts* (three issues a year).

The Society runs frequent conferences, consultations, seminars and other events. The annual conference in December is organized at and with a higher education institution. There are a growing number of networks which focus on particular areas of interest, including:

Access	Learning Environment
Assessment	Legal Education
Consultants	Managing Innovation
Curriculum Development	New Technology for Learning
Eastern European	Postgraduate Issues
Educational Development Research	Quantitative Studies
FE/HE	Student Development
Funding	Vocational Qualifications
Graduate Employment	

Benefits to members

Individual

- The opportunity to participate in the Society's networks
- Reduced rates for the annual conferences
- Free copies of *Research into Higher Education Abstracts*
- Reduced rates for *Studies in Higher Education*

- Reduced rates for *Higher Education Quarterly*
- Free copy of *Register of Members' Research Interests* – includes valuable reference material on research being pursued by the Society's members
- Free copy of occasional in-house publications, e.g. *The Thirtieth Anniversary Seminars Presented by the Vice-Presidents*
- Free copies of *SRHE News* which informs members of the Society's activities and provides a calendar of events, with additional material provided in regular mailings
- A 35 per cent discount on all SRHE/Open University Press books
- The opportunity for you to apply for the annual research grants
- Inclusion of your research in the *Register of Members' Research Interests*

Corporate

- Reduced rates for the annual conferences
- The opportunity for members of the Institution to attend SRHE's network events at reduced rates
- Free copies of *Research into Higher Education Abstracts*
- Free copies of *Studies in Higher Education*
- Free copies of *Register of Members' Research Interests* – includes valuable reference material on research being pursued by the Society's members
- Free copy of occasional in-house publications
- Free copies of *SRHE News*
- A 35 per cent discount on all SRHE/Open University Press books
- The opportunity for members of the Institution to submit applications for the Society's research grants
- The opportunity to work with the Society and co-host conferences
- The opportunity to include in the *Register of Members' Research Interests* your Institution's research into aspects of higher education

Membership details: SRHE, 76 Portland Place, London
W1B 1NT, UK Tel: 020 7637 2766. Fax: 020 7637 2781.
email: srhe@mailbox.ulcc.ac.uk
world wide web: http://www.srhe.ac.uk./srhe/
Catalogue: SRHE & Open University Press, Celtic Court,
22 Ballmoor, Buckingham MK18 1XW. Tel: 01280 823388.
Fax: 01280 823233. email: enquiries@openup.co.uk

MANAGING THE LEARNING UNIVERSITY

Chris Duke

This book debunks prevailing modern management theories and fashions as applied to higher education. At the same time it provides practical guidance for a clear and easily understood set of principles as to how universities and colleges can be re-energized and their staff mobilized to be effective in meeting the growing and changing needs of the global knowledge society. It is anchored in knowledge of management and organizational theory and in the literature about higher education which is critiqued from a clear theoretical perspective based on and tested through long experience of university management and leadership.

Chris Duke offers challenging advice for managers in tertiary and higher education – from self-managing knowledge workers who may feel themselves to be the new academic proletariat, through to institutional heads, some of whose attempts to manage using strategic planning, management-by-objectives and other techniques seriously unravel because they fail to benefit from the talents and networks which make up the rich 'underlife' of the institution. Loss of institutional memory and failure to tap tacit know-how and mobilize commitment through genuine consultation and shared participatory management inhibits organizational learning and generates apathy – or drives staff dedication and creativity into oppositional channels.

Managing the Learning University indicates how higher education institutions can link and network their internal energies with external opportunities and partners to be successful and dynamic learning organizations. It points the way to enabling an enterprising and valued university to thrive in hard times, and to be a community where it is actually a pleasure to work.

Contents
Introduction: Who manages what? – Changing universities – Managing and people in postmodern times – Managing what abiding university? – Managing through cooperation – Managing the academic enterprise – Managing people and resources – Managing communication and using information technology – Is the learning university manageable? – Bibliography – Index – The Society for Research into Higher Education.

176pp   0 335 20765 0 (Paperback)   0 335 20766 9 (Hardback)

PUTTING THE UNIVERSITY ONLINE
INFORMATION, TECHNOLOGY, AND ORGANIZATIONAL CHANGE

James Cornford and Neil Pollock

- What kind of university is emerging from the widespread adoption of new information and communication technologies in teaching, research and administration?
- What is the nature and scale of the work required to put the university online?
- What are the consequences – for academics, students, managers and others – of putting the university online?

New information and communication technologies (ICTs), and above all the internet, hold out many promises for higher education institutions in terms of flexibility, efficiency, quality and access. The vision is that of a virtual institution. *Putting the University Online* seeks to uncover what the pursuit of that vision means for an institution, its staff, students and other stakeholders, and consequences, intended and unintended, for the role and identity of the university.

This is the first book length study, based on detailed fine-grained analysis of what 'putting the university online' actually means for those involved and the wider institutions. James Cornford and Neil Pollock draw both on theories from the sociology of technology and on a large and diverse body of empirical research in order to explore how universities are attempting to build and use new ICTs to sit alongside, complement and, in some cases, replace established means of delivering, organizing and managing higher education. Their book will help sensitize policy makers, academics, university managers, and students to the limits to, and implications of, the pursuit of a virtual future for higher education.

Contents
The online imperative – Researching changing universities – Working through the work of making work mobile – The campus and the online university – The online university as timely and accurate information – Keeping up standards: the virtual university is the university made concrete – Customizing industry standard systems for universities – Campus management and the self-service student – Reflection and conclusion – References – Index – The Society for Research into Higher Education.

c160pp   0 335 21005 8 (Paperback)   0 335 21006 6 (Hardback)